Art, Rebellion
and Redemption

American University Studies

Series XVIII
African Literature

Vol. 5

PETER LANG
New York • San Francisco • Bern • Baltimore
Frankfurt am Main • Berlin • Wien • Paris

Romanus Okey Muoneke

Art, Rebellion and Redemption

A Reading of the Novels of Chinua Achebe

PETER LANG
New York • San Francisco • Bern • Baltimore
Frankfurt am Main • Berlin • Wien • Paris

Library of Congress Cataloging-in-Publication Data

Muoneke, Romanus Okey.
 Art, rebellion and redemption: a reading of the novels of Chinua Achebe
/ Romanus Okey Muoneke.
  p.   cm. — (American university studies. Series XVIII,
African literature; vol. 5)
 Includes bibliographical references.
  1. Achebe, Chinua—Criticism and interpretation. 2. Redemption in
literature. 3. Nigeria in literature. I. Title. II. Series.
PR9387.9.A3Z835 1994   823—dc20   92-43155
ISBN 0-8204-2049-2   CIP
ISSN 0742-1923

Die Deutsche Bibliothek-CIP-Einheitsaufnahme

Muoneke, Romanus Okey:
Art, rebellion and redemption: a reading of the novels of Chinua Achebe /
Romanus Okey Muoneke. - New York; Berlin; Bern; Frankfurt/M.; Paris;
Wien: Lang, 1994
 (American university studies: Ser. 18, African literature; Vol. 5)
 ISBN 0-8204-2049-2
NE: American university studies / 18

The paper in this book meets the guidelines for permanence and durability of
the Committee on Production Guidelines for Book Longevity of the
Council on Library Resources.

© Peter Lang Publishing, Inc., New York 1994

Printed in the United States of America.

To my extended family
and my mentors
Robert Wren and Michel de Verteuil.

C ONTENTS

ACKNOWLEDGEMENTS

A simple thought about the redemptive role of the writer excited my interest in 1989, and after undergoing a series of transformations, has attained the present form of a book. Through the long and elaborate process of this transformation, it became clear to me that writing a book is truly a collaborative effort. I owe an immense debt of gratitude to various people who, by way of advice, direction, and other forms of support, made it possible for this book to become a reality.

I am greatly indebted to Peter Gingiss whose timely intervention saved this work from going under during its stormy days. My special thanks to Irving Rothman for his exceptionally valuable corrections and suggestions. Through his eyes I learned to see the English language in its variety and conciseness. I have nothing but deep gratitude for my friends at the University of Houston—Anthony Collins, Lois Zamora, Elizabeth Brown–Guillory, Terrell Dixon, Lorrain Stock, Roberta Weldon, Jim Pipkin, Bill Wright, and a host of others whose support was most invaluable.

This book was completed during my 1992 Summer program as a Minority Faculty Fellow at Purdue University, and I wish to offer my thanks to the director of the program, Clara Bell, as well as the chair of English Department, Margaret Rowe, for their generous and special assistance. At Purdue, I worked closely with Professor Shaun Hughes, a very admirable character who was exceptionally generous with his books, his time, and his profound ideas. His interest and personal commitment to getting this book completed in a record time deserves special acknowledgment. It is also thanks to him that my interest in African and Postcolonial literatures has redoubled.

I am very grateful to Professor Emmanuel Obiechina for willingly sharing his profound thoughts, and for keeping me dead on track. I cannot fail to mention the moral support I received from the Rt. Rev. A. K. Obiefuna, something I needed all along.

x

Most importantly, this work depended heavily on the love and encouragement provided me by Terry Brinkman. He was my pillar of support through all my years of study in Houston. I owe him much gratitude for his intellectual and material contributions to this book.

To several others whose support made the load lighter, my simple but sincere thanks.

Art, Rebellion
and Redemption

Introduction

The creative writer, sometimes simply known as the poet, plays an impressive role in society. This study examines the fundamental question about the nature and function of the writer in society; in other words, our purpose is to explore the relationship between writers and their society, for knowledge of this relationship makes for a better understanding of literature. Our motive in venturing into this research is pragmatic: recent fiction out of Africa and many developing countries grapples with socio–political problems that currently plague third world countries. Our perspective is that this phenomenon, though not historically unique, yet in view of the African literary experience (which is relatively new), merits an investigation or an appraisal of the writer's role and involvement in society.

Africa is a continent torn apart by the aftermath of colonialism. Though rich in natural resources, Africa has remained insolvent even after independence. Devastated by internal wars, ravished by greedy and corrupt politicians, shamed by her people's inability to manage their own affairs, and recently subjected to the pains of fascist repression from political and military adventurers, the continent is left to deal with the disastrous effects of hunger, disease, malnutrition, and general unrest. Africa's humiliation is the subject of David Diop's poem "Africa":

> Africa tell me Africa
> Is this your back that is bent
> This back that breaks under the weight of humiliation
> This back trembling with red scars
> And saying yes to the whip under the midday sun.

(Quoted *Anthills of the Savannah* 123)

The corpus of literature emanating from Africa addresses itself to these problems. Most African writers see as their duty the need to concentrate on the social, economic, and political problems of their countries, and thereby precipitate a controversy regarding the role of the writer in society. Practically every major African writer is concerned about society: Ngũgĩ wa Thiong'o's novels are preoccupied with colonial and neo–colonial injustices; Athol Fugard deals with the woes of apartheid; Okot p'Bitek revolts against the "rape" of the African culture; Achebe and Soyinka contend with colonialism, corruption, and the problem of leadership in their country. African writers, by their example, are making an assertive statement that the writer is duty bound to serve his society.

The story is the same in other parts of the world characterized as third world countries, as well as in the politically destabilized countries of Europe. In these countries, writers maintain that they have an obligation to address the problems of their society. For example, in Latin American countries, where the usual means of public discussion (mass media) are silenced by the forces of oppression, literature becomes the only mirror of the people's sufferings and offers a genuine description of their problems. In "Social Commitment and the Latin American Writer," Llosa comments on the writer's responsibility in Latin America:

> In Peru, in Bolivia, in Nicaragua, . . . to be a writer means at the same time, to assume a social responsibility: at the same time that you develop a personal literary work, you should serve, through your writing but also through your actions, as an active participant in the solution of the economic, political and cultural problems of your society. There is no way to escape this obligation. If you tried to do so, if you were to isolate yourself and concentrate exclusively on your own work, you would be severely censured and considered, in the best of cases, irresponsible and selfish, or at worst, even by omission, an accomplice to all the evils—illiteracy, misery, exploitation, injustice, prejudice—of your country and against which you have refused to fight (129).

Llosa's statement is applicable to many countries. Controversial as it might be, for there are opposing views which we shall deal with later in our discussion, it nevertheless confirms a position we shall argue—that writers have an efficacious role to play in their community. In more stable and advanced societies, such as Western Europe and North America, writers assume a personal responsibility oriented toward the cultural enrichment of their society; in less stable countries, writers assume a social responsibility. Hence, in examining the role of the writer in society, we shall argue that the writer has a redemptive role to play which will often involve some manifestation of rebellion. Let us now examine these two words, "redemption" and "rebellion."

The word "redemption" is derived from the Latin word "redemptio," which means buying back, delivering or liberating by payment of a price or through a ransom (*New Catholic Encyclopedia*, 12: 136). This is the sense in which the word is used in religious contexts. Christians, for example, believe that Christ redeemed the world through the sacrifice of the cross, that is, by paying with his blood. In theology, the word redemption becomes synonymous with "salvation," "atonement," "forgiveness," and "justification."

The biblical usage has exceptions to the rule. In the Hebrew Scriptures, for example, redemption between men invariably involves either payment of a ransom or substitution of some quantity for something else, such as the sacrificial goat of the Temple; but when redemption is used in relation to God, it is only employed metaphorically and no amount is seen to be exchanged. God delivers but not by receiving payment, for "to Jahweh belong the earth and all it contains" (Ps. 24: 1). An example is the deliverance of Israel from Egypt: "Remember that you were once a slave in Egypt and that Yahweh your God redeemed you" (Dt. 15:15). The poet is sometimes likened to God metaphorically as a creator (creating the world of fiction). If the analogy holds, he can be seen to redeem society. Through the vision he provides, he guides society to the right path, and thus delivers it from the slavery of confusion, tyranny, hatred, and anarchy into a haven of order. He performs the work of redemption when he delivers society from ignorance to truth, from darkness to light, from the ugly to the beautiful. The writer does not function in society as redeemer in the strict religious sense but in the metaphorical and general sense of substitution. We must point out, however, that whereas redemption through sacrifice of one's life is rare among writers, there are times when a writer is made to pay a great price by some authority for being outspoken on behalf of an oppressed society. The case of Wole Soyinka comes readily to mind. *The Man Died* is a record of his grisly experience at the hands of a totalitarian regime which he opposed during the Nigerian civil war. Apart from such personal experience, themes of religious redemption abound in literature. The theme of the scapegoat, for example, is found in the works of Achebe and Soyinka. In Soyinka's *The Strong Breed*, it is rooted in tradition and is critically examined in the context of a society in the throes of a cultural conflict. The protagonist, Emma, ritualistically redeems his community by paying with his life.

Redemption, in its non–religious sense means improvement or "an instance of bettering." To redeem is "to change from worse to better," to purify, reform; "to put back into proper condition," that is, to repair, to restore. It also means, "to make worthwhile, to give merit to," to retrieve, to deliver, to save (*Webster's Third New International Dictionary*). Redemption, therefore, conveys such meanings as "restoration," "reformation," "deliverance," and "salvation." It is mostly in this non–religious epistemology that the redemptive role of the writer is to be defined in this study. By means of their craft, writers aim to deliver or save their society from destruction or disintegration or failure. They aim to liberate their people from ignorance and illusion and from possible difficulties and dangers that threaten them.

Rebellion, paradoxically, is also redemption. In our context, rebellion is not limited to its political meaning of insubordination against a lawful government or authority. The meaning in this study is closer to Camus' definition in *The Rebel*. For Camus, rebellion is a refusal by an underdog to continue to conform; it is saying "no" to the oppressor's injustice and affirming of one's rights. Thus, rebellion occurs when an individual who feels oppressed thwarts the oppression and insists on specific, individual rights, when "he* confronts an order of things which oppresses him with the insistence of a kind of right not to be oppressed beyond the limit that he can tolerate" (13). The oppressor could be an individual, an institution, or the society. The rebel tolerates the oppression for a period of time and, suddenly, "does a complete turnabout" (14). The goal of rebellion being freedom, rebels are prepared to stake all they have, including their life, to achieve it. Rebellion can also arise as a protest against injustice perpetrated upon someone else, in the event of which the rebel demonstrates a feeling of identity with another individual or group. Protest, defiance, resistance, refusal to accept or accommodate what one perceives as wrong, unjust, or oppressive—these are types of rebellion. The ultimate goal, of course, is freedom which, in our definition, is another form of redemption.

Rebellion "is one of the sources of the art of fiction," Camus maintains (265), and "the novel is born at the same time as the spirit of rebellion and expresses, on the aesthetic plane, the same ambition" (259). This ambition is rectification, a demand of some kind of order in the midst of chaos, of "unity in the very heart of the ephemeral," (10) a redemption. Achebe is directly and indirectly carrying out a rebellion as a form of redemption. He rebels when he refuses to comply with the norms of the establishment, norms he perceives as negative to the progress of society. He rebels when he protests against inhuman and inhumane practices in society. He also rebels when he attempts to promote awareness of the existence of an intolerable condition with a view to expunging it from society. We find rebellion in his character portrayal, in his themes, in his caricature and satire, and even in his use of language.

Two questions still remain. What is society, and, does society expect redemption from the writer? By society, we mean the universal audience or mankind, to which every human being relates. Every artistic work must extol some value which appeals to the universal mind; that is to say, enduring literature must possess universality. Society also connotes the community to which writers belong by birth or adoption. This is the primary source of writers' images and language. Their writing will relate

---

* For the most part, pronouns in quotations will be left unchanged as they are written.

immediately to a people, a community, a country, a nation and only mediately to the universal community. When Shakespeare, for example, writes about Denmark or Rome, his language and images are drawn from, and intended for, the Elizabethan England, yet Shakespeare can make claims to be universal, for he can be seen as portraying truths that transcend spatio–temporal boundaries. Achebe writes about the Igbo, Nigeria, and Africa, yet one can also claim that universality is present in the themes he explores: oppression, corruption, failure, and hope. We are mindful of Achebe and his society as our central focus, but fully recognize that our subject has a much more general application. Finally, society refers to writers' special audiences, that is, their readers, particularly those who intellectually can relate to them.

The second question deals with society's expectation. The question will receive full treatment in our theoretical discussion in chapter one and in our analysis of *Anthills of the Savannah* in chapter three. We note, in the interim, that society, especially a troubled society, yearns for redemption from its artist. Llosa has observed that "the real or potential readers" of Latin American writers

> expect novels, poems and plays to counterbalance the policy of disguising and deforming reality which is current in the official culture and to keep alive the hope and spirit of change and revolt among the victims of that policy. In another sense this confers on the writer, as a citizen, a kind of moral and spiritual leadership, and he must try . . . to act according to this image of the role he is expected to play. ("Social Commitment and the Latin American Writer," 132.)

Llosa here postulates in another form our key proposition, namely, that the writers' duty to their society is summed up in rebellion and redemption. Achebe confirms and illustrates Llosa's position by making reference to the numerous complimentary letters he received from African readers who would often identify with the characters and situations explored in his novels. One young reader from Northern Nigeria wrote to him:

> I do not usually write to authors, no matter how interesting their work is, but I feel I must tell you how much I enjoyed your editions of *Things Fall Apart* and *No Longer at Ease*. I look forward to reading your new edition *Arrow of God*. Your novels serve as advice to us young. I trust that you will continue to produce as many of this type of book. With friendly greetings and best wishes. ("The Novelist as Teacher," *Morning Yet*, 68 [56].*)

Morning Yet on Creation Day is cited from the Anchor Press/Doubleday (hardcover) edition (1975) followed in brackets by page references to the Anchor Press/Doubleday (paperback) edition (1976).

This young writer seems to speak for millions who have high expectations of their writers. These read novels and poems and watch plays not only for the entertainment value to be derived, but also for the solutions of life's problems. More recently, Gabriel Okara referred to the exciting response he gets from children who cheer and applaud him at street corners in recognition of his contributions to children's stories ("Of Tortoise, Man and Language," 101).

We have deliberately chosen Chinua Achebe as our sample case for our close study of the writer's role. Achebe proves a paradigmatic choice because he has shown a zeal to discuss in conferences and journals the writer's social responsibilities. His novels address the historical, social, and political issues of his country. He hails from Nigeria, a developing country where the role of the artist and the growth of his community are closely linked. Achebe's works in this study shall be restricted to his novels (five) which are structurally related by one subject matter, the story of his people.

The topic and content of our study require a historical and thematic approach. We shall first establish the role of the writer and next demonstrate through analysis how Achebe fulfills this role in his novels. Although the theme of rebellion and redemption sums up the writer's role, we still need an elaboration and improved definition of his role in order to understand the identity and involvement of writers in society and to comprehend Achebe's definitive contributions to society through his novels.

The work is divided into two major parts—theoretical and analytical—which are subdivided into three chapters and a conclusion. Part One consists of chapter one which has two major sections: (a) a theoretical discussion of the writer's identity and role in society and (b) a study of theoretical issues involving literature and commitment. The first section serves a double purpose: it briefly provides an overview (thematically presented) of our perception of the duties of the writer. It sums up some of the critical views frequently held about the nature and role of the writer. The section also serves as a critical backdrop for examining Achebe's role in his works. Achebe is not included, or shall we say, not made visible in our discussion in this section because he will receive full attention in the section immediately following, which deals with the African scene.

Section two of chapter one, "Literature and Commitment" looks first at the African writer's role and commitment. This section concentrates on theoretical issues concerning the role of the writer in society, mostly seen from the African perspective. From a wide angle of theories, the discussion then shifts to the narrower focus of Achebe's views on his role and commitment as a writer. Chapter one therefore gives a clear overall picture of the redemptive role of the writer from several perspectives; the next step is to show how Achebe accomplishes redemption in his novels.

Part two looks at the novels of Achebe. Chapter two deals with rebellion, and after a general historical introduction, presents Achebe's rebellion against colonialism, Negritude, corrupt politics, and dictatorship. The inclusion of Negritude requires a brief explanation. Achebe's simple style and relatively transparent plots belie the complexity of his narrative art. His novels are written in plain style in which are woven subtleties, nuances, and hidden significations which we are bound to overlook unless we read between and beneath the lines. His treatment of Negritude is typical of his subtlety. The word "Negritude" appears but once in his novels. It is casually mentioned in *Anthills of the Savannah* in Mad Medico's sarcastic statement: "This is negritude country, not Devonshire" (52). Yet, an informed reader can discern Achebe's undeclared war against Negritude, his subterranean attack on the movement in *Things Fall Apart* which was written in the heyday of the movement. It is our contention that in *Things Fall Apart,* Achebe is at once rebelling against two ideologically opposed systems that have distorted the African image—colonialism and Negritude; the one has denigrated it, the other has romanticized it. Both are attitudes of equal falsity; hence, Achebe opposes them. His rebellion against Negritude is perhaps less explosive but no less destructive; hence, both rebellions merit our consideration.

Chapter three concentrates on the theme of redemption. Here we examine several suggestions and options that are thrown open to Achebe's society as possible means of redemption in his work. This chapter analyzes each of Achebe's five novels as a means of exploring this theme in detail. The Conclusion acts as a final chapter which summarizes the central arguments and enforces the theme of optimism and hope in Achebe's novels.

PART ONE

THEORETICAL DISCUSSION

CHAPTER ONE

THE ARTIST AND SOCIETY

THE WRITER'S IDENTITY AND ROLE IN SOCIETY

Writers are uniquely prominent in society, for, among other reasons they have the capacity to offer unique perspectives. That is, they are capable of rendering order, or, in reordering events in chaos, to give a semblance of understanding. They possess the capacity to express intense feelings more than ordinary people, and their affections, sympathy, and passions run deeper than we are normally accustomed to expecting. Their extraordinary sensibility distinguishes them from the general population, and in addition to this, they possess some divinity for which they are generally revered.

The belief in poetic inspiration is as old as poetry itself. Behind every writer or poet, some *Agwu* (Achebe), some "divine furor" (Plato), some "force of a divine breath" (Sidney), is at work. The prophetic role of the poet has always been recognized and discussed, for which the poet was regarded as "vates," which means, diviner, foreseer, or prophet (Sidney, 21). In Achebe's terms, writers, with their tongues dipped "in the brew of prophecy," "can sit under [their] thatch and see the moon hanging in the sky outside" (*Anthills*, 115). These seers see things not partially but wholly; they see the divinity beneath the visible world; hence, Emerson calls this "a high kind of seeing" which "reattaches things to nature and the whole," a noetic or visionary imagination which sees connections, analogies, correspondences, where prosaic vision sees only disorder, distortions, differences, and multiplicity. This prophetic imaginative seeing "finds meaning in apparent meaninglessness of ordinary experience" (Waggoner, 168). Thus, for Wordsworth, the poet–seer sees in a new way, and his special vocation is "to liberate the vision of his readers [and of society at large] from bondage of physical eye, habitual categories, social custom, and caste prejudice, so that they may see the world he has come to see" (Abrams, *Mirror and the Lamp*, 406–07). Hence, the writer is someone capable of "seeing through appearances into the realities of life . . . [someone] with the inner eye, with the probing eye, with the all–knowing eye, who sees it all" (Obiechina, "The Writer and his Commitment," 2–3). So equipped, writers are therefore qualified to perform a redemptive role for society, a role which requires proper sensibility and insight into the realities of life.

There are several other characteristics that define the writer's redemptive role. Like Christopher Okigbo's priest of Idoto, artists are "the ambassador[s] of the gods to men" (Lowell, "The Function of the Poet," 4) revealing the Eleusianian or divine mysteries to the world, and dispensing God's wisdom in such form as their age requires. The true artist is "the light of the world, the world's Priest :—guiding it, like a sacred Pillar of Fire, in its dark pilgrimage through the waste of Time" (Carlyle, *Lecture V,* 157).

Writers are also bards, which makes their role even more community oriented. Sometimes in the history of the Greeks, the Romans and, indeed, in some European and certainly African nations, poets featured in public gatherings and feasts where they performed as bards or griots. Through songs and epic recitals they told the history and exploits of their people; they praised national heroes, and in the words of the old man in Achebe's *Anthills of the Savannah,* they "take over and recount the [national] story" after the battle is over (113), thus keeping "redemptive" memory alive and active.

The relationship between artist and divinity has given rise to the notion that the poet is a creator, a notion that, in the western tradition, originated from the Greeks, with its correspondence in African tradition. The Latin word *poeta* is related to the Greek *poietes* which literally means "a maker." The verb *poieo* means "to make, to create, to compose." The poet, like God, is a maker, a creator, but the poet is a finite maker whose power is contingent on the Infinite Maker. Thus, the *mbari* artists, though a community of creators, are mere partakers in the creative enterprise initiated and presided over by Ana, the Earth goddess, who in Igbo pantheon functions as the "fountain of creativity" (Achebe, "African Literature as Restoration of Celebration," 1–2). Though designated as apprenticed co–creators (by no means mechanical robots of the goddess), these artists aim to create things anew, to represent reality or truth with a message for the good of the society. They thus become interpreters and dispensers of God's everlasting wisdom or truth, explaining the nuances and complexities of life in society, which is why a good source of knowledge about values and activities of any society is its literature where writers deal with individuals, their day–to–day experiences, their lives, hates, and hazardous fortunes.

In concentrating on the lives of individuals, writers become moral legislators, the judges and critics of their society. Being a moral legislator is a major role for writers who, as a result of their insight into reality, are capable of discerning the good from the bad, the beautiful from the ugly, the true from the false. Artists, both modern and ancient, profess the essentially moral purpose of their art. According to Schiller, art (poetry) ennobles character, and the artist gives people art to imitate and to ennoble their character; hence, art transforms mankind from natural state to moral state. The role of the artist therefore is to shape mankind, liberate people from animal state and elevate them to a moral state (Simons, 20). The writers' prophetic and moral role, to a large extent, explains the superlative degree of reverence accorded them in society. According to Ngũgĩ wa Thiong'o in an interview with Wilkinson:

> the singer and the poet were very highly respected in Gikuyu society and they were seen as prophets, their words were listened to very, very keenly and what they had to say was important. In other words people took notice of what they had to say about so many problems in the land, about the morality of the different people or about the good life as opposed to the bad life . . . So the singer, the poet, the man of words was often seen as a prophet (130).

We recall Shelley's famous saying that poets are the "unacknowledged legislators of the world" (Preface to "Prometheus Unbound," 134). By this he means that poets are institutors of laws in society, laws of order and laws of moral behavior. Through art, the poet creates order out of chaos. "He not only beholds intensely the present as it is," he also "discovers those laws according to which present things ought to be ordered" (482–83). This is a very important source of authority for the redemptive role the writer plays in society. The writer knows how life ought to be, thanks to the writer's insight into truth, and how society, especially when fractured, should be restored, and those needed values efficacious to any particular time.

This is not to argue that all poets aspire honorably to this noble and sacred office. Swinburne underscores the point in distinguishing between the supreme poets and the giant poets, or the higher order and the lower order of poets. Both groups are capable of achieving the perfection of human reason, but the supreme poets excel by soaring beyond human reason to attain spiritual harmony with the universal essence by which they express spiritual passion in their poetry (Connolly, 37–38). A young Nigerian writer, Odia Ofeimun who published a collection of poems entitled, *The Poet Lied*, has strongly defended in an interview with Wilkinson his position that some writers betray their role as society's moral guide by their distortion of truth. "I must confess I am quite married to this Shelleyan position that writers are actually unacknowledged legislators in a lot of ways . . . ," he says. However, believing that J. P. Clark had, for personal reasons, distorted historical facts in his civil war poems, *Casualties*, Ofeimun condemns writers who "allow political propaganda to distort experience" (67–68). Although we are critically aware of the operations of charlatans, propagandists, bigots, and all kinds of pseudo–artists, as well as the pollution or corruption of art for political or religious reasons, nevertheless, our study is strictly concerned with the higher order of poets whom, for want of better description, we may call "true poets."

By virtue of their position as the moral legislators in society, poets are the critics and watchdogs of society. Part of their duty is "to take sides against injustices" and to denounce "violations of formal and personal liberties or material oppression or both" (Sartre, "What is Literature?" 229). In criticizing and judging, their aim is not to destroy but to improve society : "Sometimes also this sensitive creature [the writer] criticizes [society's] way of life, takes it to pieces, shakes it up and down or tears it apart, in order to test its consistency and to vitalize it, for the sake of those who subsist within it" (Obiechina, "The Writer and His Commitment" 2). Shelley's insistence is worth remembering at all times, namely, that the true poets must be critics of their age, and that being also prophets, they cannot expect honor and approbation from their society (Lucas, 13).

As persons of inspiration and heightened sensibilities, as critics and judges of society, and as people living in the world of crumbling values and abuses, writers are often driven to promote reform and revolution. This propensity to reform or change a world falling apart often compels writers to resort to rebellion (in the sense we have earlier discussed the concept). The writer must remind the people of their power to change circumstances for the better, that is, of their power to challenge and transform their oppression. The writer should seek out the people in their milieu and "examine their servitude with them" and "teach them both that they are victims and that they are responsible for everything, that they are at once the oppressed, the oppressors, and the accomplices of their own oppressors" (Sartre, "What is Literature?" 234). Writers are therefore prophets of social change. They play a significant role when their exposure leads the reader to awareness and possible action. It is no wonder then that writers are often at the vanguard of social revolutions, as was the case during the French and Russian revolutions, and more recently in Africa, during the Biafran struggle when Okigbo, Achebe, Soyinka, and Okara played very significant roles.

Eagerness for change relates to another role: the quest for freedom. Artists seek freedom for themselves and for others. As Sartre points out:

> Thus, whether he is an essayist, a pamphleteer, a satirist, or a novelist, whether he speaks only of individual passions or whether he attacks the social order, the writer, a free man addressing free men, has only one subject—freedom (Sartre, "What is Literature?" 68).

The writer's quest for freedom has its psychological and political ramifications. In Romantic terms the writer helps to liberate our vision from the tyranny of distortion coming from the external world or resulting from internal division of the self. Such freedom, in the opinion of Schiller, makes us "complete" and enables us to transcend necessity, for freedom is to act more than necessity dictates (Simons, 24). Psychologically, therefore, the writer helps us achieve freedom, and consequently restores to "broken worlds" and broken selves, unity, order, and beauty.

The writers' commitment to political freedom is a role they are constantly called upon to play in society. Sartre maintains that the duty of the writer is to take sides with the oppressed against the oppressor; indeed, writers should ally themselves with the members of the working class. Writers should create awareness in their readers by which they will be moved to act in the interest of freedom. This sounds Marxist and leftist, yet to a certain degree, it truly defines the position taken by many African writers, including Achebe, Ngũgĩ wa Thiong'o, Soyinka, La Guma, Serote, as well as Nwapa, Emecheta, Dangarembga, and, indeed, practically all the women writers in the continent. In "The Writer in a Changing Society," Ngũgĩ wa Thiong'o articulates the position of the African writer thus :

> I believe that African intellectuals must align themselves with the struggle of the African masses for a meaningful national ideal. For we must strive for a form of social organization that will free the manacled spirit and energy of our people so we can build a new country, and sing a new song. Perhaps, in a small way, the African writer can help in articulating the feelings behind this struggle (50).

Writers also play a Promethean role in society. The mythical Prometheus provided fire to man and laid the foundation for man's progress and transformation. The writer enlightens and illuminates society in providing the "fire" of vision by which society is ordered. Without such vision, observes George Awoonor–Williams, social life would become "sterile" and a "very futile exercise" ("From the Discussion" 31). The Pro–methean role of writers extends beyond enlightenment : sometimes, by virtue of their commitment to society, they are made to suffer. Just as Prometheus was chained to a rock and punished by Zeus, so have many writers been incarcerated by authorities for their courage to speak out against injustice. Wole Soyinka and Ngũgĩ wa Thiong'o's prison experiences speak to the point. Suffering is an inevitable messianic attribute in writers. Lucas explains that "the poet must suffer . . .because it is an essential part of his divine mission, and the one way by which he can become a worker and a builder for his fellow men" (36). Concerning the ultimate value and inevitability of this victimization, Obiechina writes: "He should be a man who is found in the thick of combat, who, when the occasion demands it, makes personal sacrifices, and in extremity, pays with the most precious thing he has to sustain the integrity of his calling" ("The Writer and his Commitment," 3). In *Anthills of the Savannah*, Achebe portrays a typical Promethean figure in the character of Ikem, a character who seeks to enlighten society and in the process is made to sacrifice his dear life. Details of Ikem's redemptive role will be discussed in the penultimate chapter.

Redemption therefore ultimately embodies the various roles the artist plays in society, some of which we have briefly discussed. The writers' prophetic role, their quest for freedom, their sacrifices, their unique perception, etc, are all forms of redemption. We shall now proceed to discuss how the African writer defines this redemptive role in terms of commitment.

LITERATURE AND COMMITMENT:

THE AFRICAN WRITER'S ROLE AND COMMITMENT

The artist's urge to make a commitment is a twentieth–century phenomenon, but in actual fact committed literature or "literature engage" has existed all through the ages. Writers are committed when they consciously use their art to explore or reveal the world they know. As Sartre, the chief exponent of the theory, points out what distinguishes the committed from the others is not just that they are involved in the world—(they are, and others are too) for to write is to reveal some aspect of the world—the difference is that such individuals are aware of their involvement. Such a committed writer "tries to achieve the most lucid and the most complete consciousness of being embarked, that is, when he causes the commitment of immediate spontaneity to advance, for himself and others, to the reflective" ("What is Literature?" 77). The issue of commitment in literature is however very controversial and has been widely misunderstood and misinterpreted. Some have described it as Leftist, some have termed it propaganda literature. The basic intention remains, and, as defined by Chinweizu *et al.*, artistic commitment is "a matter of perceiving social realities and of making those perceptions available in works of art in order to help promote understanding and preservation of, or change in, the society's values and norms" (253). For writers therefore the call to commitment is a call to bear the full burden of social responsibility, indeed, a call to redemption.

Chinweizu *et al.* have defined the African writer's role and commitment thus:

> the function of the artist in Africa, in keeping with our traditions and needs, demands that the writer, as a public voice, assume a responsibility to reflect public concerns in his writings, and not preoccupy himself with his puny ego. Because in Africa we recognize that art is in the public domain, a sense of social commitment is mandatory upon the artist. That commitment demands that the writer pay attention to his craft . . . it also demands that his theme be germane to the concerns of his community (252).

Its dogmatic overtone notwithstanding, this view is fairly representative of the African opinion. African writers need to be, and often are, committed to the social and political realities of their society. The question really is not whether they should be committed in their writing, as that is generally expected of them; the question is the extent of their commitment; that is, whether or not they should be personally committed to the social and political issues of their time—what is now banteringly referred to in African writers' circle as "gun–running" and "holding up radio stations," terms derived from real incidents involving African writers. A middle–of–the–road answer sometimes given is that writers, as citizens of their country, like any other individual, reserve the right to choose between personal commitment and indifference.

This answer fails to take into account the special position and role of the writer in society. Writers are not "any other citizen," but special human beings (thanks to their unique endowment) called to a special role in society. This special role is also prophetic and, therefore, even by analogy, public. One of the ways of fulfilling this public role is by writing. Creative or artistic writing is only one of the many forms writers may use to articulate their redemptive impulse. Wole Soyinka, for example, has employed many forms to address the burning issues of his time: writing, film directing, theatre productions, public speeches, and civic functions (he was once a special marshal in the Oyo State Road Safety Corps). By using more than one form, the writer obviously reaches more audiences. Sartre in "What is Literature?" argues that the writer must go beyond the use of the pen in addressing free men on the one and only subject of freedom, for "[a] day comes when the pen is forced to stop, and the writer must then take up arms" (69). So, when for one reason or another words fail, the writer's redemptive role for society does not end. The poetry of words then yields to the poetry of action (Sartre's "arms") both of which originate from one source. A priest's role and commitment in society is not limited to the pulpit or the altar but has to be shown in many other ways. In like manner, the writer's role is not restricted to writing only, he should use other ways available to him to move society. The relevance and morality of those other ways however remain a different question.

African writers see themselves as continuing the traditional role of their predecessor, the griot or the traditional story–teller. Griots were court artists who functioned as a "necessary accessory" to the ruler. They were people of great eloquence, the transmitters of oral history and the mentors and teachers to the younger generations. As national poets and the traditional historians, griots used their art to celebrate the deeds and exploits of rulers and national heroes. As would be expected, they also condemned, even if in subtle terms, the evils prevalent in society. It is significant that traditional African artists defined their role within the society. They were not solitary artists, not "exiles," not privatists whose artistic goal was to please themselves. They were involved and committed in the affairs of the community whose past and present they had knowledge of, and whose future they helped to shape through their art. In *The Writer Written*, Durix testifies:

> Certainly in Africa, the idea that the artist strives first and foremost to-
> wards personal integrity runs against every tradition. Like the political
> leader who must find legitimacy among his people, the artist has to jus-
> tify his presence by his positive role in the service of the community
> (14–15).

In traditional African society, therefore, griots defined their roles in the service of the community.

The rapid transition to modernity in Africa has created new situations and new challenges for the writer. So has the demand for the writer's involvement in the affairs of the community increased. Addressing a convention of Nigerian authors at Nsukka on June 27, 1981, the Federal Minister of Social Development, Youth, Sports, and Culture, P.C. Amadike assumed the writers' commitment to their society:

> When [the artist] paints, or writes, his purpose is to externalize his sub-
> conscious and share his philosophy and sensibility with others . . . it is
> wrong for the artist to remain indifferent to events around him . . . The
> artist's responsibility is to make inputs of a positive nature for influenc-
> ing government . . . indifference by the artist to happenings around him
> may save his neck but it may result in the approval of misdirection
> through acquiescence. (*Okike*, 20 [1981]: 4–5).

The obligation devolves upon the writer to serve society. African writers are them-selves aware of their responsibility; they know the literature they create must concern itself with the realities of Africa. To illustrate, we shall turn our attention to writers who spoke at the African–Scandinavian Writers' Conference held in Stockholm in February 1967.

Presenting the South African picture where oppression is sanctioned under the anomalous laws of apartheid, Alex La Guma asserts that the South African writers must reckon with the existence of so much inhumanity around them and must be pre-pared to do all in their power to achieve liberation, even if it entails "run[ning] guns and . . . hold[ing] up radio stations" ("From the Discussion" 22). Ngũgĩ Wa Thiong'o, a socialist, insists that writers must be directly involved in social reconstruction in Africa, in order to contend for the rights of the suffering masses. He accuses African writers and intellectuals of belonging to the bourgeois class. They wield power and are not concerned for the eighty percent of the people living below poverty level:

> So my feeling is that, so long as we have not changed the social structure
> in Africa so that at least 80% of the people can live above the bread–line
> standard and indeed so that those 80% of the people can also participate

in the work of social and economic reconstruction, so long shall we continue to have impotent intellectuals and writers ("From the Discussion"
26).

Dan Jacobson sees the role of the writer in Africa as one in which politics will be "a
constant factor," as happened in Russia in the nineteenth century ("From the Discussion 29). George Awoonor–Williams stresses the need for the writer to provide the
right vision by which society is to be guided through the realities of the twentieth
century in which Africa confronts new issues—ballot–box, parliament, political parties, etc. ("From the Discussion" 32). For Dennis Brutus, the exiled South African
poet, the writer must be committed:

> . . . whether we are Finns or Swedes or Norwegians or whether we come
> from any part of Africa, we are all committed, at least to one value, the
> assertion of human value, of human dignity, and that is why we have a
> special function when we see human dignity betrayed. When we see hu-
> manity being mutilated, we have a function as human beings to stand up
> against these things. . . . No matter how we choose our form . . . at the
> heart of the form must lie the same statement, and that is the assertion of
> human value ("From the Discussion" 34).

The "form" in question is the shape of an activist writer's response to the betrayal
of human dignity. It is not necessarily limited to the literary "form"; it could extend to
"running guns and holding up radio stations," which also comes from the writer's
instinctive desire for freedom. Eldred Jones also believes that the African writer cannot but be committed: "The writer today in Africa must see around him bad politics,
bad religion, the misleading of ordinary people, and he is bound to write about all this
if he writes about his environment" ("From the Discussion" 34–35). And these writers are not unaware of the harsh consequences of being committed: ". . . the role of the
writer to–day is in fact just offering himself for one generation a willing victim to
those forces which are subversive of human dignity and morality" ("From the Discussion" 35). The need to identify with the community, especially the masses and the
oppressed, and the need to join in the struggle for liberty, justice, peace, and progress
is often profound. There is no doubt therefore that most African writers are keenly
aware of their redemptive role in society.

Before we go into a detailed discussion of Achebe's novels, we shall take a quick
look at Soyinka's position on the role of the writer. A key figure in African literature,
his views are relevant to our study. Soyinka is always conscious of the messianic role
of the African writer. An ardent believer in the social function of literature, his first

attempts at play writing were directed toward the racial problems in South Africa. Those early attempts were not successful mainly because he was "experiencing the situation vicariously" ("Introduction," *Six Plays*, xii). Soon he would learn that the enemy he sought to combat in distant South Africa was "within," strongly entrenched in his own country, as indeed is the case all over the continent of Africa. Soyinka expects African writers to draw from their own experience and plumb the depths of the human condition. In examining the human condition, the writer has the duty to point out the prevalent tragedy in human life, using the rich resources of art and literature. Life is not all pessimistic; there are moments of victory and times of celebration, and these must also be reflected in the writer's work. There are those in society who confront reality headlong and are able to override the negative side of life. As Soyinka puts it in his introduction to the *Six Plays*, such people "arise from the total fragmentation of the psyche, the annihilation of even their ego, and yet succeed in piecing them together . . . to emerge and enrich us by that example" (xvii–xviii). Such heroes are worthy of celebration in literature as models of hope for the suffering humanity. This heroic acceptance of responsibility—in other words, commitment—is also demanded of writers, in order for them truly to experience life's tension in their work and express it appropriately for the benefit of society. Most of Soyinka's thought on the role of the writer is contained in his essay "The Writer in a Modern African State" which merits further study.

In this essay, Soyinka examines the sad situation of the African writer in the politically fast evolving continent. African writers have not lived up to expectation and consequently there has been a discrepancy between literary concerns and existing political reality in African states. The political status of Africa has radically changed from colonialism to independence. During the struggle for independence, the African writer joined forces with the politician to oppose colonialism. At the wake of victory, these writers neglected their role of reflecting on reality and allowed themselves to be made "the very prop of the state machinery" ("The Writer" 15). As part of the elite enjoying the status of privilege they denied their very souls as writers. The struggle against colonialism had kept them in direct contact with reality for which they were able to produce poetry of insight, but after independence, they became isolated by their very position in society, lost touch with reality, and consequently began to misread their own personal predicaments for those of their society. Furthermore, especially in reference to the Negritude movement, they endeavored to impose on society an identity it never lacked. They began to produce a literature of "cultural definitions" (17) and "metaphysical abstractions" (18). The curiosity and misguided admiration that accompanied the new literature did not however hide the fact that the average writer in the first few years of independence "was the most celebrated skin of inconsequence to obscure the true flesh of the African dilemma" (17).

A stage arrived, late as it did, when writers woke from their lethargic "opium dream of metaphysical abstractions" only to discover that the politicians had taken advantage of the writers' isolation from reality to consolidate their own positions of power in politics (18). Meanwhile the writers' contentment to seek cover–up solutions in the splendors of the past, "to turn [their] eye backwards in time and prospect in archaic fields for forgotten gems which would dazzle and distract the present" (17), prevented their correct search inwards and a thorough examination of the present for the real solution to society's problems. We note that Soyinka does not spare words in pointing out the dangers of over–fascination with the past. His attack on Negritude as a "camouflage" (20) and an "evasion of the inward eye" (escapism) (21), is consistent with his generally negative attitude toward the movement, details of which we shall see in the next chapter. When however writers attempted to "express new wisdoms" (18), to challenge the politician, they were faced with the consequences of the politician's anger: exile and incarceration, as was the case with Soyinka himself. In reaction, some writers (for example, Christopher Okigbo) took to violent resistance, and others to "gun–running and . . . holding up radio stations" (18). Often they were compelled by disaster, rather than foresight, to come to grips with reality. Soyinka finally appeals to African writers to play their role in society:

> When the writer in his own society can no longer function as conscience, he must recognize that his choice lies between denying himself totally or withdrawing to the position of chronicler and post–mortem surgeon. . . . The artist has always functioned in African society as the record of the mores and experience of his society *and* as the voice of vision of his own time. It is time for him to respond to this essence of himself ("The Writer 21).

Soyinka blames African writers for neglecting their duty to society, for selling their birthright for a mess of elitist comfort, for their petty concern with aesthetic problems, especially with the African personality, and for their total disregard of the burning political issues of the day. He calls upon them to confront these issues and to reassume their role as the conscience of society and the arbiter of vision, and this is a call for writers to play their redemptive roles.

There are other African authors who define the writer's role from a totally different perspective; for example, those who insist that art should steer clear of politics and social activities. John Nagenda, Lewis Nkosi, J.P. Clark, Dan Izevbaye and Ali Mazrui belong to this group. John Nagenda, believing that "ultimately we do not change anything" ("'From the Discusssion' to Soyinka 'The Writer'" 24) by involvement or commitment and that "our only responsibility is to ourselves"("'From the Discussion' to Nkosi 'Individualism'" 54), recommends that writers must stick to "the sensuous feel of the written word" ("'From the Discusssion' to Soyinka 'The Writer'" 25). Exhibiting what we might call an extreme purist position, Nagenda makes the following statement which would prove an anathema to many on the opposing side:

> I want to suggest that dealing with the individual in society is the primary consideration; as far as I am concerned my part in society is not necessarily to make the society better than I found it . . . but essentially . . . to live my life in this world before I die . . . And if it came to a point at which all the rest of the world was being murdered and I could escape to a little cave and still manage to find a private 'explosion,' I would do that, and to hell with the rest of the world! ("'From the Discussion' to Nkosi 'Individualism'" 54).

The sincerity of those who firmly hold this opinion and yet strive to publish their works is questionable. Lewis Nkosi, another purist, is not on such extreme edge, but holds that artists are citizens of "a special kind of republic, the republic of letters" ("Individualism" 48) and therefore their commitment should be "a commitment to craft" ("'From the Discusssion' to Soyinka 'The Writer'" 27). Such total commitment is, it seems, hard to imagine, for, as Eldred Jones has observed, even Jane Austen, who wrote as if unaware of the Napoleonic wars that raged during her time, was concerned with the human foibles of society and criticized pride and snobbishness("'From the Discusssion' to Soyinka 'The Writer'" 34).

Ali Marzui is the one African writer who strongly argues this purist position in a book. In his novel *The Trial of Christopher Okigbo*, now turned into a play by Opiyo Munna and retaining the same title, Marzui creates a scenario in which Christopher Okigbo, the Igbo poet who died in the battle field fighting for Biafra, is placed on trial and accused, among other charges, of having "descended from the mountain of human vision to the swamp of tribal warfare" (71). In the main, Marzui's position is a recommendation that art should not be committed to political and social ends. The artist should leave politics, economics, warfare, and other public affairs to those best suited to handle them. The aesthetic activity is the particular concern of the artist. The irony of *The Trial of Christopher Okigbo* is that the author undermines his own argument by his very act, for his novel, written as an historical narrative, is suffused with highly controversial political ideas. The author's religious and political beliefs obviously interfered with his handling of history. No true purist could have written *The Trial of Christopher Okigbo*, for it is a case of an artist's commitment to politics. The difference between Okigbo and Marzui is negligible: both are politically involved but fight with different weapons.

The foregoing presentation of the purist's view is relevant to our discussion because we need to be aware of the principal objection that could challenge the foundation of our argument, which is, that writers, by virtue of their calling, are at the service of society, and the kind of service they render is redemptive. The view that art should exist for its own sake and that the writer should have no social responsibilities seems misguided in view of the fact that literature in itself is a social institution. As Glicksberg observes, it may be personal in its origin, yet "it represents the socialized working out of some personal problem" (*Literature and Society*, 3). It "transforms emotions seeking release into some socially meaningful pattern" (Ellison, 39). Glicksberg further comments:

> the writer as artist struggles to preserve his integrity; he must satisfy himself first in his work and in releasing his deepest powers of imagination create what is of urgent importance to himself; only then does he discover that by probing his own obsessions and embodying his private vision, however singular in expression or rebellious in content, he has spoken for others as well (1–2).

Literature, no matter how private its claims are, is a social preoccupation. Stephen Dedalus in Joyce's *A Portrait of the Artist as a Young Man,* struggling to resolve the conflict between the demands of society and his creative self, may suggest a contrary view in his famous statement:

> I will not serve that in which I no longer believe, whether it call itself my home, my fatherland, or my church: and I will try to express myself in some mode of life or art as freely as I can and as wholly as I can, using for my defense the only arms I allow myself to use, silence, exile and cunning (291).

The rebellious Stephen here utters the language of the purists—he will not serve society, will not concern himself with home, fatherland, and church; he will rather express himself. But this is not the whole truth about Stephen, for in the end, this "persona" of James Joyce goes into the world resolved to face "the reality of experience and to forge in the smithy of my soul the uncreated conscience of my race" (299). This final resolution is one geared toward commitment, and one can well argue that it is messianic.

The writer's role is therefore not defined in silence, exile, privatism or seclusion but in the service of society. Writers do not exist in a vacuum, nor do they draw their experience from nowhere. They are products of society on whom they largely depend for their literary sustenance. They write for the public, and often on matters concerning the public—the human condition—as Doris Lessing explains in her essay "The Small Personal Voice":

> The image of the pretty singer in the ivory tower has always seemed to me a dishonest one. Logically he should be content to sing to his image in the mirror. The act of getting a story or a novel published is an act of communication, an attempt to impose one's personality and beliefs on other people. If a writer accepts this responsibility, he must see himself . . . as an architect of the soul, and it is a phrase which none of the old nineteenth–century novelists would have shied away from.
>
> But if one is going to be an architect, one must have a vision to build towards, and that vision must spring from the nature of the world we live in (190).

It is true that writers sometimes treat a subject that is strictly private. For example, in their responses to nature, their material could be based solely on personal experiences. Wordsworth sees, for example, a cloud and his heart leaps for joy, Keats experiences stages of transformation in response to a bird's song, and Christopher Okigbo returns from exile as a "prodigal" to assume his new role, his new kind of poetry. In each of these instances, poets become both individuals and representatives of society (whose spokesman they are), which is why we can read their poems with empathy and enjoy them. Strictly speaking, therefore, there is no such thing as asocial literature, and as Glicksberg rightly observes, the so–called asocial literature, the literature of social criticism, and the literature of commitment all "shadow forth different versions of the life of man in society" (*Literature and Society*, 6).

ACHEBE ON THE WRITER'S ROLE AND COMMITMENT

In his essays and interviews Achebe ranges widely over a number of vital issues. One of his preferred subjects is the role of the creative writer in society. His theory on the writer's role and commitment can be summed up under the following propositions:

(a)   Art, including literature, is a communal celebration in Africa.
(b)   The African writer cannot but be committed, for there is no room for art for art's sake, given the African situation.
(c)   Writers, as individuals exceptionally gifted, carry with them so–cial responsibilities, among which is rendering vision and a sense of order to a non–perfect society.
(d)   The special role of the writer is to teach.

Achebe's theory of art is founded on the African belief in the indivisibility of art and society. The *mbari* ceremony found among the Owerri Igbo of Nigeria has been constantly used by Achebe as a point of departure to show that art functions as a communal celebration of life. As Achebe explains in "African Literature as Celebration," celebration does not simply mean a remembrance of blessings and happy events, it includes other experiences: "all significant encounters which man makes in his journey through life, especially new, unaccustomed and thus potentially threatening encounters" (52).

The *mbari* example demands a total involvement of the participating artists who work in holy seclusion with selected members of the community to produce art works that reflect the life of the entire community in its diversity—gods, men, women, animals, historic events (the coming of the white man, for example), the village scandal, etc.—all are represented in the final ensemble. What is interesting about *mbari* ceremony is that it is initiated by Ala,* the Earth goddess and patron of morality and creativity. When she calls for the ceremony of images, her priest assembles a selection of people from the community, and they work under the supervision of master artists and craftsmen. These artists and their aids represent the entire community, and in a sanctified vicinity they endeavor to reproduce the community's life experience. Since most of the hands involved in this creative process are not "artists" but a random choice of the goddess, it follows, according to Achebe, that:"*There is no rigid barrier between makers of culture and its consumers. Art belongs to all and is a 'function' of society*"

---

* *Ala, Ana, Ani* are the expression of the same concept in different Igbo dialects.

("Africa and Her Writers," *Morning Yet*, 34 [29]). African art, as represented in the *mbari* culture, is therefore not an individual affair but a "creative communal enterprise" in which the community functions both as the "beneficiary" and the "active partaker" of the experience (*Morning Yet*, 35 [30]).

Achebe has also pointed out that even the griot and the traditional storytellers operate within the matrix society. They are conscious performers for the society; that is, they are aware of their playing a definite role for their community—they are "the continuity of the generations," "the memory that is necessary" for the survival of the community (Moyers, 5). The modern African writer, Achebe maintains, is essentially continuing the role of the traditional artist: "He remains like the griot of Sundiata, a practitioner of the art of eloquence for the benefit of the people, present and future" ("The Uses of African Literature," 12).

The theory of the story as a vehicle for transforming the human consciousness is important in understanding Achebe's literary vocation. The story is for him an indispensable medium for cultivating virtue and ideal values. It is not mere entertainment, nor simply a mode of conveying experience, but more functionally, a means to redeem the human system, to give it a soul, to transform it.

Since the cosmology of the Igbo is based on tradition that is fluid rather than fixed, "anyone seeking an insight into their world must seek it along their own way," among which paths is the medium of the folktale ("Chi in Igbo Cosmology," *Morning Yet*, 161 [132]). The centrality of the story in Achebe's literary practice is revealed in the words of the Old Man, the head of the delegation from Abazon in *Anthills of the Savannah*: "It is the story . . . that saves our progeny from blundering like blind beggars into the spikes of the cactus fence. The story is our escort; without it, we are blind" (114). Experience, therefore, is essential for mobilizing the intellectual, emotional and ethical resources of a people; it is essential for the functioning of both literate and non–literate peoples, for the continuity of their sensibility, and this explains why Achebe uses fiction for reforming the inadequate structure of society.

A difference exists between European writers and their African counterparts. In Achebe's observation, it is marked by the way they relate to their communities. In "The Novelist as Teacher" he writes, "We have learned from Europe that a writer or an artist lives on the fringe of society—wearing a beard and a peculiar dress and generally behaving in a strange, unpredictable way. He is in revolt against society, which in turn looks on him with suspicion if not hostility" (*Morning Yet*, 67 [55]). The European writer is not accountable to the community, the African is. Again, European art "exists independently of us, of all mankind," whereas the African art exists "to serve a down–to–earth necessity," "to minister to a basic human need" in society. Achebe continues in "Africa and Her Writers":

> Our ancestors created their myths and legends and told their stories for a
> human purpose . . . they made their sculptures in wood and terra cotta,
> stone and bronze to serve the needs of their times. Their artists lived and
> moved and had their being in society and created their works for the good
> of that society (*Morning Yet*, 29 [25]).

Achebe is here concerned with one aspect of the European view on art for art's sake
which has left its imprint on the contemporary European literary scene. The comparison with the European attitude only serves to underscore one point, that art and society are inseparable in Africa, past and present, which explains why African writers
must devote their creative energy to the service of society.

Achebe further argues that art for art's sake has no place in the African world. He
once began a lecture on this tone of denunciation: "*Art for art's sake is just another
piece of deodorized dog shit*" ("Africa and Her Writers," *Morning Yet*, 29 [25]). He
has since tried to modify this extreme position. He now acknowledges the importance
of individual talent and artistic eloquence, but he feels that the importance of such
gifts is highlighted by a recognition of the "seminal potentialities of the community"
(35 [30]). He now explains how and why the European art and literature should experience a phase of despair and thus be preoccupied with the "sickness of the human
condition": Europe may have "overreached [herself] in technical achievement without spiritual growth" (38 [32–33]). Achebe insists that, given the African situation,
aloofness and escapism should have no place in the African writer. He must be committed.

On the writer's commitment, Achebe's stand is unflinching. In "The African
Writer and the Biafran Cause" he states:

> It is clear to me that an African creative writer who tries to avoid the big
> social and political issues of contemporary Africa will end up being
> completely irrelevant—like that absurd man in the proverb who leaves
> his burning house to pursue a rat fleeing from the flames (*Morning Yet*,
> 137 [112]).

Achebe made this statement when the Nigerian civil war was raging. He had identified fully with the Biafran cause, functioning as the Biafran P.R.O. abroad. The poet,
Christopher Okigbo, Achebe's close friend, had also translated his commitment into
action by taking up arms in the war only to perish from his wounds. Further, Wole
Soyinka had been imprisoned for taking a stand contrary to that of the Federal military government. With all this in mind, Achebe, in response to an interviewer's ques-

tion regarding the writer's role in the war, declared: "I decided that I could not stand aside from the problems and struggles of my people at that point in history. And if it happened again, I would not behave differently" (*Research in African Literatures,* 12 [1981]: 8). Such boldness, shown particularly at the end of the war when some prominent Biafrans were already denying their roles, marks the degree of Achebe's sincerity. His statement demonstrates the kind of resolve Soyinka requested when he addressed writers in Stockholm in 1967, which we have already discussed.

Achebe defined commitment as "the sense of social obligation or strong attachment to a cause, and the use of art, in this case literature, to define that obligation and advance the cause" ("The Uses of African Literature," 12). His own writings are an application of this concept, which all the more makes him a committed writer. His major works relate to the history of his people, in which their problems, successes and failures are addressed. *Things Fall Apart,* his first novel, examines the Igbo society prior to and at the point of confrontation with colonial rule. *Arrow of God* shows the same society as it tries to accommodate the new system. These two novels are devoted to the past, a past that had its glories as well as its disappointments, a past in need of definition because of the distortions by which the colonialists had portrayed it. *No Longer at Ease* examines life in Nigeria at the threshold of independence when the noble values of the past suffered terrible recidivism as two cultures met and engaged war in the protagonist, Obi Okonkwo. *A Man of the People* turns the light on the politicians of post–independence Nigeria. They are found wanting in many ways and are seen to be incapable of giving the people the right leadership. A military intervention ends the novel—an event that coincidentally took place in Nigeria nine days after the novel was published. Achebe's most recent novel, *Anthills of the Savannah* focuses on the country under the military. He alerts the reader to the cultural, social, and political life of a fictitious West African country which is no other than Nigeria. *Girls at War,* a collection of his short stories, and *Beware Soul Brother* (poems) are set in the Nigerian civil war. In Achebe's novels, society is fully alive; it moves and breathes. Many Africans who read Achebe's novels easily identify with the characters and events as is evident from the numerous letters the author received after the publication of *Things Fall Apart.* In his essay, "The Uses of African Literature," Achebe writes, "A writer who feels a strong and abiding concern for his fellows cannot evade the role of social critic which is the contemporary expression of commitment to the community" (17). This commitment, he maintains, has always been at the essence of African literature. It is no wonder that practically all his works are concerned with the affairs of his community.

Achebe may not have used the word redemption to describe the role the writer plays in society, yet his position, when closely examined, comes to this, that the writer's duty is to change society for the better. Achebe's "post–lapsarian" conception of the world is at the basis of his definition of the writer's responsibilities. He believes that we live in an imperfect world, a world that is evolving through crises. He expressed his view in an interview with Kalu Ogbaa:

> If things were perfect, there would be no need for writers to write their novels. But it is because they see the possibilities of man rising higher than he has risen at the moment that they write. So, whatever they write... would be in essence a protest against what exists, against what is (*Research in African Literature*, 12 [1981]: 4–5).

The redemptive role of the writer introduces a note of optimism in a world that is made more complex by what Achebe calls the "powers of event" (that is, that which we cannot control—accident or chance) and man's wrong deeds.

The Nigerian society stands as an example of a world driven to the edge by man's greed and selfishness. In his television interview with Moyers, Achebe laments that the numerous blessings God has showered on the country have been "squandered," with the result that the country has achieved little since independence (3). Corruption, bribery, violence, vulgarity, rigged elections, etc., are painfully common practice, and it is understandable why Achebe remarks in *The Trouble with Nigeria*: "We have given ourselves over so completely to selfishness that we hurt not only those around us, but ourselves even more deeply, that one must assume a blunting of the imagination and a sense of danger of truly psychiatric proportions" (30). Africa, too, has her multiple problems. He sees Africa as a continent much debased and insulted by colonialism and post–colonial dictatorship. To Chinweizu he discloses in an interview: "The crisis of colonialism in Africa had reached a point where we either had to do battle—a battle of the mind—with colonialism or perish" (*Okike,* 20 [1981]: 29). Beyond Africa, Achebe finds the entire world suffused with problems. The world is "stifling" as a result of man's inhumanity to man (Moyers, 2). Again to Chinweizu he confides, "There is a crisis in every society, but sometimes the crisis is particularly severe, and this has to be resolved" (*Okike* 20 [1981]: 29). It is the duty of the writer to resolve this crisis, and in that resolution lies Achebe's redemptive role.

Like God the Creator who created order out of chaos and saw that his work was "good" (*Morning Yet,* 28–29 [25]), the writer, according to Achebe, renders vision and order to our chaotic world. It is the special office of the writer to "recreate the world for the advantage of humanity," a task which also involves creating the "new man," that is, a society guided by solid moral principles, for as Achebe attests in a presentation he made with Baldwin, African art is morally based (Hill–Lubin, 3). Hence, the writer does not concern himself with mere aesthetics; he has to provide society with "something solid and permanent," external values that will underlie the moral consciousness of the "new man." With African societies caught at the crossroads of cultures as a result of colonialism, the modern African writer would have to retrieve from the past worthy ancestral values and attitudes—respect for age, for parents, emphasis on the family, etc.—which are capable of redeeming an already confused society.

The writer is a teacher, and African writers feel they have a special mission to change their society by the process of education. Achebe will be remembered by generations for his new emphasis on the educational role of the writer. Certainly, he is not the first to expound the concept; Tasso, Sidney, Carlyle, Lowell, Sartre, all mentioned it in their works. Wordsworth was known to have said, "Every great Poet is a Teacher; I wish either to be considered as a Teacher, or as nothing" (Zall, *Literary Criticism of William Wordsworth,* xv). Wordsworth taught his audience that the common man is a worthy subject for poetry. Achebe also regards himself as a teacher, but what is even more important is the prominence he has given this role in the African world.

African writers will educate their society to understand the proposition that reality is at once simple and complex. Like a prophet, they will call society's attention to the inevitability of the unforeseen, the "powers of the event" which can intervene in human affairs and create change. Even when life seems smooth and undisturbed for the individual or the community, there is always some danger lurking, sooner or later to undermine our optimism. Writers as prophets can perceive the danger through their imagination, and knowing that "it can't all be that great," they come "up when things are going very well and . . . [start] proclaiming doom" (Interview by Jeyifo, *Contemporary African Literature,* 11). On the other hand, where we think life is so simple, the writer sees deeper and points up complexities, thus "a writer comes into the relationship and dredges up all kinds of frightening possibilities. And then what seems a simple thing is made not so simple" (12). In drawing attention to the presence of the unforeseen, writers thereby prepare us for the battle against it. They teach society that life is not an unending day of joyous celebration; it has its nightmare.

This nightmare which is partially responsible for life's complexity could be made "not so terrifying" by the writer's revelation of the past as a metaphor. The writer simplifies life by presenting the past analogously, "as if saying to us, 'if this has happened before, and our ancestors have coped with it, then there's no reason why we of this generation could not deal with it'" (12). Such demonstrative analogies contain possible solutions, one would expect, for when the present generation sees how the past handled their problem, they are equipped with one or more alternatives. It is also the duty of the writers to "dramatize" humanity's predicament in order to reveal to it hidden possibilities or "choices" or "alternatives" at its disposal so it can choose correctly (Interview by Kalu Ogbaa, *Research in African Literatures*, 13). Okonkwo's terrible error, if we take the world of *Things Fall Apart* as an example, is to approach life single–mindedly as if there cannot exist any alternatives. But Obierika, who Achebe concedes to relate to the writer himself, represents the alternative.

The most important lesson African writers need to teach their people is self–esteem. They must teach them "that their past—with all its imperfections—was not one long night of savagery from which the first Europeans acting on God's behalf delivered them" ("The Novelist as Teacher," *Morning Yet,* 72 [59]). The aim of writing *Things Fall Apart* and *Arrow of God* could not be more explicit. In these two novels, in particular, Achebe makes the strong case that the Igbo culture and institutions possessed beauty and substance. Igbo life and society were not the grotesque creations that the colonialists had made them out to be. Furthermore, the image of the African has suffered terribly in the hands of European colonizers and writers, and it is the duty of the writer, "a human being with heightened sensitivities" to correct this distorted image and "restore to his people a good opinion of themselves" ("The African Writer and the Biafran Cause," *Morning Yet*, 139, 142 [115, 117]). In the same essay Achebe writes:

> Whether we like to face up to it or not, Africa has been the most insulted continent in the world. Africans' very claim to humanity has been questioned at various times, their persons abused, their intelligence insulted. These things have happened in the past and have gone on happening today. We [writers] have a duty to bring them to an end for our own sakes, for the sake of our children, and indeed for the safety and happiness of the world (138 [114]).

The irony of the situation is that even the victims of the colonial denigration ultimately came to accept colonial life–style with awe and admiration, and to perceive everything African "as something to be ashamed of and snapped at the earliest opportunity." As a writer whose duty is to teach and correct, Achebe reacts thus in "The Novelist as Teacher":

> Here then is an adequate revolution for me to espouse—to help my society regain belief in itself and put away the complexes of the years of denigration and self–abasement. And it is essentially a question of edu-

cation, in the best sense of the word. Here I think my aims and the deepest aspirations of my society meet *(Morning Yet,* 71 [59]).

Achebe carefully selects his words in this quotation. It is a question of education and,
although not directly mentioned but implied, teaching.

The significance of "teacher" to the African is worth mentioning. The one who
teaches provides knowledge and insight to the taught. In African communities, especially in the 50's and 60's, teachers were highly revered not only because of the
knowledge and insight they provided but also because they were looked upon as a
individuals of dignity and authority, and as social ambassadors or representatives of
society. Like the ancient Jewish priest who knew the Jewish law and ritual and had
authority to interpret them, the teacher in Africa was expected to be knowledgeable
about the society, including its norms and values. The relationship between teachers
and their community was often based on love and trust. When Achebe chooses to use
the word "teacher" to explain the role of the writer, he is well aware of the strong
connotations the word carries.

Toward the end of "The Novelist as Teacher" Achebe makes it clear that the writer's role does not end with teaching Africans about their moral goodness and the nature of creation, teaching them that "there is nothing disgraceful about the African
weather, that the palm tree is a fit subject of poetry" (71 [58]); there needs to be "re–
education and regeneration" (72 [59]). The education involved is an on–going process, as C.D. Narasimhaiah rightly observes, and it must be amenable to readjustments
as society changes with the times (228).

AN EXCURSUS ON COMMITMENT IN
THE WORKS OF SOYINKA AND ACHEBE

Soyinka and Achebe share a common ground in their views on the role and commitment of the writer, although differences exist. Both writers believe that art, including literature, is a social phenomenon. Both profess that it is the function of art to
provide a visionary reconstruction of the past and that the writer must provide the
sagacity for social direction. A proper sense of history is therefore required of him.
Both agree that the writer has a duty of exploring in depth the human condition with a
view to changing the society for the better. Although raised with the doctrine of art for
art's sake, Soyinka and Achebe are vehemently opposed to the writers' indifference

to the social and political issues in their society. Both writers not only preach the need for commitment in arts, they are intensely committed in their writing to the socio–political affairs of their country. Like Achebe, Soyinka's major theme holds that, in an ailing society, the writer's mission is reconstruction, redeeming a collapsing humanity. As Ogungbesan rightly observes:

> [Soyinka's] persistent call to African writers to demonstrate that they have a vision shows that he sees the literary artist as a redeemer. He believes that the writer possesses an inner light unavailable to the mass of his people, and that it is his duty to use this inspiration and insight to guide his society towards a beautiful future (*New West African Literature*, 7–8).

One or two differences between the two writers deserve our notice. First, Achebe lays much emphasis on the need for writers to reach back in time to restore lost dignity and rebuild self–esteem in their peoples. Soyinka is not opposed to a writer's journey into the past, but he is not inclined to be nostalgic because the past denies the writer the more urgent task of projecting society into the future. "[I]t is about time," he says, "the African writer stopped being a mere chronicler and understood also that part of his essential purpose is to write with a very definite vision. . . . he must at least begin by exposing the future in a clear and truthful exposition of the present" ("'From the Discussion' to Nkosi 'Individualism'" 58). In "The Writer in a Modern African State," he is even more explicit and says that "[t]he African writer needs an urgent release from the fascination of the past" because such an "escapist indulgence" leads to the "destruction of the will to action" ("The Writer" 19). The difference seems a matter of emphasis, especially considering that Soyinka resorted to the past in his play *A Dance of the Forests*.

Second, Achebe opposes "the human condition" syndrome. There is need for writers to examine the human condition not as an ultimate goal but as a means to a solution. Achebe condemns as hypocritical any attempt to impose on a society a false human condition and its effect, as the Ghanaian novelist Ayi Kwei Armah does in *The Beautiful Ones Are Not Yet Born*. According to Achebe, this novel fails by attempting to explore the sickness of the human condition—alienation, despair, etc.—in Ghana "where no such ailments exist." Achebe decries the "enormous distance between Armah and Ghana" ("Africa and Her Writers," *Morning Yet,* 40 [34]). Achebe's stand is that people are aware of the human condition in their society; the writer's duty is to truly explore this condition to present possibilities of solutions. Soyinka's position is somewhat complicated because he emphasized the so–called human condition earlier in his career, although not as existentially as did Armah, but later shifted emphasis. In his early writing, Soyinka insisted on having writers deal with contemporary reality by analyzing the prevalent mood in society with the expectation that society would be made to confront its real problems. This kind of philosophy informed the action in *The Interpreters* where young intellectuals in a newly independent African nation are continually frustrated in their attempts to match their visions with the claims of society. African critics and writers highly criticized Soyinka's position. The most notable was Ngũgĩ wa Thiong'o who sees *The Interpreters* in the light of a revolutionary Africa devoid of colonial interest:

> It is not enough for the African artist, standing aloof, to view society and highlight its weaknesses. He must try to go beyond this, to seek out the sources, the causes and the trends of a revolutionary struggle which has already destroyed the traditional power–map drawn up by the colonialist nations ("Wole Soyinka," 65–66).

Soyinka later changed his emphasis, especially after a series of direct involvement in political action culminating in his detention in 1967. He then began to see literature as a "political weapon" and the writer as one with a duty to restore to society "the permanent values—justice, freedom, human dignity" that it ought to have. He would even go further to acknowledge the impotence of literature to achieve all these and to suggest that there might be need for the writer to be "spurred" to taking other positive actions in defense of these ends.

Achebe and Soyinka at first seem to differ on the teaching role of the writer, but are, in actuality, in accord. In an interview by Lewis Nkosi in 1962 Soyinka says: "I don't believe that I have any obligation to enlighten, to instruct, to teach. I don't possess that sense of duty or didacticism" (173). This statement, in the light of its context, is not sufficient grounds to build up a difference of opinion between Achebe and Soyinka. Soyinka was here addressing the issue of the playwright/director and his audience relationship whereby he felt it was not his duty to teach the audience as Brecht would do, but simply to offer them an excellent theatre (173). In the fuller analysis, Soyinka and Achebe are not opposed on this issue; indeed, both see the need for the writer to create awareness, which precisely is Achebe's meaning of "teach." Soyinka's obscurity in his works, coupled with his statement that he writes for people on the same wave–length as his, for "a thousand people" who share some feeling about an issue as he, is the reason why many wonder if Soyinka truly believes the writer has a duty to teach. Yes, he does believe. Obscurity in Soyinka is only a matter of personal style, not intended to hinder meaning but to artistically challenge the mind—a common characteristic in modern plays and poetry. Then concerning communication, a narrow audience appeal is still an appeal, much more so since every writer reserves the right to appeal to a wider or lesser audience. After all, Jesus Christ, though not a writer, chose to appeal immediately to only twelve apostles, and with time his message reached millions.

At this point we shall end our theoretical discussion and devote the rest of the work to Achebe's novels. With the foregoing theories in mind, we shall examine Achebe's five novels to see how the writer's rebellion and redemption function in practice.

PART TWO

THE NOVELS OF CHINUA ACHEBE

CHAPTER TWO

REBELLION

INTRODUCTION

In his articles and interviews Achebe has repeatedly said that the writer's works express the spirit of a people's civilization. As we saw earlier, he maintains also that the primary duty of a novelist is to teach. One of the ways novelists teach is through a thorough diagnosis of the problems of society whereby they open our awareness to the follies of humanity. Their criticism of humanity's social institutions and people's attitudes (protest or rebellion) could lead to changes in our life styles. Achebe believes that protest is an "assumed mission" of the artist. It is the duty of writers to protest against the distortions in what they are given. Roles, histories, human conditions, the world are full of distortions. According to Achebe, the need for protesting will never end, and writers must continue their protests seeking for truth and "better alternatives."

Achebe's position is valid, for fiction is humanity's attempt to rebuild its world. As Camus points out in *The Rebel,* "The world of the novel is only a rectification of the world we live in, in pursuance of man's deepest wishes" (263). Many times this attempt at rectification of the world (or reconstruction) leads to rebellion which Camus has rightly identified as "one of the sources of the art of fiction" (265). In "The Novel as Subversion," Frederick Karl convincingly argued that from its inception in the eighteenth century the novel was subversive, protesting against "closed forms" and advocating for a community "based on dignity, acceptance, equality, and virtue through achievement, not birth." It became socially oriented, and overturned feudalistic world view by presenting the view that society is constantly changing and should therefore be open to "the possibilities of endless variations and changes." It became rebellious, especially in its "nearly always testing out the received and the given, attacking hypocrisy, and demonstrating alternate ways of action and response" (*A Reader's Guide to the Eighteenth Century English Novel*, 39). Rebellion in literature is, however, not necessarily destructive; it is, after all, a manifestation of one of fiction's basic roles in society, which is, to illuminate society's inadequacies with a view to finding solutions. The novel is therefore at once rebellious and redemptive. Before we examine rebellion in Achebe's works, we shall first take a cursory survey of events in Nigeria, the society of Achebe's primary concern.

BACKGROUND EVENTS IN NIGERIA

Given the explosive situations in Africa past and present, it is not surprising that her literature is largely characterized as protest literature. Chinua Achebe's protest is a direct response to the social and political events in Nigeria. We shall briefly examine some of the events in order to appreciate Achebe's reactions to them.

Before it became a British colony, what we now know as Nigeria had embraced all sorts of political systems ranging from large kingdoms and emirates to tiny independent clan–states, some of whose inhabitants had little or no contact whatsoever with one another. Cultural, religious, linguistic and even environmental differences made it almost impossible for them to fuse together as one nation. Something historically dramatic needed to happen to bring together these separate political units. The coming of the British unified the area. Following the Berlin Conference (1884–85), Britain laid claims to territories north and south of what she later named Nigeria. The two entities were amalgamated in 1914 under Lord Lugard. But the differences among the component ethnic groups persisted, and in some cases multiplied, and account for the numerous tensions and conflicts that have plagued the country ever since.

Colonialism, which created and sustained the country until independence, was nonetheless perceived by the people as an imposition. Its rejection even in its initial stages is well represented in Achebe's *Things Fall Apart* where we read about rumors of resistance and reprisals, particularly the massacre at Abame related by Obierika during Okonkwo's exile (97–99 [127–130]*). The novel itself dramatizes the initial

---

* Citations to *Things Fall Apart* are first from the Heinemann African Writers Series edition (reset 1976) and then from the Fawcett (paperback) edition (1969).

contact of Umuofia clan with the British and how Okonkwo's belated effort to mobilize the people for resistance proved fatal. Colonialism advanced with ruthless force, inflicting "punishments" and imposing brutal "pacification" as it pushed toward the Igbo hinterland. Robert Wren in *Achebe's World* refers to two of such punitive expeditions carried out by the British between 1900 and 1920: the Aro expedition and the Bende–Onitsha Hinterland Expedition (26–31). Although in general "the white man's power was wielded only with difficulty," Wren observes, "when wielded it was implacable" (27). Collective punishment authorized by the Collective Punishment Ordinance of 1912 became one of the obnoxious means of "pacification." This means that if a crime were committed against a colonial officer, or if there were resistance to colonial rule, there was no effort to identify the individuals responsible, rather a collective punishment was inflicted on a whole group, village, or clan. Besides violence or ruthlessness, another reason for colonial resentment was what Nigerians often refer to as "colonial mentality," that is, the colonialist's disdainful attitude toward his subjects and their culture.

As a challenge to colonial rule, two movements emerged:

    (a)   *Negritude*—a cultural and literary revolution initiated by the

        Francophone writers, and

    (b)   *Nationalism*—a political movement that spread mostly in

        Anglophone African countries.

Negritude was no big issue in Nigeria. Much as it affected the thoughts of some Nigerian writers, it was indeed intellectually opposed by major Nigerian writers like Soyinka and Achebe. Nationalist movements led by politicians like Oged Macauley, Nnamdi Azikiwe, Nduka Eze, and others picked up momentum in the late 40's and the 50's. It was mostly through their efforts that independence became a reality in 1960. The spirit of revolt, which informed Nationalist movements, also inspired the literature of the time. Writers joined hands with politicians to challenge British rule. At this time, the politician was depicted in literature as a hero who sacrificed everything to redeem his people from oppression and misrule. Onitsha market pamphleteers exulted in their works such nationalist heroes as Zik and Awolowo, and among them, foreign nationalists as Nkrumah (Ghana), Patrice Lamumba (Zaire), and Jomo Kenyatta (Kenya). Cyprian Ekwensi, an early Nigerian novelist, dedicated his novel *Beautiful Feathers* to Léopold Senghor, the Sengalese president and chief African exponent of Negritude, and Abubakar Tafawa Balewa, the Prime Minister of Nigeria.

Shortly after independence, this unholy wedlock between the writer and the politician ended. The departure of the colonial master had created a power vacuum which the politician had neither the wit nor manners, nor even the goodwill, to fill up. During the struggle for independence, he had created great expectations in the minds of his people with promises of freedom, equality, and peace. When he came to power, he gave the people greed, corruption, graft, thuggery, election–rigging, and despair. The people were totally disillusioned and disappointed and felt betrayed. Many joined hands with the politician to rape the country, while others expressed anger, cynicism, and despair, earnestly waiting for some kind of redeemer to come. The writer who, according to Soyinka, had been carried away by the euphoria of independence and his newly acquired elitist status, when he realized that his politician partner was a rogue, turned against him and began to cry foul. Achebe and Soyinka in particular were vocal in their condemnation of the politician. *A Man of the People* and *Kongi's Harvest* became classic examples of works that portrayed the kind of monster that replaced the colonial master.

Barely six years after independence, the army stepped into power (1966) in an apparent move to redeem the country. Like the politicians they too promised a paradise. Hopes raised were soon to be dashed, for the man in khaki had not kept a peaceful home nor had he rid himself of the greed and corruption that had been the bane of the politician. Coups, counter–coups, and assassinations followed his path, and soon he turned the country upside down, armed the people and shoved them into a civil war to slaughter each other. One question that perplexes the Nigerian mind today is: the politician and the soldier, who is the greater rogue? Meanwhile, a "literature of trauma," as Lindfors calls it, resulted from the military experiment. It exposed the horrors and sufferings in the military era. In some cases it portrayed the soldier in mock–heroic terms. Achebe's war poems and short stories as well as his latest novel *Anthills of the Savannah* deal with events under military dictatorships. Soyinka's A *Shuttle in the Crypt* (poems), *The Man Died, Madmen and Specialists, Season of Anomy*, etc. show him reacting even more than Achebe to the military intervention. In this passage from "Named for Victoria, Queen of England", Achebe gives us a summary description of the whole situation:

The nationalist movement in British West Africa after the Second World War brought about a mental revolution which began to reconcile us to ourselves. It suddenly seemed that we too might have a story to tell. "Rule Britannica!" to which we had marched so unself–consciously on Empire Day now stuck in our throats.... But things happen very fast in Africa. I had hardly begun to bask in the sunshine of reconciliation when a new cloud appeared, a new estrangement. Political independence had come. The nationalist leader of yesterday (with whom it had not been too difficult to make common cause) had become the not so attractive party boss. And then things really got going. The party boss was chased out by the bright military boys, new idols of the people. But the party boss knows how to wait, knows by heart the counsel Mother Bedbug gave her little ones when the harassed owner of the bed poured hot water on them. "Be patient," said she, "for what is hot will in the end be cold." What is bright can also get tarnished, like the military boys.

One hears that the party boss is already conducting a whispering campaign. "You done see us chop," he says. "Now you see *dem* chop. Which one you like pass?" And the people are truly confused (*Morning Yet*, 123–124 [102]).

The people are confused in every sense of the word, but not the writers, especially Achebe and Soyinka. They possess the right vision to see through the events, and refuse to be intimidated. And so they rebel. Achebe hints at this response when he refers to an inscription in a coffee shop in Amherst that reads (124 [103]):

> Take care of your boss
> The next one may be worse.

Achebe's response reveals the position of writers: "The trouble with writers is that they will often refuse to live by such rationality" (124 [103]).

AGAINST COLONIALISM

Achebe's first novel, *Things Fall Apart* was published in 1958, two years before independence. Although Achebe came late, he was not left out in the battle against colonialism. On the whole, Achebe is not a fanatical opponent of colonialism. He considers colonialism as part of a historical process which has its own positive side (see chapter three). But he protests against colonial abuses, especially in colonial literature, colonial administration, and Christian evangelization.

In *Culture, Tradition and Society in the West African Novel*, Emmanuel Obiechina classifies colonial literature into three groups:

(i)   Works in which the writers use Africa merely as an exotic setting. Graham Greene and Joseph Conrad, for example, use Africa as "an allegorical setting within which to explore European civilization" (22). Greene's *The Heart of the Matter* and Conrad's *The Heart of Darkness* readily come to mind.

(ii)   Works in which writers deal with authentic local themes. Such works are often distorted by their authors' ignorance of the African culture and the African mind. "These writers," Obiechina contends, "are not interested in reality and authenticity. They are exploring the Africa of tribal and communal violence" (23). Examples are: Joyce Cary's novels, especially *Mr. Johnson*, Elspeth Huxley's *The Walled City*, and William Loader's *The Guinea Stamp*.

(iii)   Works used by European writers to present "an attitude, a sociological theory, or a psychological statement." A common theme here is the impact of Western culture on the African culture. With little or no knowledge of African culture, the writers end up distorting African values.

An exception to this trend, according to Obiechina, is *Stormy Dawn* by Margaret Field (writing as Mark Freshfield). Field, an ethnologist who spent many years in Ghana, was writing as an insider. In her novel she uses the character of the District Commissioner to satirize Europeans who came to Africa with stereotyped ideas of the continent.

Achebe's first novel, *Things Fall Apart,* was written partly as a reaction to the caricature of the Africans in colonial literature. Achebe wrote "'to set the score right about [his] ancestors'" (Awoonor, 252). In an interview with Lewis Nkosi in 1962, Achebe explained why he set about to write:

> I was quite certain that I was going to try my hand at writing and one of
> the things that set me thinking was Joyce Cary's novel set in Nigeria, *Mr.*
> *Johnson,* which was praised so much, and it was clear to me that this was
> a most superficial picture of . . . not only the country, but even the Nige-
> rian character and so I thought if this was famous, then perhaps someone
> ought to try and look at this from the inside (4).

Mr. Johnson is a novel set in northern Nigeria in the colonial era. The main character, Johnson is a semiliterate civil servant possessed of self–delusions of grandeur. As he pursues his naive and vivacious life in the African bush, he is full of praises for the King of England and proudly endeavors to equip his wife with clothes and shoes to exalt her to the status of the colonial officials' wives. His buffoonery however leads him to the gallows at the end of the novel. This grotesque caricature is used to portray life in the African bush as disorganized, primitive, violent, and lawless. Achebe re-bels against this misconception in *Things Fall Apart* by presenting life as lived in Igboland before the arrival of the Europeans. As one who understands the people and their customs, he makes a good case for Igbo culture and institutions. *Things Fall Apart* reveals that the African world before the arrival of the Europeans was inhabited by men of honor, and dignity, and self–pride. Men of character like Okonkwo lived side by side with indolent men like Unoka. They cultivated their fields, took titles, observed laws, worshiped their gods, and celebrated their feasts. The way their sys-tem functioned might radically differ from that of the Europeans, yet it had its own logic.

Besides rebelling against colonial literature, Achebe also revolts against the ad-ministration for its arrogance, high–handedness, double standard, and ignorance of the indigenous people and their culture. The District Commissioner in *Things Fall Apart* is a typical example of a colonial official with these faults; he is arrogant, unin-formed, and ruthless. We see all this in the way he handles the *egwugwu* crisis. After the zealot Christian convert Enoch unmasks the *egwugwu* or masked spirit, a band of *egwugwu* sweeps through the church premises and sets fire to the mission church. On hearing these events, the District Commissioner invites six elders of the clan under the pretense of a meeting and he imprisons them without a hearing. As soon as they are safely handcuffed, he lectures them on the Pax Britannica:

> We have brought a peaceful administration to you and your people so that you may be happy. If any man ill–treats you, we shall come to your rescue. But we will not allow you to ill–treat others. We have a court of law where we judge cases and administer justice just as it is done in my own country under a great queen. I have brought you here because you joined together to molest others, to burn people's houses and their place of worship. That must not happen in the dominion of our queen; the most powerful ruler in the world (137 [178]).

Achebe uses this incident to expose the weaknesses of the colonial administration. The District Commissioner has had "a long discussion" with Mr. Smith the church leader but has made no attempt to investigate the matter. When he invites the six elders, he is not prepared to listen to the their side of the story, and yet, ironically, he assures them that he will come to their rescue if any man ill–treats them. Achebe is here attacking a colonial practice which assumes the people wrong and punishes them unfairly without a hearing. Refusal to listen leads to misunderstanding and misrepresentation.

Achebe returns to this theme of misunderstanding toward the end of the novel. After Okonkwo's tragic death by suicide, and after the District Commissioner orders that his body be taken down, we read about the book the Commissioner intends to write:

> The Commissioner went away, taking three or four of the soldiers with him. In the many years in which he had toiled to bring civilization to different parts of Africa he had learnt a number of things. One of them was that a District Commissioner must never attend to such undignified details as cutting down a hanged man from a tree. Such attention would give the natives a poor opinion of him. In the book he planned to write he would stress that point. As he walked back to the court he thought about that book. Every day brought him some new material. The story of this man who had killed a messenger and hanged himself would make interesting reading. One could almost write a whole chapter on him. Perhaps not a whole chapter but a reasonable paragraph, at any rate . . . He had already chosen the title of the book, after much thought: *The Pacification of the Primitive Tribes of the Lower Niger* (147–48 [191]).

Ajofia, the leading *egwugwu* of Umuofia had earlier remarked about Mr. Smith, "He does not understand our customs, just as we do not understand his. We say he is foolish because he does not know our ways, and perhaps he says we are foolish because we do not know his. Let him go away" (134 [175]). The point he makes about each side's not understanding the other is right, and it explains the friction between the natives and the new comers. The irony however is that the District Commissioner makes such outlandish claims about his knowledge of the "primitive tribes" whom he actually does not understand. It is repulsive that he is going to write a book on them.

In this way Achebe subtly attacks those Europeans, as mentioned earlier, who write about Africa, knowing little or nothing about its people. To feel the full weight of the irony intended by Achebe, one must examine his timing: he drops it at the very last paragraph of the novel. Having presented the picture of pre–colonial Africa to his reader, he ends with a slice of a colonial official's view and leaves the reader to judge the truth for himself. Achebe has written an entire novel exploring the whole cultural truth behind the suicide of an obscure African man; the District Commissioner is willing to concede that the whole event merits a single paragraph. Perhaps, the irony is extended in that Achebe, who is not a contemporary of the early Colonial period, has had to use the basic tools of research to rediscover a past long since forgotten in his own time, and sees more clearly than an eyewitness to the events.

There is more than a suggestion that the proposed book by the Commissioner will present a distorted picture of the people, as really happens in *Arrow of God* where we see the book already published. Achebe is suggesting that the District Commissioner is not qualified to render a reliable account of Africa because he does not know the people and cannot know them having obstructed the means of knowing them. He has, for example, surrounded himself with soldiers and corrupt court messengers (all strangers) who carry out the dirty work of repression for him. Furthermore, he is vowing not to "attend to such undignified details" so as not to "give the natives a poor opinion of him." The studied intellectual distance that was meant to communicate an air of dispassionate judgment on the part of the District Commissioner (as something he consummately desired) is seen to be little more than making himself so aloof that, while being an eyewitness, he is at best myopic. To him the very details of history (and one can presume the people and customs themselves) are "undignified" in comparison to the vision of "bringing civilization."

In *Arrow of God* the proposed book by the District Commissioner (George Allen) has been published under the proposed title. A newly arrived, unbiased colonial officer, Tony Clarke, is reading it. He finds it "dull" and "too smug" and later tells his boss, Captain Winterbottom, that the author is "a trifle too dogmatic." He adds, "He doesn't allow, for instance, for there being anything of value in native institutions. He might really be one of the missionary people" (35*). Winterbottom, long in the colonial service, totally disagrees: "I see you are one of the progressive ones. When you've been here as long as Allen was and understand the native a little more you might modify some of your new theories" (35).

Ironically, Winterbottom's claim that he and Allen know the people very well is immediately debunked. His version of the war between Umuaro and Okperi, details of which the reader has already heard from the third person omniscient narrator (14–28), is inaccurate. The reader already knows that the war was fought over a piece of land claimed by both clans, and that it could have been avoided but for the tempestuous nature of Akukalia, the head of the Umuaro delegation. In Winterbottom's version, an Umuaro man visited his friend at Okperi and, after he sated himself with palm wine, destroyed his host's *ikenga* (which represents his ancestors) and this led to a fight that later involved the two clans (37). Winterbottom has much in common with George Allen. Both falsely claim to know the natives. Also, both are too conscious of maintaining their dignity by keeping a distance from the indigenous people. Winterbottom is very insistent on the Europeans keeping a respectful distance from the natives. On one occasion he had cause to warn Wright about his relationship with native women. And we read that "it was absolutely imperative, he told him, that every European in Nigeria, particularly those in such a lonely outpost as Okperi, should not lower themselves in the eyes of the natives" (32).

Some colonial policies were carried out without respect to native customs. Indirect Rule is a good example. This was a policy that would enable the British to grant limited authority to native rulers and to control the natives through them. Achebe considered such a policy in Igboland as obnoxious, unrealistic, and oppressive. The political system in Igboland before the colonial rule was, by most African standards, peculiar. According to Robin Horton as reported in Wren's *Achebe's World,* the Igboland was a conglomeration of "stateless societies" (83). In such societies, no one wielded authority as a "specialized, full–time occupation." The communities functioned under "agreed rules"; they met in assemblies and made decisions on issues under the leadership of elders, titled men, and priests. While many African societies were characterized by states or kingdoms ruled by kings or emirs, the Igbo had no

---

* Citations from *Arrow of God* are to the second (revised) edition, Anchor Books/Doubleday (paperback) edition (1974).

king, except in exceptional cases as in Onitsha and Nri where kings (*Obi* and *Eze* respectively) existed but never operated as absolute monarchs. The Obi of Onitsha was elected, while the Eze of Nri was considered the highest religious titled man in Nri; his function was therefore mostly religious. *Igbo enwe eze* (the Igbo have no king) is an old Igbo adage that is still current. Achebe makes this point in *Things Fall Apart* in the first encounter of the missionaries and the people of Mbanta, Okonkwo's home of exile. The missionaries "asked who the king of the village was, but villagers told them that there was no king. 'We have men of high title and the chief priests and the elders,' they said" (105 [138]). Earlier in the novel we learn that "among these people a man was judged according to his worth and not according to the worth of his father"(6 [11]). It is a society in which social mobility was determined by prowess, wealth, and merit. For example, by sheer hard labor Okonkwo climbs the social ladder from mere pauperism to become "one of the greatest men of his time," with a rich barn full of yams, three wives, and two titles, not to mention the number of human heads credited to him from war (6 [11–12]). He fulfilled the saying among his people that "if a child washed his hands he could eat with kings" (6 [12]).

The Igbo communities were ruled not by Kings and chiefs but by *mmo* ("spirits living and dead"), as Wren explains in *Achebe's World*:

> The *ndichie* [elders], and *ozo* title holders . . . "ruled" collectively. Thus, the community was a community of *mmo*, spirtits living and dead. The community was ruled by *mmo*. It was sometimes manifest in oracles, sometimes in priests, sometimes in the *egwugwu*—the masked actual presence of the ancestral spirits, as in *Things Fall Apart*—but it was manifest most of all in the collective will of the clan itself, of which the *ndichie* were the orators, spokesmen, and the common voice (85).

With this complex system of government the Igbo societies were unprepared for the colonial imposition of chieftaincy under the policy of Indirect Rule.

Indirect Rule was the brainchild of Lord Frederick Lugard, the first governor of Nigeria (1914). The policy had worked in the feudalistic North directly ruled by autocratic emirs. Through this policy Lord Lugard required colonial administrators to create chiefs where there were none, so as to "hasten the transition from the patriarchal to the tribal stage, and induce those who accept no other authority than the head of the family to recognize a common chief" (quoted by Afigbo, 138). Lugard's successor as High Commissioner of the Northern Protectorate (1907), Sir P. Girouard explains the need for the policy in these words:

> It was felt that there was need of an increased knowledge on our part of
> methods of rule and native law and customs before any dislocation of
> institutions should take place—institutions which however faulty had
> the traditional sanction of the people. Insofar as the Residents were con-
> cerned they were to be Administrators in the true sense of the word; not
> direct rulers. Direct personal rule of British officers would not be accept-
> able to the people who look to their natural leaders for guidance . . .
> (quoted by Greary, 277).

Certainly the system that obtained in the North was suited for Indirect Rule, but not
the system in the East, particularly in Igbo societies. The "transition" ordered by
Lugard failed in the East because the chiefs were forced on the people and also because their role was civil and governmental. As Wren explains in *Achebe's World,*
"These 'chiefs' by appointment were made to serve as committees of judges in matters of civil conflict . . . and as administrators in seeing to the demands of government
for work crews and the like" (118). They lacked the religious and traditional authority
of the village leaders as we can infer from the account of a retired warrant chief:

> It would be wrong to compare the Native Court's with village assemblies
> of the people. The chiefs were employed by the white man to try cases
> according to the white man's laws. We [chiefs] were government work-
> ers, or at least that was what we thought. When I tried cases in my house I
> followed traditional law and custom, but in the Native Court it was a dif-
> ferent matter: this was why we used to rely on what the clerk told us was
> the white man's law (Afigbo, 208).

The colonial policy of Indirect Rule is treated at length in Achebe's third novel
Arrow of God. Achebe sees the policy as a political blunder. His perspective comes
through in the reaction of Captain Winterbottom whose duty is to effectively implement the system in his district. The memorandum he receives from the Lieutenant–
Governor, though fictional, reads as if taken out of a colonial record:

> My purpose in these paragraphs is limited to impressing on all Political
> Officers working among tribes who lack Natural Rulers the vital neces-
> sity of developing without further delay an effective system of "indirect
> rule" based on native institutions. . . . In place of the alternative of gov-
> erning directly through Administrative Officers there is the other method
> of trying while we endeavor to purge the native system of its abuses to
> build a higher civilization upon the soundly rooted native stock that had
> its foundation in the hearts and minds and thoughts of the people and
> therefore on which we can more easily build, moulding it and establish-

ing it into lines consonant with modern ideas and higher standards, and yet all the time enlisting the real force of the spirit of the people, instead of killing all that out and trying to start afresh. We must not destroy the African atmosphere, the African mind, the whole foundation of his race ... (56–57).

Winterbottom regards all this as rubbish: "words, words, words," and thinks the Lieutenant–Governor should be told that "the whole damn thing was stupid and futile" (57). His strong opposition to "the stupid trend" (59) had cost him his promotion in the Civil Service, and although he is "under orders" to carry it out, he remains completely skeptical. To Clarke he confides: "Unlike some of the more advanced tribes in Northern Nigeria, and to some extent Western Nigeria, the Ibos never developed any kind of central authority. That's what our headquarters fail to appreciate" (37). At times he becomes highly critical of the British colonial method: "We flounder from one experiment to its opposite. We do not only promise to secure old savage tyrants on their thrones [a reference to the feudalist chiefs and emirs of the North] ... we now go out of our way to invent chiefs where there were none before" (36). Citing the case of chief Ikedi, who after being appointed chief, went ahead and made himself *obi* or king, Winterbottom lashes out against the British administration: "This among a people who never had kings before! This was what British administration was doing among the Ibos, making a dozen mushroom kings grow where there was none before" (59). The frequency of repetition of the idea of inventing chieftaincy where none had existed, not only indicates the degree to which Winterbottom abhors this type of governance, but also reveals an important colonial error which Achebe is protesting against using a fictional character.

Achebe is not satisfied with merely criticizing the policy as a political error; he goes on to show how difficult it was to implement. He illustrates with two examples: (a) the case of Chief Ikedi and (b) the case of Ezeulu. Under pressure from his authorities, Winterbottom had appointed James Ikedi, an intelligent christian convert, as the Warrant Chief for Okperi. It took Ikedi only three months to abuse this office. He was "high–handed," "set up illegal court and a private prison," and committed what amounted to a grave scandal in Igboland by taking to himself any woman he liked without paying the customary bride–price. In this way Chief Ikedi took advantage of his office to abuse traditional values. For his scandalous behavior, Winterbottom had him suspended for six months, but being a smart "rascal" he went through a Senior Resident and had himself reinstated. The suspension had no lasting effect on Chief

Ikedi. He continued his scandalous practices. In collusion with the road construction overseer, he blackmailed his people, especially wealthy villagers. He took money from them to forestall the demolition of their compounds for the construction of the new road even if the road had never been planned to encroach upon their boundaries. His corruption was beyond limits, yet he proved too clever to be incriminated, having covered all possible loopholes. For Achebe, just as for Winterbottom, Ikedi's case is a typical example of what is bound to happen when the colonial administration imposes a man or a system on a people. The result is bound to be disastrous, as the Secretary for Native Affairs discovered after an official inquiry into Paramount Chieftaincy. According to Winterbottom: "The fellow came over here and spent a long time discovering the absurdities of the system which I had pointed out all along. Anyhow, from what he said in private conversation it was clear that he agreed with us that it had been an unqualified disaster" (109). The Secretary's official report was never published, which is a commentary on the administration's preoccupation with ineffectual inquiries. According to Clarke: "We set up a commission to discover all the facts, as though facts meant anything. We imagine that the more facts we can obtain about our Africans the easier it will be to rule them" (109). Winterbottom disagrees with his junior officer's criticism saying: "Facts are important . . . and Commissions of Inquiry could be useful. The fault of our Administration is that they invariably appoint the wrong people and set aside the advice of those of us who have been here for years" (109). In this dialogue Achebe attacks colonial administration with a pointed irony. The colonials seek to gain knowledge of the people and their culture through bureaucratic red tape: they can obtain only facts and not true knowledge. As Winterbottom rightly suggests, they should go through officials who by their long experience in the field [presumably] know the people. Earlier in his reaction to the Lieutenant–Governor's memorandum, Winterbottom had ruminated thus in his mind: "The great tragedy of British colonial administration was that the man on the spot who knew his African and knew what he was talking about found himself being constantly overruled by starry–eyed fellows at headquarters" (57). Ironically, even the so–called Old Coasters —as we have seen earlier, as evidenced in the wrong choice of Ikedi—lack true knowledge of the people and their culture, which is also a great obstacle to the successful implementation of Indirect Rule.

The appointment of Ezeulu, the priest of Ulu, as the Warrant Chief of Umuaro also betrays a lack of understanding on the part of the Administration. The choice of Ezeulu is based on a false impression: he witnessed against his people in the land dispute between Umuaro and Okperi. Such singular candor is uncharacteristic of the natives and so Winterbottom attributes it to "some pretty fierce tabu working on him" (37). Further, Winterbottom misinterprets Ezeulu's authority in his conversation with Clarke: "I've gone through the records of the case again and found that the man's title is Eze Ulu. The prefix 'eze' in Ibo means King. So the man is a kind of priest–king" (107). His explanation is very literal and thus we suspect that his understanding of Ezeulu's authority is secular. In reality Eze–Ulu means Chief Priest of Ulu (26), and the authority associated with the title is spiritual and sacerdotal. The authority Winterbottom intends to confer on him is administrative and purely secular, and will be resisted by the people. Already Ezeulu is under fire from his detractors, accused of overreaching his authority, as is evident in Nwaka's address to the Umuaro assembly:

> Nwaka began by telling the assembly that Umuaro must not allow itself to be led by the Chief Priest of Ulu. "My father did not tell me that before Umuaro went to war it took leave from the priest of Ulu. . . . The man who carries a deity is not a king. He is there to perform his god's ritual and to carry sacrifice to him. But I have been watching this Ezeulu for many years. He is a man of ambition; he wants to be king, priest, diviner, all. His father, they said, was like that too. But Umuaro showed him that Igbo people knew no kings." (26–27).

Long as Winterbottom may have been in the colonial service, it is obvious that he does not understand the basic custom of Umuaro, in particular, that the priest of a god is not a king.

He does not understand Ezeulu's character either, even though he bases his appointment on that perception. He thinks Ezeulu is a worthy candidate for chieftaincy simply because he did not "perjure" himself, but hardly did he know that the traditionally conservative and headstrong Ezeulu could muster courage to say, "Tell the white man that Ezeulu will not be anybody's chief, except Ulu." And once he made up his mind, nothing could change it, not even weeks of detention in Captain Winterbottom's guardroom. In the end, the well–intentioned offer backfires when Ezeulu feels insulted by the white man's patronage and henceforth regards him as an enemy, though in his fight with his own people, the white man still remains his ally (176).

We see then that Achebe's rebellion against colonial policy is portrayed in the reaction of his major characters, Winterbottom and Ezeulu, both representing the rulers and the ruled. The contempt with which they receive the news of the failure of the policy is a further indication of Achebe's opposition. In his sick bed Winterbottom reads the Lieutenant–Governor's directives that no further appointments be made until a decision is taken on whether or not to continue the policy. He reacts with disgust, muttering under his breath "something like: shit on the Lieutenant Governor!" (180). On his own part, Ezeulu reacts to the news of his release both from the jail and from the burden of chieftaincy with cynical laughter: "He broke into his rare belly–deep laugh" (178). Laughter is his best weapon to express contempt at the white man's futile attempt. "So the white man is tired?" he asks, as if he knew all along that the white man was wasting his time.

Achebe ends his attack on Indirect Rule with an irony. After the release of Ezeulu, Mr. Clarke picks up his mail and reads a Reuter's telegram and a letter. The telegram carries the news about Russian peasants rebelling against the Communist regime and refusing to grow crops. Mr. Clarke, who apparently is anti–Communist, reacts by saying: "Serve them right." He will post it on the notice board in the Regimental Mess for all to read. Clarke is aware of the futility of forcing a system (communism) down the throat of a people. Ironically, the same thing is happening in his district where chieftaincy is being resisted. The second letter is a report by the Secretary for Native Affairs. It enjoins the Administrators to withhold enforcement of Indirect Rule until further notice. Thus, Achebe likens the colonial government to the Russian Communist regime: both impose unpopular policy on the people and both are failing in that regard.

One should, at this point, clarify what Achebe is attempting to portray. First, it needs to be stated that Achebe is not rebelling against the British per se. Rather, though wrongheadedly, the British were attempting to accomplish what had not even been conceived of by the Nigerians themselves. These were separate tribes, cultures, and peoples who never thought of themselves as being joined under the umbrella of a single national group. For better or worse, for Achebe Nigeria is a nation of separate peoples who must learn to become a nation. This is about the best thing that the British did, though unknowingly. Second, as to the question of Indirect Rule, it is clear that Achebe depicts the system for what it is—simple subjugation. What is more denigrating is the use of the native in the effort of total domination of one cultural power over another. There are some tacit but real assumptions that are made by the British characters in his novel. It comes in what was said previously about "facts." We have seen that Achebe has illustrated the British attitude toward gathering "facts" as a messy if not unwholesome chore. Of more importance, is that "facts" are useful only if they are ordered. Hence, it is this passion for order, the superstructure into which the "facts" fit, that Achebe rebels against. It is clear, as we had previously pointed out, that the British ignorance of knowing the "facts" has blinded them from understanding the African, but further, there is an inferred theory in the British attitude toward "primitives." The British seem to believe that there is a sort of evolutionary continuum to political administration. At the lowest level is the patriarchal model, higher still is the system of elders, still higher is the feudal model, and finally the full blown monarchy as the pinnacle of the evolutionary chain. Achebe's ongoing chant that there is "no king among the Igbo" serves almost as a Greek chorus concerning the impending tragedy being perpetrated on the Igbo and their culture. It was simply the presumption by the British that because the Igbo had no king, elder system, etc., they were only a patriarchal society, hence at the lowest echelon of the evolutionary chain. It was this "ordering" itself that further blinded the British Administrators from understanding the Igbo. It never occured to a single British official to ask why they have no king. Since their faith in the evolutionary theory of authority had attained the unassailable position of dogma, it was an unquestionable law of societal development. Had they examined the Igbo system of titles and their relation to wealth, they would have seen the extraordinarily complex system of checks and balances in the Igbo "a–political" system that separated raw power from rule through wisdom. They would not have been so arrogant in their presumption to rule over anyone but themselves. The balance between wealth and titles in the Igbo system kept the Igbo from exercising the common inclination to dominate or exploit others for one's own personal gain. In the case of Ikedi and Ezeulu, we see this balance upset. This is Achebe's ironic humor in action. What is a perfectly *ordered society* is upset in the *name of order*; what truly civilizes individuals in society through the system of *balances* is overturned by an alien culture by the imposition of monarchical (meaning *mono* or single) tyranny. There is no resistance to the forces within the individual toward exploitation (and ultimately chaos) when a societal order is removed that had kept those inclinations tethered. Things simply fall apart. Rational, civilized men are made to become savages. Basically, he asks us to consider whether the "treatment of the disease was worse than the disease itself?" For him Indirect Rule is no rule at all.

Achebe also rebels against the missionaries who, like the Administrators, have also contributed to the denigration and disintegration of the Igbo people and their culture. In keeping with his style of balanced treatment of his subjects, Achebe presents us with the positive and negative sides of missionary activities. We shall deal with the positive results of Christian evangelization in the next chapter; here we are concerned with their faults.

In their excessive zeal to proselytize, the missionaries distorted the tribal values and customs of the Igbo. In the words of David Carroll: "The missionaries, like the administrators, had an occupational need to consolidate the image of savage Africa. The more barbaric were the tribal gods and rituals then clearly the more praiseworthy were the attempts to reform and convert" (*Chinua Achebe*, 9). In *Things Fall Apart,* for example, the first missionaries in Mbanta attack and discredit the deities worshiped there. The white preacher tells his audience that "they worshipped false gods, gods of wood and stone" (102 [134]). These "gods of deceit . . . tell you to kill your fellows and destroy innocent children" (103 [135–36]). His own God is the "only one true God" who rules the earth, the sky and everything (103 [136]). The preacher's antagonistic method of conversion is explained by his ignorance of the true beliefs of Mbanta people. He does not know, for example, that his audience also believe in the supreme God as he does. If only he had come closer to the people as Mr. Brown did, he would have been better informed. Achebe sometimes uses subtle contrasts to reinforce his criticism. Here he uses the good example of Mr. Brown to attack the faults in other missionaries.

Mr. Brown is highly respected by the whole clan "because he trod softly on its faith" (126 [163]). His friendship with the people, Christians and non–Christians, enables him to dialogue with someone like Akunna from whom he learns much about traditional beliefs: "'You say that there is one supreme God who made heaven and earth,' said Akunna on one of Mr. Brown's visits. 'We also believe in Him and call Him Chukwu. He made all the world and the other gods'" (126 [164]). The result of such a dialogue is significant: "In this way Mr. Brown learnt a good deal about the religion of the clan and he came to the conclusion that a frontal attack on it would not succeed" (128 [166]). He then proceeded to build a school and a hospital for the people, and went from house to house to persuade the people to send their children to school. Before long his efforts yielded a tremendous result in terms of conversion.

Mr. Brown's humane, and indeed, Christ–like approach contrasts sharply with the arrogant and uncompromising method of Smith and the unnamed preacher at Mbanta. Smith had replaced Mr. Brown, and as soon as he took control of the mission, he replaced Brown's policy of "compromise and accommodation" with that of aggression. His aggressive policy inspired such zealots as Enoch to violent extremes. Enoch is believed to have killed and eaten the royal python considered sacred by non–Christians. His unmasking the *egwugwu* in public immediately set off a chain reaction of violence that led to a showdown between Christians and non–Christians, and finally led to the death of Okonkwo.

In *Arrow of God* we meet indigenous missionaries who, although two decades apart from their predecessors in *Things Fall Apart*, have retained their style of evangelization. Achebe sees them as equally guilty of distortion. Again, as in *Things Fall Apart*, he exposes the prevalent belligerent approach by contrasting it with a milder and more realistic approach. Moses Unachukwu's compromising method, for example, conflicts with the aggressive method of John Goodcountry who is relentlessly bent on eradicating pagan superstition. Based on his literal interpretation of scripture, he urges the Christians to kill the python for "it is nothing but a snake, the snake that deceived our first mother, Eve" (47). Earlier, on his arrival at Umuaro, he had told his converts about the accomplishments of the early Christians of the Niger Delta who "fought the bad customs of their people, destroyed shrines and killed the sacred iguana" (47). He had also said to them: "You must be ready to kill the python as the people of the rivers killed the iguana" (47). With such instigation Oduche attempts to kill a royal python by imprisoning it in his box, a precipitant act that shocks everyone and hurts the cause of proselytization.

Achebe's opposition to missionaries is centered on their arbitrary condemnation of non–Christian values and beliefs. For Achebe, life is complex and truth has many angles of perception. No human institution should claim to possess the whole truth. Achebe's rebellion against a simplistic approach to life is expressed in an interview with J. O. J. Nwachukwu–Agbada in 1985:

> I am fully convinced that Igbo tradition was very sophisticated in its appreciation of this complexity of life. It was in fact the Western, the Christian tradition which was more simplistic, more naive than what the Igbo were already practicing. The Igbo were practicing a complex view of the world which accepted diversity, which accepted multiplicity of things, of gods even. For them, if the white man comes, well, he must have his own god just as they have their own. But the white man came, claiming to be the way, the light, the truth: nothing else works except him. Now this kind of thinking, this kind of simplicity and self–righteousness, wherever it is emanating from, is dangerous because it is one of the basic causes of distress to mankind today (281–82).

In his outcry against the destruction of the Igbo customs, Achebe accuses both the Administration and the missionaries with the same finger. They both claim to be saving the people: the Administration in its involvement in the "pacification" and civilization of the primitive people; the missionaries in their commitment to the deliverance of the people from savagery, "wicked ways and false gods" (*Things Fall Apart*, 102 [135]). But such claims are challenged by their actions which serve as a catalyst of destruction of an existing civilization. Achebe therefore sees colonization and proselytizing Christianity as twins of destruction, the difference being that one is armed with the gun and the other with the bible. Moses Unachukwu points this out in his address to an age group in *Arrow of God*: "As daylight chases away darkness so will the white man drive away all our customs. . . . The white man, the new religion, the soldiers, the new road—they are all part of the same thing. The white man has a gun, a matchet, a bow and carries fire in his mouth. He does not fight with one weapon alone" (85).

Achebe sees the failure at utilization of commonalities of culture as a serious weakness of colonialism (which includes Christianity). In his view, the ground was fertile for building the Christian faith upon features common to Christianity and tribal religion; for example, the concept of the supreme being. The problem of deracination is that the new faith remains alien and shallow–rooted. This is the problem with such Christian converts as the notorious James Ikedi in *Arrow of God*. He is said to be "among the very first people to receive missionary education in these parts" (57). But the tough ethical values of the past are no longer there to sustain him against the temptation of materialism, and, consequently, he flounders in error in his mad pursuit of power. Cut off from his native religious roots, from the gods of his conscience, and with nothing of equal impact as replacement, he becomes high–handed, corrupt, clever, and cruel. Achebe's expectation from the Administrators and missionaries is contained in the Lieutenant–Governor's memorandum in *Arrow of God*:

> . . . to build a higher civilization upon the soundly rooted native stock that had its foundation in the hearts and minds and thoughts of the people and therefore on which we can more easily build, moulding it and establishing it into lines consonant with modern ideas and higher standards, and yet all the time enlisting the real force of the spirit of the people, instead of killing all that out and trying to start afresh. We must not destroy the African atmosphere, the African mind, the whole foundation of his race . . . (56–57).

Failure to abide by the spirit of this memorandum spelt disaster and largely explains Achebe's rebellion against colonialism.

Yet, one needs to be more specific here to see precisely what Achebe's critique involves. There is little doubt that he despises self–righteousness, cultural blindness, irrational zealotry, and dogmatism that crushingly represses the human spirit. These are rather common to rebels in any age. Achebe's specific lament is that the cultural and religious revolution introduced by the process of colonialism not only overthrew an existing, vibrant culture but also almost completely eradicated the preceding's cultural insights into human life and its mysteries from Nigeria's memory. There were no threads of connection between the former and the latter. Surely, the cultural attainment of a people that stretches to time immemorial which could be almost totally obliterated in the span of a little more than fifty years, must be one of the great tragedies of human history, especially when it is motivated in the name of "civilization." As was mentioned at the beginning of this chapter, "fiction is man's attempt to rebuild his world." In the genre of rebellion literature Achebe must be distinguished in his effort since his rebellion is not some speculation on a utopian future nor a desire to recapture a polaroid of a situation in a paradise lost. Rather, he wishes to show that a very real historical contribution to humanity of an entire people has been expunged from history by the imprint of a civilization that was none too gentle nor appreciative of the many dynamic ways the human spirit manifests itself in all of its magnificence.

AGAINST NEGRITUDE: ACHEBE'S REALISM

INTRODUCTION

Negritude is an anti–colonial movement which attracted the attention of many African intellectuals in the 40's and 50's. Achebe was among the writers influenced by Negritude but at the same time he was repelled by some of its claims. His ambivalent attitude will be examined later after a brief overview of the Negritude movement.

Negritude had its distant origin in the rise of "The Harlem Renaissance" in the early twenties. This was a movement started by a group of young Black writers: Langston Hughes, Jean Toomer, Claude McKay (a Jamaican), Sterling Brown, and others. These writers aimed at promoting the cultural values of the Negro; as Langston Hughes put it, they wanted to express "our individual dark–skinned selves without fear or shame." Inspired by this movement, a group of Martiniquaise students in Paris launched a twenty–page radical journal in 1932—*Légitime Defense*. It never survived its maiden issue. But though short–lived, the journal awakened an anti–colonial sentiment in Parisian Black intellectuals, and it could be said to be the launching pad of the cultural revolution that came to be called Negritude. The authors of *Légitime Defense* denounced colonial exploitation and oppression and also condemned "the vain efforts of coloured bourgeoisie to integrate themselves into the class of the white oppressors" (Finn, 34).

The importance of *Legitime Defense* is that it prepared the ground for the mounting tide of the Black political and cultural rebellion in the early 1930's against colonialism and its values. It awoke Black intellectuals from their slumber, and suddenly they began to debate hot issues such as Black culture, colonialism, socialism, Marxism and assimilation [French colonial policy aimed at integrating the colonized into the culture of the mother country]. Among these awakened intellectuals were the three who really founded Negritude as a movement—Léopold Sédar Senghor (Senegal), Aimé Césaire (Martinique), and Leon–Gontran Damas (Guyana). All the three were poets. The principal goal of the movement was the liberation of the Black people from colonial injustice and the redemption of Black culture.

As defined by Senghor, "Negritude is the consciousness of being Black, the simple recognition of the fact, implying acceptance and responsibility for one's own destiny as a Black man, one's history or one's culture. It is the refusal to assimilate, to see oneself in the 'other'. Refusal of the other is affirmation of the Self" (Finn, 38). This refusal and affirmation gives Negritude its rebellious character. It is not surprising that the movement, which really was a cultural nationalism, coincided with the great nationalist movements sprouting all over the colonies in the 30's and 40's with the principal objective of reclaiming national independence from the colonies. Rejecting negative colonial stereotypes, the Negritude advocates sought for a rehabilitation of the African past, a rediscovery of the goodness in things African. But in this pursuit they beatified and glamorized not only the past but also the present. Léopold Senghor, for example, celebrates in *Chants d'Ombre* respect for the spirit of the ancestors, a longing of an exile in Europe for a return to the land of his birth in Africa, the charm of the African night, the beauty of the Black woman, the need for the Black culture to lend warmth and vitality to the European culture, and other recognitions of the virtues of Blackness.

In "Black Orpheus" Sartre, not without some justification, has described Negritude as "antiracist racism," but it is the type that will lead to the abolition of racial differences (296). In an attempt to justify this brand of racism, he argues that since the Negro is oppressed because of the color of his skin, to free himself "he must first of all become conscious of his race. He must oblige those who have vainly tried throughout the centuries to reduce him to the status of a beast, to recognize that he is a man. ... Thus ... he draws himself erect and proudly proclaims himself a black man" (296). Sartre's prediction that Negritude would be destroyed after it performed its role proved to be true. Political independence of the African countries fulfilled the spirit of nationalism which Negritude had helped promote. Then followed the moment of disillusion when it became obvious to Black Africans that Black is not as beautiful as Negritude had painted it. The negative effect on Negritude was immense.

Negritude had its many critics. Ezekiel Mphahlele, the South African writer, criticized Negritude in an interview with Egejuru for its false and extravagant claims, especially that Blacks enjoy a monopoly of emotional intensity. He also attacked the romanticization of Black and African values by Negritude writers (136). Romanticism which hides the ugly side of the African personality, he contends, indulges in half–truths and makes for bad poetry. Mphahlele was one of the first critics of Negritude but there were many others, most of whom were from English–speaking African countries. These Anglophone writers countered the claims of Negritude, in spite of the influence of Negritude in their writings.

The most vocal opponent is Wole Soyinka whose pithy statement, "a tiger does not proclaim his tigritude, it pounces" served as a death blow on Negritude. In "The Future of West African Writing" Soyinka attacked Negritude's much vaunted notion of "African authenticity" and interpreted it as a "mummification" of traditional life. For him, the truly authentic African literature was produced not by the Negritude Senghor but by the realist Chinua Achebe. Here is part of his criticism of Negritude:

> if we would speak of 'negritude' in a more acceptable and broader sense Chinua Achebe is a more 'African' writer than Senghor. The duiker will not paint 'duiker' on his beautiful back to proclaim his duikeride; you'll know him by his elegant leap. The less self-conscious the African is, and the more innately his individual qualities appear in his writing, the more seriously he will be taken as an artist of exciting dignity. But Senghor seems to be so artistically expatriate that his romanticism of the negro becomes suspect . . . I would say that poets like Leopold Senghor . . . are a definite retrogressive pseudo-romantic influence on the healthy development of West African writing (*The Horn*, 4 [1960]: 14–15).

To sum up, despite the spiritual and cultural role Negritude played in generating Black and African consciousness and despite stressing what Lindfors termed "the wholesome integrity of things African" (31), it was bound to be destroyed by the problems it created in pursuit of its goal: racial obsession, narrowness of self-definition, exaggeration and romanticization of Black culture and experience, and devotion to static norms and forms. Hence, a rebellion that started with a lofty objective was flawed by the methods it used to pursue that objective.

ACHEBE AND NEGRITUDE

Achebe and Negritude exponents share certain things in common: the spirit of rebellion, a commitment to the past, and a commitment to the restoration of the dignity of African values. But Achebe differs from them in one particular—he sees roundly where they see partially. It is a mark of Negritude that it takes only the good side of Black personality and culture and totally ignores the bad side. For example, Negritude literature failed to deal with the dark issues of the African past—intertribal wars, slavery, and the horrors of superstition. Furthermore, in dealing with the present, it glossed over poverty, sickness, tribal turmoil, and Black inhumanity to Black. As Chinweizu *et al.* observe, Negritude chose to present us with the "illusion of purity and sanctity," a "blanket praise in retort to Europe's blanket condemnation of Africa" (257–58). But in so doing it created an unbalanced picture approximating absurdity. Achebe, on the other hand, presents a realistic picture of African past and present in which the beautiful and the ugly converge and co–exist.

Such realism underlies Achebe's attitude toward Negritude. As a critic of colonialism, he lauds the role of Negritude in preparing Africans for independence and in helping to restore dignity to Africans. Negritude's propaganda and art served at a particular period as "props" fashioned "to help us get on our feet again" ("The Novelist as Teacher," *Morning Yet*, 71 [59]). In view of the prejudices against the Blacks, especially in colonial literature, Achebe justifies Negritude's extreme reaction: "In a world bedeviled by these [colonial literary prejudices] and worse beliefs is it any wonder that Black nations should attempt to demonstrate (sometimes with exaggerated aggressiveness) that they are as good as—and better than—their detractors?" ("The Role of the Writer in a New Nation," 8). In one instance, at least, Achebe defends Negritude's "antiracist racism." In "The Novelist as Teacher," he writes: "For the moment it is in the nature of things that we may need to counter racism with what Jean–Paul Sartre has called an antiracist racism, to announce not just that we are as good as the next man but that we are much better" (*Morning Yet*, 71–72 [59]).

The other side of Achebe condemns Negritude. In an interview in 1963, Achebe makes the following statement: "I am against slogans. I don't think, for example, that 'Negritude' has any meaning whatsoever. Panafricanism? Maybe. Negritude, no" (quoted in Bishop, 160). To understand this change of attitude, we need to keep in mind that Achebe distinguishes between the early and later Negritude. In an answer to Egejuru in an interview in *Towards African Literary Independence*, Achebe clearly draws the line between "historic Negritude and that of today," adding in reference to the former: "At the moment when it was created, there was a genuine need and it contributed something significant" (132). The later phase of Negritude was defined more in conferences, and became more of empty propaganda and slogans. It was a Negritude that was overtaken by historical realities. The end of colonialism and the failure, to a large extent, of Black politicians and Black rule had reduced Negritude to mere cliché.

Achebe attacks Negritude for its outlandish claims. Senghor, for example, believes that Africa can save Europe by her gifts of healing through emotion. In the poem "Prayer to Masks," Africa is portrayed as the "'leaven that the white flour needs'." Africa will "'teach rhythm to the world that has / died of machines and cannons'." In "New York" Senghor calls on New York—the symbol of Western civilization—to "'let black blood flow into your blood / That it may rub the rust from your steel joints, like an oil of life'"("Africa and her Writers,"*Morning Yet*, 37 [31–32]). Reacting to such claims, Achebe retorts saying that firstly, Africa is not healthy enough to undertake such a "messianic mission" in the world, and secondly, the world may not be interested in such salvation. Such "solicitude for the health and happiness of Europe," he says, "may indeed have a ring of quixotic adventure about it" ("Africa and her Writers," *Morning Yet*, 37, 38 [32]). An aspect of Negritude's romanticism is its dream of Africa's catalytic role in the world; another is its golden image of the past. Achebe deflates this form of idealization with his image of light and glass:

> When white light hits glass one of two things happen. Either you have an
> image which is faithful if somewhat unexciting or you have a glorious
> spectrum which though beautiful is really a distortion. Light from the
> past passes through a kind of glass to reach us. We can either look for the
> accurate though somewhat unexciting image or we can look for the glori-
> ous technicolor ("The Role of the Writer in a New Nation," 9).

Negritude opts for the glorious technicolor, with the result that the Negritude writer becomes "an unworthy witness" while the world he attempts to re–create loses credibility (9). Achebe chooses the opposite, that is, to present a "faithful" albeit "unexciting" picture of the past, strongly insisting that "any serious African writer who wants to plead the cause of the past must not only be God's advocate, he must also do duty for the devil" (9). Whereas Negritude plays only "God's advocate," Achebe consciously plays God's advocate and devil's advocate, and in this way he rebels against Negritude. We shall now proceed with a detailed example from one of Achebe's novels. We shall see how he presents the beautiful and the ugly aspects of the society of Umuofia in *Things Fall Apart*.

The beauty of Umuofia is mostly portrayed in the first thirteen chapters which deal with domestic matters, agriculture, marriage, games, festivals, and other forms of social interaction. This section is lacking in plot development, but that is because Achebe wants to concentrate first on the customs of the people and then (in the second section) on the actions of the hero. Umuofia is "goldenly" presented as a proud and stable society, vibrant with music, dance, and festivities. It is a dignified society in which law and order is preserved by a complex system of customs and traditions covering birth, marriage, and death. It is a highly competitive society in which merit rather than heritage determines one's status. In this society, a man could begin life as a pauper and rise to become one of the distinguished men of the clan. Hard work, valor, and wealth are revered. A man's prestige depends on the number of yams in his barn, the number of wives and children he has, the number of huts in his compound, the number of titles he has taken, and the number of heroic acts he has performed, especially at war.

Okonkwo fulfills all these. One of the highlights of this novel is its artistic weaving of the personal and the public levels, that is, the hero's character and destiny with the clan's. The son of the improvident Unoka, Okonkwo is determined not to be like his father—debt–ridden, poor, and effeminate. Thanks to hard work and strong will, Okonkwo who starts life through share–cropping, becomes one of the wealthiest and most respected men in his clan, thus proving that in Umuofia, if a child washed his hands, he could eat with elders; that is, the opportunity is there for anyone who wants to take advantage of it.

The strength of Umuofia society lies in its political and judicial institutions. The people are ruled not by chiefs and kings but by the will of the people determined in the people's assembly. The will of the people is the unwritten law. In their Athenian–type democracy, any opinion that carries majority support prevailes. A decision to dispatch an ultimatum to Mbaino asking them to choose between paying compensation and war is preceded by an assembly deliberation involving about ten thousand people (*Things Fall Apart*, 8 [14]). On another occasion, after the District Commissioner has detained and released six leaders of Umuofia, an emergency meeting of the clan is summoned to determine the right course of action. Okonkwo attends the meeting expecting a decision in favor of war, but his hope is dashed because the people are not inclined toward war. The point Achebe makes by this dramatic presentation of

Umuofia meeting at this time is that the precolonial Igbo had a democracy, and therefore the impression created by the Europeans that the Africans were savages enslaved by tribal chiefs was false. Powerful as Okonkwo is in his community, he fails to impose his will on his people. He then acts alone, killed the white man's messenger, and hangs himself. The will of the community remains supreme.

The role the society plays for the individual members is admirable. The members find security and protection in their community, and for that reason, they are attached to it. Internal disputes are redressed, and peace and harmony is maintained through unwritten laws and the traditional form of judicial system. An example is the marital case brought before the communal tribunal in which the ancestral spirits act as jury. The wife–beater Uzowulu had been paid in his own coin when the brothers of his wife Mgbafo beat him up and refused to return his wife or his customary bride–price. Uzowulo appealed to the tribunal. On the appointed day, the jury holds their deliberation and in the end Evil Forest pronounces their verdict. Uzowulu is to take a pot of wine to his in–laws and beg for his wife to be returned to him. He is reminded that "it is not bravery when a man fights with a woman" (66 [89]). His in–laws are to release Mgbafo as soon as Uzowulu brings the wine to them. This fair verdict, as Obiechina observes, is "conciliatory rather than contractual" (*Culture, Tradition*, 209), and underscores the familial rather than the legalistic spirit that pervades communal interactions in this society. Members derive moral support from kinship groups as is shown in the seating of the tribunal where the plaintiff (Uzowulu) and the defendant (Mgbafo) are each surrounded by their nearest kin. The extended family system provides support, especially in a crisis. Okonkwo enjoys such support from his mother's people during his exile at Mbanta. Collective responsibility and communal solidarity as displayed at joyous occasions like marriages and sorrowful occasions like funerals are precious values of the past which Achebe in this novel intends to recommend to the present generation who have lost these values.

Religion is partly responsible for this collective solidarity. Traditional religion provides the people with common beliefs and helps to mold a collective conscience. Umuofia society has a powerful religion around which the lives of the members revolve. The will of God is sought before any major decision is taken. Powerful and intimidating as the clan may be, it would never go to war against her neighbors "unless its case was clear and just and was accepted as such by the Oracle—the oracle of the Hills and the Caves" (9 [16]). Okonkwo's father, Unoka, sacrifices a cock to Ani the goddess of the earth and a cock to Ifejioku the god of yams every year before he begins planting his yams (12–13) [20]. The gods are feared and respected. Their commands must be strictly obeyed or there would follow a terrible punishment which sometimes could visit the entire community. Okonkwo is made to understand this when he breaks the week of peace by beating his third wife, Ojiugo. The priest of Ani, Ezeani, addresses these stern words to him: "The evil you have done can ruin the whole clan. The earth goddess whom you have insulted may refuse to give us her increase, and we shall all perish" (22 [32]). Although Okonkwo scrupulously discharges the penalty imposed on him—"one she–goat, one hen, a length of cloth and a hundred cowries" to be sent to the shrine of Ani—he does not escape the condemnation from the people who for some time "talked of nothing else but the *nso–ani* [abomination] which Okonkwo had committed" (22 [32, 33]). Sometimes the penalty for an offense against the gods or the community is exile or ostracism. The "female murder" Okonkwo commits by accidentally killing the son of Ezeudu is punished with seven years of exile, and the killing of the royal python by a Christian convert causes all the Mbanta Christians to be ostracized (113 [148–149]).

The family is the backbone of Umuofia society, and the cohesion in the family contributes to the orderliness and stability in this society. Some critics criticize Achebe's emphasis on domestic scenes for slowing down the tempo of the novel. They are right; nevertheless, the novel gains more by the inclusion, for through them we view the Igbo society at its very foundation. The family in *Things Fall Apart* is the basis of cultural continuity. Okonkwo is aware of this when he constantly insists on making Nwoye a man capable of upholding the family name and also of sustaining the link between the living members and their ancestors. Discipline, respect, fear of the gods, etc.—these values on which the communal stability depends, are learned in the family. The security which the individual enjoys in the community begins in the family. Okonkwo's family in particular reveals the idyllic situation in which parents exercise judicious care of their children. Except in the crises that now and then erupt, the children live happily in a stable and secure family environment. Ekwefi's tender care for her only surviving daughter Ezinma is a typical example of parental love in Umuofia. Although Okonkwo, like many fathers in this traditional society, exercises patriarchal authority over his household, "down his heart [he] was not a cruel man" (9 [16]). His great affection and concern for Ezinma and her mother is shown when Ezinma falls sick and is reported to be dying. Okonkwo is quick to find a remedy. Chielo, the priestess, later carries Ezinma off in the dead of the night to the shrine of Agbala. It is a very fatherly Okonkwo who dares the dangers of darkness to stand beside Ekwefi near the cave, and realizing such immense love, she responds with "tears of gratitude" (76 [102]).

The society in *Things Fall Apart* is lively, prosperous, self–assured, and to some extent, civilized. Yet, it is a society plagued with serious problems. Fear, death, and danger brood over it. There is "the fear of evil and capricious gods and of magic, the fear of the forest, and the forces of nature, malevolent red in tooth and claw" (9 [16–17]). Haunted by her sense of insecurity, often arising from her fear of the gods and the unknown, this society performs some outrageously cruel deeds. Whatever is identified as a threat to Umuofia's security or any possible cause of the wrath of the gods is expeditiously and often ruthlessly disposed of. On the basis of this, twins are abandoned to die in evil forests. Uchendu's daughter, Akueni, is said to have lost many twins (95 [124]). *Ogbanje* children (who are regarded as viciously plaguing their mothers by their cycle of birth and death) are mutilated at their death to prevent them from coming back. Swelling sickness is regarded as an abomination to the earth goddess and those who suffer from such are tied to trees and left to languish in evil forests and sometimes to be devoured by vultures. Unoka, Okonkwo's father, falls victim to this horrible practice. Nor does Okonkwo escape the fate of abandonment. Suicides are buried by strangers in the evil forest, and Okonkwo who hanged himself is so treated. *Osu* people are denied normal relationships with other citizens, and at death, are buried by their kind in the evil forest. [The *osu* are people or their descendants who were originally sacrificed or consecrated to a god. They thus become sacred possessions of the god. As possessions of the god, they are now the god's special servants or, more strictly speaking, the god's slaves. And as the god's slaves, in human society, they are marginalized and alienated because they have the stigma of slavery attached to them.] Human sacrifice is practiced. Ikemefuna, the innocent boy, is thus sacrificed for an offense committed by his people.

These examples and others are presented as cruel and horrible practices in the pre–colonial society. Here and there Achebe drops comments questioning and challenging such practices. An example is his viewpoint expressed through Obierika after the destruction of Okonkwo's property following his crime and exile:

> Obierika was a man who thought about things. When the will of the god-
> dess had been done, he sat down in his *obi* and mourned his friend's ca-
> lamity. Why should a man suffer so grievously for an offense he had
> committed inadvertently? But although he thought for a long time he
> found no answer. He was merely led into greater complexities. He re-

membered his wife's twin children, whom he had thrown away. What crime had they committed? The earth had decreed that they were an offense on the land and must be destroyed. And if the clan did not exact punishment for an offense against the great goddess, her wrath was loosed on all the land and not just on the offender. As the elders said, if one finger brought oil it soiled the others (87 [117–18]).

In *Things Fall Apart*, Achebe creates a strong and stable society, rich in culture, producing a heroic personality. He also shows that the "cracks and weaknesses" in this traditional society make it impossible for the center to hold together. Achebe intends that the positive aspects of this society should inspire his contemporary society while its weaknesses leading to its collapse should serve as a lesson. In this educational role, Achebe seriously departs from Negritude's narrow perspective. Like the sons of the prophets of old, Negritude gives the people only what pleases their ears in order to affirm their pride and dignity. Like Elijah the prophet, Achebe gives them the sweet and bitter truth in order to save them. Achebe's departure from Negritude is not only rebellious but also redemptive.

AGAINST POST INDEPENDENCE CIVILIAN POLITICS

In fighting colonialism the African nationalist leaders had rallied the support of the people with promises of a free democratic country marked by peace and prosperity. After independence, the new leaders failed to make good their promises. Instead of the paradise they had promised, they produced a government riddled with bribery, corruption, nepotism, violence, and murder. People were disillusioned. For writers like Achebe, "the great collusive swindle that was independence showed its true face to us. And we were dismayed" ("Colonialist Criticism," *Morning Yet*, 23 [20]). In "Named for Victoria, Queen of England," Achebe also complains about the new changes in Africa where the nationalist leader of yesterday has become "the not so attractive party boss" (*Morning Yet*, 123 [102]) Having observed this party boss for six years, and not content to sit back while the system decayed, Achebe fought back with a satiric novel, *A Man of the People,* which exposed the political mess in the newly independent Nigeria. Achebe explains in his own words why he wrote this novel:

> Within six years of independence, Nigeria was a cesspool of corruption and misrule. Public servants helped themselves freely to the nation's wealth. A certain professor has described the government of many African countries as a kleptocracy. Nigeria could certainly be called that. Elections were blatantly rigged. (One British weekly captioned its story of a Nigerian election NIGERRIMANDERING.) The national census was outrageously stage-managed; judges and magistrates were manipulated by politicians in power. The politicians themselves were manipulated and corrupted by foreign business interests.
>
> This was the situation in which I wrote *A Man of the People*. ("The African Writer and the Biafran Cause." *Morning Yet*, 143–44 [118–19]).

In *A Man of the People*, Achebe presents us with a picture of political life in a typical newly independent African country which evidently is Nigeria. Irony which had served him well in his rebellion against colonialism now gives way to ridicule and satire. The novel deals with the political activities of Chief Nanga, a semi–literate, corrupt, opportunistic politician who maneuvers his way to the post of a Minister in the government of an unnamed African country. Once in that lucrative position, he uses his power and ill–gotten wealth to ensure his re–election. All his politicking is however aborted by a military "coup d'etat" which topples the government. We watch the activities of Nanga through the eyes of a first person narrator, Odili who is a college graduate and a former pupil of Chief Nanga. Odili is a critical observer but also an interested participant in the action. Although the whole story is told from his viewpoint, there are times when he himself is made the object of Achebe's satire. Achebe uses him to indict and ridicule institutions and people, but he often finds occasions to laugh at him too. In this novel Achebe evaluates not just Chief Nanga, Odili, and their types, but the entire Nigerian community. He questions their ability and desire to govern themselves properly. As they fumble from one form of corruption to another, we see the terrible consequence of the corrupting power of money, position, and power on a people who have lost touch with traditional values needed for a stable government. The society represented in this novel has lost sight of its past and has consequently fallen an easy victim to materialism. As we proceed to examine Achebe's reaction to the political muddle in the post independent Nigeria, we shall focus on two key figures—Chief Nanga and Odili, and on the Nigerian community as well.

In portraying Chief Nanga, Achebe carefully restrains himself from the temptation of making him a villain. Nanga has some admirable qualities. He is "a man of the people." The irony associated with this title notwithstanding, Nanga is in every sense popular among his people. The novel begins with a huge reception in his honor during his home visitation. A female singer likens his popularity to that of "the proverbial traveller–to–distant–places who must not cultivate enmity on his route" (1*).

Chief Nanga's popularity can be explained by a number of factors. To begin with, he is handsome and impressive. Odili remembers him as he was sixteen years ago: "a popular, young and handsome teacher, most impressive in his uniform as scoutmaster" (2). His portrait on the school wall depicted a "faultlessly handsome scoutmaster wearing an impeccable uniform" (2). When we meet him in Anata Grammar School, we are attracted by his features as we learn from Odili that "the man was still as handsome and youthful–looking as ever" (8). Nanga has more than his physical features to his advantage.

He has a compelling personality which is capable of charming even his critics such as Odili. His exceptional charisma gains more by his affable qualities. He smiles and jokes with everybody, and when it suits him speaks pidgin English, a popular dialect

---

* Citations from *A Man of the People* are to the 2nd ed., Heinemann African Writers Series edition (1988).

among common folks. Chief Nanga is able to mix with people of all classes; "he had a jovial word for everyone. You could never think—looking at him now—that his smile was anything but genuine" (8). His generosity is outstanding. Contrary to Odili's fears, Nanga recognizes him after sixteen years of separation. He openly expresses his joy and embraces Odili. He is concerned about Odili's progress in life, and is quick to promise his assistance. It is much to his credit that he keeps the promise he made to Odili: harbors him in his luxurious government house at Bori intending to help him obtain a post–graduate scholarship to continue his studies abroad. Their relationship is suddenly broken by Nanga's reckless interference with Odili's girlfriend, but Nanga shows remorse, apologizes and wins our sympathy. Although his motive is political, he does make a fresh move to reconcile with Odili through Odili's father. In all this, we cannot fail to admire the positive qualities that Chief Nanga commands.

But beneath this outward charm and sometimes genuine generosity lies the corrupt and crafty nature of Nanga. His lively humor, affability, and generosity always serve his political ambition. One of the ways he gains his popularity is by pandering to the people. At the reception in Anata Grammar School, seeing himself surrounded by teachers, he expresses nostalgia for the teaching profession. "True to God who made me . . . I use to regret it. Teaching is a very noble profession," he tells the teachers (9). The cynical laughter he receives is enough reminder that teachers all over the country were in a restive mood. Nanga sensing his error quickly makes it up by giving the teachers what they wanted. With a more serious face he confides to them: "You can rest assured that those of us in the Cabinet who were once teachers are in full sympathy with you" (9–10). And this does the magic. The teachers are full of praise for him. Again, during the parliamentary crisis, when the general outcry was directed against the "Miscreant Gang," Nanga seized the opportunity to please the people and win a political advantage for himself. The "gang"—some members of the Cabinet—had dared suggest a reduction in the money paid to coffee planters who were the power base of the P.O.P. party. In the crisis that ensued, Chief Nanga gainfully led the "hungry hyena" of back benchers in demanding the neck of the "Miscreant Gang" (5). His dramatic interruptions of the Prime Minister's speech with acrimonious condemnation of the "gang" were obviously publicity stunts for cheap popularity. And surely, he impressed many. His contributions—the interruptions—were entered in the Hansard, and the Prime Minister rewarded him by incorporating him into the reconstituted Cabinet.

Politicians all over the world are wont to condescend to any level to gratify the people and win their votes. Achebe shows Nanga's ostentatious gratifications as rather cheap and ridiculous. During the Anata reception, for example, as Chief Nanga and his party walked toward the Proprietor's Lodge, groups of dancers resumed their performance. "The Minister danced a few dignified steps to the music of each group and stuck red pound notes on the perspiring faces of the best dancers. To one group alone he gave away five pounds." (14). Right after this spending fit, Chief Nanga settled down to a cold beer and complained about the Minister's burden: "I no de keep anini for myself, na so so troway. . . . Minister de sweet for eye but too much katakata de for inside" (15). Of course, nobody believed him, certainly not Josiah, who said openly that he would not mind being a Minister and putting up with such ministerial "katakata" (problem). Achebe is indirectly attacking Nanga's self–serving extravagance characteristic of post–independence Nigerian politics. Such wastefulness is unnecessary and only leads to corruption. It is too obvious that Nanga was spending "a fortune" he acquired through corruption, and the more recklessly he spent it, the more he needed to replenish his pocket. The impression he tried to create, that he was penniless, is farcical. A couple of pages later Achebe warns us not to believe Chief Nanga because he says one thing and means another. Achebe reveals this prevarication through Nanga's mistress, Mrs. John, who, we expect, knows him very well. Nanga has just promised to lodge Odili in his comfortable self–contained guest–room in the capital. Mrs. John cuts in: "Make you no min' am, sha–a . . . I kin see say you na good boy. Make you no gree am spoil you. Me I no de for dis bed–room and bath–room business–o. As you see dis man so, na wicked soul. If he tell you stand make you run" (18). This is Achebe's way of telling us early in the novel that Nanga is not the "good guy" he presents himself to be. His cosmetic actions should not deceive us because he is simply an actor.

One of the problems facing newly independent African countries was that semi–literate politicians edged out well educated ones from government and began to pose as intellectuals. Empty titles and honorary degrees were madly sought for to boost their egos. Idi Amin of Uganda and others like him lined up chains of titles and degrees after their names. The unquenchable appetite for degrees and titles among African leaders was the subject of Soyinka's burlesque in *A Play of Giants*. In *A Man of the People*, Achebe ridicules the efforts of politicians to use titles and degrees to create a false image. We meet such outlandish names as: "Chief the Honourable Alhaji Doctor Mongo Sego, M.P." (18); "Alhaji Chief Senator Suleiman Waganda" (100);

and, of course, "Chief the Honourable D[r]. M.A. Nanga, M.P., LL.D." (19). Of all the characters in the novel, Nanga is the most intellectually postural, but Achebe deflates him through satire. Nanga's library reveals his level of education. The set of an American encyclopedia on his shelf is said to be decorative, and the rest of the books—*She, The Sorrows of Satan, Speeches: How to Make Them*—are low class books popular among traders and semi–literate masses in Nigeria (40). Achebe's satire cuts deeper in the episode in which Chief Nanga, as Minister of Culture, is invited to open the book exhibition of works by local authors. We discover that the intellectually bloated Minister of Culture has not heard of Mr. Jalio the country's leading novelist, and that he mistakes Jalio's novel, *The Song of the Black Bird*, for a song (61–62). Such ignorance personified is the people's Cabinet Minister and their idol. The people are greatly impressed by degrees and titles and other forms of posturing. When Nanga announced that an American university was going to award him Doctor of Laws, the people cheered. The journalist spoke their minds when he compared Chief Nanga's new impressive address with Mongo Sego's and found Nanga's more impressive (18–19). The politicians are not the only ones who try to impress with whatever objects are available. During the book exhibition, one of the prominent guests set out to make an impression with his expensive traditional robe on which the manufacturer's advertising label was boldly and proudly displayed: "100% WOOL: MADE IN ENGLAND" (64). Such a boorish show of superior foreign textile in a traditional robe proudly worn for a cultural occasion can only come from a society uncertain about its values. Besides, it shows Achebe's dark humor in force, dark because the politicians and the people have wattled interests, which implies that when the politicians are overthrown, the problems of the nation will not disappear.

Achebe's satire slashes with a sharp edge as Nanga unknowingly betrays his affectation of knowledge in public and the people applaud him. The appalling ignorance in Nanga's speech is revealed in Odili's criticism:

> For how else could you account for the fact that a Minister of Culture announced in public that he had never heard of his country's most famous novel and received applause—as indeed he received again later when he prophesied that before long our own great country would produce great writers like Shakespeare, Dickens, Jane Austen, Bernard Shaw and—raising his eyes off the script—Michael West and Dudley Stamp (65).

The renowned authors are obviously familiar to Nanga's speech–writer, while the obscure writers whom Nanga improvises are those he is familiar with. Michael West is the author of text books such as *English Words for All Occasions* and (together with James Endicott) the *New Method English Dictionary*, a beginner's mini English dictionary used in West African primary schools in the 50's and 60's. Dudley Stamp's geography book, *An Intermediate Commercial Georgraphy*, was also a primary school text. Chief Nanga's knowledge has not gone beyond what it was sixteen years ago when he taught in primary school, and that explains the basis of his "erudite" comparison.

Corruption is endemic in the new nation. Chief Nanga's corruption clouds the entire novel. He is indeed an epitome of the uncontrolled corruption of the first Nigerian republic (1960–66). Nanga struggles to see that the road that passes through his village is paved because it will serve as part of "the national cake" he has grabbed for his people, and will surely ensure his re–election. A more personal reason is that his ten luxury buses will ply that route (43). Bribery over government contract awards has fetched him large sums to enable him to buy those buses, and, in addition, set up rows of blocks of luxury flats in the capital (99–100). Bribery for Chief Nanga is like a fun ticket. A "dash" of five pounds to the Editor of the *Daily Matchet* is a guarantee against any publication of "rubbish about [him]" (66). When threats fail to dissuade Odili from running against him at the elections, Nanga tries to bribe him off with two hundred and fifty pounds and a scholarship (118).

Bribery and corruption permeate the entire fabric of the society affecting not only politicians but also policemen, journalists, thugs, and school teachers. Even ideologues like Max and his party members are not free of the evil of bribery and corruption. Max, to our utmost disappointment, accepts a bribe of one thousand pounds from Chief Koka, and, sadly, he rationalizes about it (126–27). When such loud critics of Nanga cave in to bribery, we clearly understand the point Achebe is making, namely, that the evil of corruption is endemic in this society. Foreign interests are also contaminated. The British Amalgamated pays four hundred pounds to P.O.P. to promote their election campaign and also to safeguard the company's interests. We are told that the Americans "have been even more generous" (126). These international companies, no doubt, hope to receive their dividend after the elections.

No part of the country is free of corruption, not even the villages. Edna's father is a typical example of village corruption. He exhibits a greed hardly surpassed by any other character in all the works of Achebe. This avaricious man knows only one creed: "bring that I may eat!" He says to Odili: "Leave me and my in–law. He will bring and bring and bring and I will eat until I am tired" (91). Material benefit is the only reason he wants to force his daughter Edna in marriage as second wife to Chief Nanga. He hates Odili with a passion because he sees Odili as a threat to his source of material gain. Edna's father, Chief Nanga, Chief Koko, Max, and the entire populace are all tarred with corruption. They are all swayed by their stomach and not by solid moral values.

Consequently, the country's stability is in jeopardy. Greed breeds violence. It is much more so in this novel where greed for power and "the national cake" results in election malpractices and the collapse of the civilian regime. More specifically, corruption and scandal involving the Minister of Foreign Trade, Alhaji Chief Senator Suleiman Waganda, and the British Amalgamated plunge the country into a political crisis leading to preparations for new elections. Given the spirit of unrestraint in the political and social life of the country, we expect a very bitter contest among the political parties for the control of power. The election is prefaced with waves of violence. Odili is assaulted by his audience at the launching of his party in Anata (101–02); the whole country is littered with thugs who masquerade as bodyguards and youth vanguards and molest people. A clash between Odili's bodyguards and the "Nangavanga" [Nanga's youth vanguard] results in destruction of property (112–13); and Odili's intrusion in Nanga's campaign rally earns him a rain of blows that split his skull and leave him half dead in the hospital (140–41). The climax of the election violence culminates in the killing of Max. Chief Koko's driver, under the direction of Koko himself, runs over Max with Koko's car. A reign of terror engulfs the entire country and only ceases with sudden intervention of the military. The soldiers take over the country and lock up the members of the government. The military intervention proves conclusively that the post colonial regime has been a failure. "The man of the people" has not proved himself to be better than his colonial predecessor. The Chief Nangas have been a disappointment, but so too have been their critics, as will be seen in our close study of Odili and his role.

Achebe shows that Odili's idealism cannot succeed because it lacks moral integrity. At the beginning of the novel, Odili is very bitter about the poor state of the economy in his country which he blames on the politicians:

> As I stood in one corner of that vast tumult waiting for the arrival of the
> Minister, I felt intense bitterness welling up in my mouth. Here were
> silly, ignorant villagers dancing themselves lame and waiting to blow off

their gunpowder in honour of one of those who had started the country
off down the slopes of inflation (2).

He has no reason to be enthusiastic about meeting Chief Nanga, and when it comes to
shaking hands with him, he holds out his hand stiffly. But soon Chief Nanga wins him
over with charm and warm embrace. Odili's inconstancy strikes us as he gets excited
over the recognition and prestige he gains from the occasion. From his adversary position he turns completely around and accepts Chief Nanga's invitation to Bori. And
when he gets there, he settles down to the comfort of the ministerial palace, as can be
seen from his comments:

> I was simply hypnotized by the luxury of the great suite assigned to me.
> When I lay down in the double bed that seemed to ride on a cushion of
> air, and switched on that reading lamp and saw all the beautiful furniture
> anew from the lying down position and looked beyond the door to the
> gleaming bathroom and the towels as large as a *lappa* I had to confess
> that if I were at that moment made a minister I would be most anxious to
> remain one forever (36–37).

What we understand from this comment is that if given the power, Odili, like Nanga,
will do everything in his power to retain it. Thus, the idealistic Odili who has despised
and condemned the cynical morality of the crowd which maintains that a sensible
man would not "spit out the juicy morsel that good fortune placed in his mouth" (2), is
now prepared to defend this point of view. In his defense he restates the crowd's viewpoint in different words:

> A man who has just come in from the rain and dried his body and put on
> dry clothes is more reluctant to go out again than another who has been
> indoors all the time. The trouble with our new nation—as I saw it then
> lying on the bed—was that none of us had been indoors long enough to
> be able to say "To hell with it" (37).

He rightly identifies this analogy as the trouble with the new nation; however, it has
become clear to us that Odili has succumbed to the temptations of materialism. This
exemplifies Achebe's position, namely, that when idealism lacks moral foundation, it
crumbles in the face of reality. One of the themes in this novel is the corrupting power
of privilege. In this new nation, ideals yield easily to privilege and rise to prominence.
Odili who chose not to sell his soul for the privilege of going to Europe, now loses his
ideals in the midst of comfort. This makes us distrust his ability to change the political
realities if voted into power.

Politically, Odili is not reliable. His decision to enter politics is not motivated by high principles but by revenge. He had come to Bori to try further his studies. When he loses his woman, Elsie, to Chief Nanga, he decides, as his first act of revenge, to "go back, seek out Nanga's intended parlour–wife and give her the works, good and proper" (76). His second act of revenge is to join the Common People's Convention, a new political party formed to challenge the ruling party, the P.O.P. Joining this party, as Odili puts it, "would add a second string to my bow when I came to deal with Nanga" (78). This leaves us questioning the kind of leadership Odili would provide. It is true that he remained incorruptible by refusing to be bribed and refusing to endorse Max's acceptance of a bribe from Chief Koko. Nevertheless, he is tarnished in other ways: his interest in women, which gives him out as lacking in the proper morality for a leadership role, and his weakness for material comfort.

An incident at the end of the novel leaves us further in doubt as to Odili's qualifications for leadership and the messianic roles he seeks to fulfill. With the civilian regime dissolved and the fate of Nanga in question, Edna's father becomes more tolerant toward Odili whom he now sees as a secure prospect. He is now ready to allow his daughter to marry Odili on condition that Odili pays three hundred and fifty pounds to cover the cost of Edna's education and the customary bride–price. The custom is that when a woman re–marries, the former husband is paid back his bride–price, the funding for this usually comes from that paid by the new husband. Odili does not have enough money to cover such expenses, and so he decides to "borrow" from C.P.C. funds still in his keeping. Odili describes the matter lightly, yet we know that since all political parties have been abolished, Odili is simply appropriating the money. This act further enhances our suspicion that this educated critic, who is corrupt on a minor scale, will be no better, were he to be elected, than those he criticizes. It is Achebe's ironic way of attacking the intellectual elite who talk glibly about the ills of the country and criticize the politicians whereas they themselves have their own guilt. We can see Achebe's pessimism at work: he is implying that there is no hope in the very group we are inclined to believe will save the country if allowed to govern. That does not mean, however, that there is no expectation whatsoever for salvation in this novel; there is; and we shall see how that could come about in the next chapter.

Achebe's revulsion to the role played by "the people" in post independence Nigeria invites discussion. In this novel, the people compare with the chorus in Greek tragedy. They are constantly in the background playing a supportive role, but unlike the chorus in Greek drama, never criticizing the system. Occasionally Achebe turns the spotlight on the people and exposes the dearth of spiritual values as a result of their propensity to greed and acquisitiveness. He also reveals that the Nigerian society after independence was a sick society plagued with ignorance, resignation, and cynicism.

An ignorant people easily falls victim to political intrigue. In *A Man of the People*, we get the impression that the people are unaware that they are being used by the Nangas of the country. At the beginning of the novel, Odili cannot contain himself watching "silly, ignorant villagers" lavishing out of ignorance "fulsome praises" on most unworthy Ministers, including the Prime Minister (2). Odili confesses that in his student days he had himself acted in ignorance. When the Prime Minister dismissed the Minister of Finance, "no one knew the truth at that time," and so the radio, the newspapers, the Students' Union, all fell behind the Prime Minister, and "[p]rotest marches and demonstrations were staged up and down the land" (3–4). The students passed a vote of confidence on the Prime Minister, and called for the detention of the "miscreants". In all of this, the people proved to be ignorant and gullible.

Achebe goes on to show, to his utter dismay, that even when they know the truth about politicians' misdeeds, they fail to raise an outcry. For example, there was "already enough filth clinging to [Nanga's] name to disqualify him for the second term of office, and the C.P.C. publicly did its utmost to expose every scandal associated with him and his colleagues, and yet no one could say: 'No, Nanga has taken more than the owner could ignore!'" (109). Interestingly, the newspapers daily exposed the scandals committed by the leaders, but "far from causing general depression in the country—[they] produced a feeling akin to festivity" (100). This inaction and, especially, the festive response to the terrible spread of misconduct provoke Achebe's condemnation of the people. We can then understand Odili's harsh tone in relating the general response to Max's exposition of the corruption in the outgoing government. Max accused the government of swindling and corruption, and gave an example of how some of the leaders rose from the state of paupers to states of near–millionaires within five years in office. This anomaly evoked laughter from the audience, which Odili recognizes:

> But it was the laughter of resignation to misfortune. No one among them
> swore vengeance; no one shook with rage or showed any sign of fight.
> They understood what was being said, they had seen it with their own
> eyes. But what did anyone expect them to do? (123–24)

One would have expected them to rise with one voice to denounce the wrong done, as the villages of Anata did when Josiah took away a blind beggar's stick. Josiah used the stick to "make juju" in order to charm people into his shop. The whole village rose to condemn him, and in their customary way, they ostracized him (84–86). The acquisitive society of the new nation cannot do what the villagers did, not only because they have lost sight of traditional values but also because they have become too materialistic, too swayed by their stomachs, to condemn such corrupt acts. We see, therefore, a people who are not only resigned to corruption but also have become cynical toward it. Hence: "The greatest criticism a man like [Nanga] seemed capable of evoking in our country was an indulgent: 'Make you no min'am'" (65). Roughly translated, this is like saying "poor boy" when a five year old child steals from his mother. Referring to his incognito appearance in Nanga's campaign rally, Odili tells us that if he marched up to the dais where Chief Nanga's virtues were being enumerated and announced to the people that Nanga was "an Honourable Thief," it would not be news to them; they would simply laugh and say: "What a fool! . . . Was he not here when white men were eating; what did he do about it? Where was he when Chief Nanga fought and drove the white men away? Why is he envious now that the warrior is eating the reward of his courage? If he was Chief Nanga, would he not do much worse?" (138). Achebe is here showing the extent of the deterioration in the people's guiding principle which has shifted from the age–old traditional ethics based on the people's collective will, to the new ethic of the national cake, or crudely put, "you–chop–me–self–I–chop" ethic. They "had become even more cynical than their leaders and were apathetic into the bargain." Their new philosophy rings this way: try to outlive the present trying moment, for "if you survive, who knows? It might be your turn to eat tomorrow. Your son may bring home your share" (144). Achebe seems to be suggesting by the emphasis on "eating" that a nation which depends on the crude principle of sharing and eating rather than on building and contributing, will sooner than later come crashing down. And the new nation did crumble with the military intervention.

Judging from the people's behavior immediately after the military take–over, there are grounds to suspect that military intervention will only serve as a temporary relief. This is the impression created in the following passage which is Odili's analysis of the situation:

> What I found distasteful however was the sudden, unashamed change of
> front among the very people who had stood by and watched [Max] die.

> Overnight everyone began to shake their heads at the excesses of the last regime, at its graft, oppression, and corrupt government: newspapers, the radio, the hitherto silent intellectuals and civil servants—everybody said what a terrible lot; and it became public opinion the next morning. And those were the same people that only the other day had owned a thousand names of adulation, whom praise–singers followed with song and talking–drum wherever they went. Chief Koko in particular became a thief and a murderer, while the people who had led him on—in my opinion the real culprits—took the legendary bath of the Hornbill and donned innocence (148).

It is disturbing to see the people wash their hands in innocence and siding with the military, ready to condemn the politicians. Such a Protean attitude by "the real culprits" further complicates the country's problems, for it is likely that in their clean–up efforts the military will leave the people untouched; hence, the problem will in time resurface.

To end this section, we must address Achebe's prophetic role demonstrated in the writing of this novel. Barely nine days after the Nigerian military coup in January 1966, *A Man of the People* was published. This caused some people to wonder if Achebe had foreknowledge of the coup. Achebe has denied any knowledge of the coup, arguing that any close watcher of the events in Nigeria in the few years before the coup could easily have told that some catastrophe was imminent. Yet, we are impressed by the details of the coup which happened as narrated in the text, for example, the rounding up of politicians, the people's mercurial attitude, and most importantly, the counter coup (147). In his prophetic role Achebe foresaw the coming disaster and forewarned the people about it. In *A Man of the People* he examines the new Nigeria, sometimes in mocking terms, sometimes in a tone of bitterness and rebellion, but on the whole, with a prophetic vision.

AGAINST MILITARY DICTATORSHIP

The failure of politicians in post–independence African states was a drum signal for military intervention in politics. In Nigeria, military intervention has become a common feature. Out of thirty years of the country's independence, twenty has been under military rule. Coups and counter–coups punctuate the political history of the country. Each military intervention comes as a new attempt to salvage the country from greedy politicians or soldiers. Ironically, the self–styled military messiahs often end up more destructive of the country than their predecessors. Nigerian writers have reacted more quickly against the military than against the politicians, because military corruption and dictatorship tend to be brash and ruthless and so provoke a quicker response. Besides, after being fooled by the politicians in the early period of independence (as was shown in Chapter One of this study), writers have become more vigilant. *A Man of the People* ended with the military overthrow of the civilian government. Twenty–one years lapsed between that work and Achebe's latest novel, *Anthills of the Savannah*; yet in his latest novel Achebe continues the saga of Nigeria from where he left it in *A Man of the People*. *Anthills of the Savannah* is a story of an African country under military dictatorship. Although the novel is set in a fictitious African country, the subject matter and the names of the characters identify the country as Nigeria.

In *Anthills of the Savannah*, Achebe presents the story of three boyhood friends —Sam, Chris, and Ikem—who attended the same local school and later trained in England in their separate careers. At the beginning of the novel, Sam, the graduate of Sandhurst, has become head of state following the military overthrow of a corrupt civilian regime. Chris is his Minister of Information, and Ikem, the poet, is the editor of the *National Gazette*, a government–owned paper. As events develop in the novel, we see how Chris and Ikem react as their friend Sam slides from his initial reluctance to rule to an absolute dictatorship in which he literally terrorizes his subjects. His paranoia, served by a colonial left–over bureaucracy and his efficient security service (the Bureau of State Research), soon preys on Ikem, his outspoken critic, and brings about his death. Chris, who aligns with Ikem in opposition, flees to avoid a similar fate, but he does not get too far before he is cut down by a power drunken policeman right after the news of Sam's overthrow in a bloody coup. The story ends as the "anthills" of this savannah country—Beatrice and her group—in an ecumenical gather–

ing, perform a naming ceremony of Ikem's daughter, born posthumously, and share their views on a number of issues.

To read *Anthills of the Savannah* in isolation from Achebe's novels, particularly *A Man of the People*, is to harvest only a part of its fruits. The failure of the politicians to provide a stable, progressive, and uncorrupt government in *A Man of the People* results in a military take–over. In this latest novel, Achebe shows that the military, corrupt, dictatorial, and estranged from the people, is as bad as, if not worse than the politicians. *Anthills of the Savannah* may therefore be read as a continuation of *A Man of the People*, although with notable changes in Achebe's approach. Whereas in the earlier novel he tells his story in a highly satirical and grotesque language, in the latter he is more serious and realistic. We no longer judge events through one man's perception (Odili's), but through a multiple, although sometimes complicated, points of view. The events in Kangan are explained and interpreted to us through the impressionistic testimonies of Ikem, Chris, Beatrice, and a third person omniscient narrator. This admixture of the narrative voices, newly experimented in Achebe's novel, adds color and authenticity to the tale of power, corruption, and tyranny in a newly independent African state. To attack corruption and misuse of power and privilege by the military, Achebe gives us the story of three main characters which, in Chris's opinion, represents the story of the entire country (60*). It is the story of the rise and fall of a tyrant; it is also the story of resistance to tyranny. Achebe's rebellion is thus defined in his manner of portraying tyranny and its effect on the people. He exposes tyranny in such a way that it becomes morally justifiable to resist.

Sam represents the military in government. Emulating the military in Africa, he begins as a "green virgin" endeared to the people, but later he turns into a monster brutalizing them. Achebe obviously is still exploring the theme of the corrupting power of privilege, a theme that he treated prominently in *A Man of the People*. Initially, Sam was a fine fellow. At Lord Lugard College he was "the social paragon," an "all–rounder," good in sports, in academics, and in manners. For such attractive qualities, young girls flocked to him. As a young officer training in England, he was an admirable fellow, as Mad Medico, who knew him then, testifies:

---

* Citations to *Anthills of the Savannah* are to the Anchor Press/Doubleday editions (1987) and (paperback) (1988).

> ... he was such a nice fellow in those days. He had a wholesome kind of
> innocence about him. . . . He was morally and intellectually intact—a
> kind of virgin, if you get my meaning. . . . He was more assured, knew a
> lot more than his fellow English officers, and damn well spoke better
> English, I tell you (54).

Sam sought perfection in everything, and this may have affected his cultural outlook. He was imitative of the customs of the English gentlemen which have always been regarded in England as a model. On a Sunday morning, for example, he was seen by Ikem dressed in a morning coat "lounging in a sofa with sundry papers scattered around him on the floor a half–smoked pipe on a side table," enjoying Mozart's music (45).

In addition to his gentlemanly deportment, Sam was a smart fellow. Ikem may well criticize the level of his intelligence, but he still concedes that Sam is not a block-head: "To say that Sam was never so bright is not to suggest that he was a dunce at any time in the past or that he is one now" (44). Perhaps, as part of his protest against the fawning devotion Sam receives from his Cabinet members and other sycophants, Ikem is hard pressed to praise Sam directly; hence, Ikem accords Sam only deferen-tial recognition, as is evident in his following statements: "Not very bright but not wicked" (45); "The Emperor may be a fool but he isn't a monster. Not yet anyhow." (42). In truth, Sam was neither a fool nor a dullard. He was, as Chris says, "a very intelligent person" (11). So aware was he of his limitations that after being suddenly chosen to head the government by the coup makers, he knew he had "pretty few ideas" about government, and so called his friends together to solicit their help (11). He was sensible enough to choose Chris and Ikem to help him to set up his govern-ment and to continue to rely on them for the first six months. Sam proved himself smarter than most of his Cabinet Ministers. Only Chris could oppose him and stand his grounds in the Cabinet; none of the rest could rationally oppose him. One incident illustrates his early image as a good man with a bright mind. When the doctors re-volted against Mad Medico and wanted him repatriated, Sam recognized that Mad Medico was being victimized for strongly opposing medical malpractice. He sup-ported legal action against the corrupt doctor whose greed superseded his medical integrity. With Ikem, Sam stood solidly behind Mad Medico until the crisis passed. In presenting Sam as a virtuous person at the start, Achebe is only being realistically true to the trend in African military politics: the military rulers always begin as ennobled persons celebrating an altruistic mission. So, Sam, like his counterparts in Africa, began as a benevolent man and an astute fellow.

But the season of goodness ends after His Excellency attends his first Organization of African Unity Conference where he is patronized by the African President–for–Life, Ngongo. On his return, Sam begins to dramatize his role as Head of State more imperiously, thus signaling the end of his socializing. He begins to "withdraw into seclusion" and to maintain a distance from his former friend and confidant, Chris. He relies, instead, on his vicious Head of Security, Major Johnson Ossai. Gradually he transforms himself into a full–blooded tyrant. Achebe dramatizes aspects of his tyranny and in so doing unravels the nature of tyranny in contemporary Africa. First, in the opening scene, we see the picture of an authoritarian ruler during a Cabinet meeting. This is not a meeting in which the members debate to arrive at a consensus; it is not anything near the free and open deliberation in the traditional Umuofia of *Things Fall Apart*; it is rather a forum in which His Excellency brandishes his authority while the rest shuttle in and out of themselves frightened. The Attorney–General stutters and misses his words: instead of "flout" he says "flaunt." The Chief Secretary is thrown into "utter confusion and inelegance of speech" when questioned by His Excellency. He is too nervous to make a clear statement, not even after he summons courage to address His Excellency: "But Your Excellency, if I may—erm—crave your indulgence—erm—Your Excellency's indulgence—erm—put in a word for the Honorable Commissioner" (6). When the members are not frightened out of their wits, they are depicted applauding him, flattering him, or grovelling before him. His Excellency thoroughly enjoys the fruits of his intimidation. As long as he is able to keep his ministers cowered, his supreme authority is sustained.

To foster his knack for intimidation, His Excellency delights in acting. His dramatic skill is shown in the closing of his Cabinet meeting. The members are purposely kept standing and waiting in dead silence while His Excellency performs the slow ritual of putting on his shoes. As he leaves, Chris notices "a smile or the radiance of a smile from the back of his head like the faint memory of light at the edges of an eclipse" (8). Acting and the effects of para–language, Achebe seems to point out, are an indispensable strategy by African tyrants for bolstering their authority. In his capricious mood, in bullying his Cabinet, in surrounding himself with stern–faced orderlies—in all these, we see Sam consciously acting to prop up his authority.

Sam is not only power conscious, he is also corrupt. The Presidential Retreat symbolizes the corruption that links the defunct civilian government to the military administration. This connection is overtly revealed in Beatrice's statement about the Retreat: "The rumoured twenty million spent on its refurbishment by the present administration since the overthrow of the civilians who had built it at a cost of forty–five million may still be considered irresponsibly extravagant in our circumstances . . . " (67). To spend such a huge amount in refurbishing the Presidential Retreat in a country plagued with bad roads, poor housing, poor sanitation, lack of drinking water, and lack of electricity (191–93), is to be corrupt. And furthermore, there is no difference between Sam's enjoying the luxury of the Presidential Retreat away from the rough and tumble in Kangan and Chief Nanga's enjoying the comfort of the Minister's "palace" in the midst of the slum and stench of the capital. In the plushy Presidential Retreat Sam lavishly entertains his cronies and associates with representatives of foreign business. The bird, which to Achebe signifies wisdom, vigilance, and by inference, the writer himself, sings and questions, according to Beatrice, the safety of the King's [the country's] treasury. For Beatrice, in this Presidential Retreat, Sam allows "the King's treasury" to be "broken into" and lets "all his property carried away—his crown, his sceptre and all" (99). His association with Lou Cranford, the American journalist who represents (in her view at least) multinational interests, is questionable. Sam's "real" Cabinet, as opposed to the rubber stamp Cabinet we meet at the beginning of the novel, comprises eight men and six women of uncertain character, and these include the ruthless head of the Security, Major Johnson Ossai, and in particular, the withdrawn multi–millionaire, Alhaji Abdul Mahmoud who is the chairman of the Kangan/American Chamber of Commerce. In a country hard–hit by shortages of the basic amenities like good water, housing, and food (67), Mahmoud owns eight ocean liners, private jets, a bank, and some fifty odd companies. And we are told he made his fortune in a corrupt way: "No customs officials go near his jetty . . . he is the prince of smugglers" and has monopoly over government fertilizer imports (107). As His Excellency dissociates himself from his close friends Chris and Ikem, he depends on such ruthless people as Major Ossai and the corrupt Alhaji Abdul Mahmoud, with grave consequence for the country.

As the novel progresses, His Excellency becomes more intoxicated with power, more sinister, and more blood–thirsty. His ambition for absolute power (he wants to be President–for–Life) grows side by side with his paranoia for security. In his obsession for power and security he misinterprets goodwill gestures from Abazon ex–rebels, gags the press, summarily dismisses Ikem from his job, and uses his security officers to arrest and torture him to death. The death of Ikem precipitates a national crisis in which the forces of oppression unleash their hounds against intellectuals like Chris and the student leaders. The country is turned into a police state as the six Abazon delegates are arrested for marching on the Presidential Palace without police permit, Beatrice's apartment is brutally invaded by the Security Police, and road blocks are mounted all over the country in search of dissidents. In his narrative, Achebe creates a chilling picture of tyranny in Kangan. In the end, the tyrant Sam is overthrown in a coup. He is killed and buried in a shallow grave and thus made to pay the price of tyranny. His lieutenant, the Chief of Security Police suffers a similar fate. Although Sam's dictatorship ends abruptly, we are not comforted by his successor Major–General Ahmed Lango, Sam's former Army Chief of Staff, himself a member of the Presidential Retreat "Cabinet," nor do we easily forget that Kangan is still full of "cannibals" like the brutal sergeant who searched Beatrice's apartment and the drunken policeman who killed Chris and escaped. We cannot fail to be haunted by their presence and the continued presence of the military.

The military dictatorship in Kangan evokes a variety of responses, and in pointing them out, Achebe does not hide his condemnation of military dictatorship. Some intellectuals with selfish motives and cowardly reactions submit slavishly to the dictator. There is a tinge of irony in Achebe's portrayal of such intellectuals as Professor Okong who gratifies the dictator to win favor, but his loyalty is misdirected, for he is debased when he goes privately to discuss one of his Cabinet colleagues. His Excellency addresses him thus: "That's fine, Mr. Okong. I deal with facts not gossip," and dismisses the Professor with a "loud impatient buzzer" (18–19). The Attorney–General, too, is reduced to the role of the sycophant as he flatters His Excellency saying, "We have no problem worshipping a man like you." He will play any string to please His Excellency, including playing up his rural background. He tells his boss that he was never blessed with golden opportunities as was his boss; for example, while his boss attended a prominent school, Lord Lugard College, he himself only went to a bush grammar school (22). His fawning however fails to impress His Excellency who shabbily dismisses him as he had done to Prof. Okong. In presenting these two intellectuals as flatterers, and in treating them in mocking terms, Achebe displays his contempt for a whole range of African intellectuals who, in spite of themselves, are willing to "worship" dictators, if only to keep their jobs. These intellectuals are as guilty as their "heroes" in damaging the cause of freedom in Africa.

The failure of the African intellectuals is one of the major concerns of the novel. When the Chief Nangas and Chief Kokos—semiliterate politicians—failed to provide good leadership in *A Man of the People*, their critics were intellectuals, thus suggesting that given the opportunity, these intellectuals would lead the country properly. But as we have seen, Achebe dampens our expectation by exposing the weaknesses of the two intellectuals, Max and Odili. In *Anthills of the Savannah* he reinforces this theme of the failure of educated Africans to deal with the problems facing their nations. It is significant that the four key figures in *Anthills of the Savannah* are well educated people. Sam is a graduate of Sandhurst; Chris, Ikem, and Beatrice also studied in England. Beatrice earned a first class in English. These four hold responsible government offices and represent the educated elite in power. Despite their intellectual prowess, as the courteous, urbane, and intelligent President embarks upon the road to despotism, Chris and Ikem hardly seem to notice. Chris fails to perceive the change because he is too close to the situation and is "blinded by the elation of playing politics." Ikem, too, is preoccupied with investigating public abuses and exposing them in his "crusading editorials" in the *National Gazette*; he is also busy with his fictional works. Ironically, it is a group of uneducated villagers that rouse Ikem's awareness. Ikem's involvement with the Abazon demonstrators signals his awakening to the possibility of an open rebellion because of Sam's totalitarian tactics. Chris, however, continues longer in the state of "inertia" and "curiosity" which he earlier confessed were responsible for his conformity (2). For a time he remains captious toward Ikem; for example, he criticizes his editorial urging the President to decree against public execution. Here is how Ikem reports it:

> Chris was critical of my tone and of my tactlessness in appearing to command His Excellency. But when the said Excellency proceeded to do exactly what I had demanded Chris had to come up with a new tune. My editorial suddenly had nothing whatever to do with the new decree. His Excellency had quite independently come to the conclusion that he could earn a few credits by reversing all the unpopular acts of the civilian regime. And the Public Executions Amendment Decree was only one of them. And this was the same Chris who had just rebuked me for not knowing that public executions were such a popular sport (39).

In defending the system, Chris is obviously playing the role required of him in the totalitarian regime. As the Commissioner for Information, he is required to rationalize the President's actions. With Ikem's opposition, the reader is aware of Achebe's ironic twist. Chris, as the Minister of Information and clearly the most capable in the Cabinet, is the most misinformed, refusing even to believe Ikem's editorials, which, at the same time, he must acknowledge as truthful. The point is that the intellectual elite initially fails to perceive, challenge, and arrest a tyrannical trend. However, when some of them finally begin to confront tyranny, they become full–blown rebels. We shall now examine how Achebe uses their rebellion to further expose and condemn dictatorship in Africa.

Ikem's rebellion is first directed toward social issues. He revolts against injustice perpetrated against individuals or the society at large. He regards his neighbor who works for the Posts and Telegraphs as a "disgusting brute" because he takes delight in beating his wife: "There is an extraordinary surrealistic quality about the whole thing that is almost satisfyingly cathartic." For after the beating in the night, the husband and wife could be still "outrageously friendly and relaxed! She especially" (32), to Ikem's amazement. Wife–beating is so tolerated in this society that once, when a concerned neighbor phoned the police to report the Posts and Telegraphs man was battering his wife, "the Desk Sergeant asked sleepily: 'So Therefore?'" (32). We can see the double irony here: the police who sleeps at work is totally unconcerned about a victim who has been denied her comfort and right to sleep; in other words, the one who should stay awake is sleeping, while the one who should be sleeping and protected is kept awake. Achebe's revulsion is directed against the society that accommodates and seems to enjoy such a breach of social justice as the maltreatment of women. He also directs his attack on the government whose machinery fails in its essential duty. More importantly, underlying this episode is the suggestion that one man's wife–beating foreshadows another type of beating carried out on a larger scale: the tyrant's subjugation of the entire country. Soon the problem will no longer be that of the "masochistic" wife, but that of the masochistic society "relishing" the oppression of a brutal dictatorship. Chapter four of the novel contains a catalog of crimes and anarchy in Bassa which revile Ikem: armed robbery rampage, "loose women for Bassa who no de sleep for house" (33), the unswept and unlit stairs in apartment buildings (33), reckless driving on Bassa roads, and unbearable traffic hold–ups. These social problems are neglected by the government whose rulers have removed themselves from the people and who hardly notice them. In pointing out the problems, Ikem does not spare those who are responsible, as in his discernment of public executions.

The public execution of criminals, specifically armed robbers, was a "spectacle that turned [Ikem's] stomach" not only because he was absolutely opposed to capital punishment, but also because of the terrible revelations that event made about his society. The most painful and horrifying thing about the execution was that it was perceived by the people as an entertainment and recalled the worst excesses of the ancient Roman gladiator games in the amphitheater. Tickets were purchased for special seating areas, while the most comfortable seats were reserved for the VIPs. The seating arrangement was indicative of the wide gap between the common people and their oppressors. These affluent ones were given "nicely spaced–out numbered seats" in a raised and sheltered platform, while the poor masses were scattered around and left to bake under the sun. Commenting on this, Ikem asks Achebe's questions:

> Isn't the great thing about a VIP that his share of good things is always waiting for him in abundance even while he relaxes in the coolness of home, and the poor man is out there in the sun pushing and shoving and roasting for his miserable crumbs? Look at all those empty padded seats! How does the poor man retain his calm in the face of such provocation? From what bottomless wells of patience does he draw? (37)

These are perennial and universal questions, although here the context, steeped in irony, enhances their rebellious overtone. Achebe is implying that the authorities are executing people whose crimes are the result of the social conditions created by the authorities themselves. Oppression and exploitation have driven these prisoners to commit petty crimes for which they are paying with their lives. They are unfairly singled out to be punished for crimes which their oppressors commit routinely though they escape punishment. As a matter of fact, the whole country is infested with "robbers"; hence, when the defiant prisoner stoutly proclaims, "I shall be born again," Ikem believes that the prophecy of his reincarnation can only be faulted in its projection into the future, for it is already fulfilled in the present. Facing the bold thief were 'his innumerable doubles' "who daily stole more from us than mere lace and terylene"; these include "leaders who openly looted our treasury, whose effrontery soiled our national soul" (39). Again, by dramatizing the punishment through public execution, the authorities were downgrading the sanctity of life, creating a situation whereby the people enjoyed the sight of blood and became blood–thirsty. Public execution is not corrective, and if so intended, it is failing because already pick–pockets were in the very scene of the execution having a busy day even as four men were being shot. For Achebe, therefore, public execution of criminals is not going to solve the problems that created them in the first place; rather, it will increase crime in society. In short, Achebe uses this scene significantly. A "nation of robbers", at every level of society, beheld the spectacle of the punishment of a single crime, not of stealing (a phenomenon rampant in this society); these individuals were being executed for the crime of being caught. And, where does the patience of the poor masses arise in response to Ikem's question? It is easily inferred—"there, but for the grace of God, go I." In other words, many were guilty, but not everyone had yet been caught. The public execution was a semi–cathartic experience that ritually semi–absolved the spectator, which absolution changed the national character not a tad since it did not address the social ill of mismanagement itself. Rather, it only made the "nation of robbers" more crafty and set the nation, as a whole, on the path to always looking for a scapegoat than reforming itself from within.

Ikem is also concerned about the people's reaction in the face of oppression. They bear oppression with a sense of humor. To save himself from total dejection, the oppressed has "learnt to squeeze every drop of enjoyment he can out of his stony luck" (37). But he gets carried away in his humor and forgets the cause of his suffering. As the people make jokes and laugh during the execution, Ikem worries about the laughter becoming a sign of resignation. "That afternoon he was punished most dreadfully at the beach and he laughed to his pink gums and I listened painfully for the slightest chink of the concealed weapon in the voluminous folds of that laughter. And I didn't hear it" (37). Their laughter is mere escapism and therefore unhealthy. It is also tragic, for they "laughed at their own humiliation and murder."

In confrontation with the authorities, Ikem manifests his rebellion. He is vocal in his editorials in which he attacks social evils, including those committed by the government. He believes that Sam could be saved from all "the petty interests salaaming around him all day" and making it difficult for him to reach right decisions. It is therefore the duty of Ikem and Chris to let Sam "glimpse a little light now and again through chinks in his solid wall of court jesters." One way of doing this is through his controversial editorials. Sam tries to gag him through censorship, but failing, dismisses him as the editor of the National Gazette. Ikem reacts by taking his case directly to the people—the university audience, and thus he fulfills Sartre's view earlier stated, that when the pen is stopped, the writer should resort to other forms of expression in his fight for freedom ("What is Literature?" 69).

Ikem, no doubt, is Achebe's persona, and in him we see the writer's role in society best exemplified. It is not by accident that Achebe makes him a poet, a novelist, a playwright, and a newspaper editor. Part of his role is to supply Sam and society a "glimpse of little light." Earlier in our discussion we observed that the writer seeks to enlighten the reader. Ikem is also passionately engaged in a struggle for freedom, justice, and fair–play, in short, in setting the country in order. But he has many obstacles to surmount before achieving his noble goal, obstacles created by the beneficiaries of the corrupt and oppressive regime. Waging war against a dictatorship involves much risk and could lead to death. In his role as a writer, Ikem boldly accepts the course of rebellion, suffers for it, and eventually dies for it.

Chris's rebellion against Sam's dictatorship begins slowly and belatedly. At first he is torn between loyalty to his job and fidelity to his personal conviction. He claims that he stayed on in his job, the "silly observation post" where he makes "farcical entries in the crazy log–book of this our ship of state," in order to observe fully and write (2). As a writer and as a witness to the events, he is Achebe's spokesman and exemplifies the role of the writer. Being an insider, although a moderately detached and rebellious one, he knows much about the oppressive regime he serves. From him we learn about the servile and hypocritical Cabinet, as well as the insecurities, the posturings, and the power plays that are present in Sam. All the while, he observes critically and does not openly confront the tyrant, although he is sometimes able to stand by his independent opinion. In those moments he is not cowed by His Excellency's threat; for example, when he insists that His Excellency visit Abazon (1–4). Occasionally, for fear of rocking the boat or creating "stupid problems," we find him opposed to Ikem's radical editorials (40). On such occasions, he rationalizes the President's position as a defense to the system. For example, he tries to argue in favor of dictatorship, believing that it is a baptism by fire which developing nations must endure. Sophistry might best describe his argument for the system, especially when he labors to defend the rationale for gigantic government projects such as the Presidential Retreat:

> Nations were fostered as much by structures as by laws and revolutions. These structures where they exist now are the pride of their nations. But everyone forgets that they were not erected by democratically–elected Prime Ministers but very frequently by rather unattractive, blood–thirsty medieval tyrants. The cathedrals of Europe, the Taj Mahal of India, the pyramids of Egypt, and the stone towers of Zimbabwe were all raised on the backs of serfs. Our present rulers in Africa are in every sense late–flowering medieval monarchs, even the Marxists among them (67–68).

Chris's argument represents the position of some intellectuals who believe that, as a realistic means of solving her crucial political problems, Africa needs some kind of benevolent despotism for a limited number of years. This is the continent's solution to the persistent failing of democratic governments in African states. Achebe is nevertheless aware that in Africa, as in other parts of the world, absolute power corrupts absolutely, and what starts off as a benevolent dictatorship often turns awry, becomes self–serving and bloody. This is the case with Sam's dictatorship. With the arrest of the six Abazon delegates, the deportation of Mr. Kent (Mad Medico), and the abduction of Ikem by the State Security Police, the signs are too visible for Chris not to see that this is not the case of benevolent despotism. He finds himself dealing with a bloody tyrant who is prepared to spend lives to prop up his corrupt regime. The moment of full realization is reached during his confrontation with Sam over the suspension of Ikem. "Well, Your Excellency, for once I am turning you down. I will not carry out this instruction and I hereby tender my resignation" (133). With this act of defiance, Chris proclaims his rebellion, and plunges deep into it. He resigns his post, goes into hiding, and secretly grants an interview to a BBC Bassa correspondent, explaining the circumstances of Ikem's violent death in police custody. He further instigates the Students' Union to protest the death of Ikem. He tells their leader Emmanuel, "This country counts on you" (158).

On a lesser scale, Beatrice, herself, rebels against Sam's dictatorship. Her rebellion emerges at the "small private dinner" at the Presidential Retreat. His Excellency had personally invited her on the phone but the sole reason for this gesture was his need to display Beatrice as a mantlepiece [i.e., "the woman's angle"] to the American woman, Miss Cranford. The manner in which His Excellency introduces her to Miss Cranford reveals his intention to use Beatrice as a show piece to impress others: "Lou, this is one of the most brilliant daughters of this country, Beatrice Okoh. She is a Senior Assistant Secretary in the Ministry of Finance—the only person in the service, male or female, with a first–class honors in English. And not from a local university but from Queen Mary College, University of London. Our Beatrice beat the English to their own game. We're very proud of her" (68). The irony of this invitation is that Beatrice turns out to be not an object of adornment, but an instrument of rebellion.

Her "first act of rebellion" was her rejection of the "owner's corner" (a seat of honor) in the chauffeured black Mercedes provided for the occasion by the government. She preferred to sit in front with the driver. Her second act of rebellion was her greeting the driver, an act unthinkable in the highly structured and bureaucratic setting of Kangan. But these simple acts of rebellion are signals to the chauffeur as well as to the reader that this "eccentric cargo" will prove an instrument of protest. In her modest way, Beatrice describes her actions as "my puny, empty revolts, the rebellion of a mouse in a cage" (66). Chris, however, recognizes the import of her mission. He thinks Beatrice "may do some good," that she "may be of help" to His Excellency. If

Chris is right (that Beatrice had been invited to help "extricate" Sam from an undefined hopeless situation), then the outcome proves disastrous, for the kind of help she renders is a far cry from what Sam wanted. At the dinner Beatrice is repulsed by the characters operating in the inner circle, the real force behind the Presidential authority: the "reticent" Major Ossai, Joe Ibe, the Commissioner for Works, General Lango, the subservient Chief of Army Staff who is attentive to Sam like a second–class chief to a paramount chief (71), Alhaji Abdul Mahmoud, the corrupt millionaire, Miss Cranford of the American United Press, and others. This group represents brutality, corruption, and waste. Beatrice's strong objection to the American woman's presence and her intimate and seductive connections with the President is a direct criticism of African Heads of State who sell themselves and their countries cheaply to foreign interests. Greatly resenting the influence of this "Desdemona" over "the sacred symbol of my nation's pride," Beatrice confronts His Excellency with this rhetorical question: "If I went to America today, to Washington DC, would I, could I, walk into a White House private dinner and take the American President hostage. And his Defense Chief and his Director of CIA?" (74) His Excellency does not take this kindly and "storms away" calling Beatrice a racist. Truly, racism is not the issue. The voice we hear is not that of racism but of rebellion: Beatrice's rebellion and Achebe's rebellion.

The three rebellious characters—Ikem, Chris, and Beatrice—are associated with writing, and each functions as Achebe's spokesperson. Ikem, as we saw earlier, is a well known writer whom Mad Medico calls "one of the finest [poets] in the entire English language" (57). Chris is a trained journalist and former editor of the National Gazette. At the beginning of the novel, he tells us that one of the reasons he has not resigned as Sam's Commissioner for Information, despite his dissatisfaction with Sam and his colleagues, is the desire to write. "I couldn't be writing this if I didn't hang around to observe it all," he says (2). Beatrice, too, is interested in writing. Chapter seven of the novel opens with her complaint about the difficulties of writing: "For weeks and months after I had definitely taken on the challenge of bringing together as many broken pieces of this tragic history as I could lay my hands on I still could not find a way to begin. Anything I tried to put down sounded wrong—either too abrupt, too indelicate, or too obvious—to my middle ear" (75). Later, she claims that her motive for writing is to discover the truth about herself, "to expose my life on these pages to see if perhaps there are aspects of me I had successfully concealed even from myself" (77). In these three writers Achebe explores the writer's role in his society; indeed, we might say that he explores his own role. As mentioned in our first chapter, Sartre maintains that freedom is the ultimate goal of writers ("What is Literature?" 58). A commitment to the cause of freedom in the dictatorial state of Kangan has only one meaning for the writer: rebellion. The three characters we have considered approach their function differently: Chris, reluctantly, Ikem, forthrightly, and Beatrice, cautiously. Achebe here suggests that whichever approach works for a writer is acceptable, so long as it is directed toward freedom or redemption.

CHAPTER THREE

REDEMPTION

INTRODUCTION

One concept that we must keep in mind as we read Achebe's novels is that he is basically a story–teller interested in the history of his people. "What I was doing in my novels was to tell our story, our history, in fictional terms," he once declared in an newspaper article (*The Hartford Advocate*, July 24, 1989). In telling his story, Achebe was concerned not just with "the trouble with Nigeria," but also with solutions. In "The African Writer and the Biafran Cause" he attributes to the writer the prophetic duty of attempting to solve problems and attempting to restore self–confidence to his people (*Morning Yet*, 142 [117]). Achebe's own attempt has led him to point out "where the rain began to beat us," and more importantly, how best to proceed to build a happy and prosperous nation. As an image maker who feels that his duty is to educate his people, Achebe uses his novels to suggest, and sometimes directly portray, the "adequate man" and the "adequate world" of his vision. In his novels he provides the image, the conception, and the correct ethical values for a healthy society. Chapter two of our discussion has dealt at length with Achebe's preoccupation with the problems in his society; chapter three will deal with suggestions he has adduced toward the realization of the "adequate" society.

We shall preface our detailed discussion of redemption in Achebe's specific novels with a brief consideration of certain concepts that inform some of his views and relate to redemption: duality, moderation and balance, gender, and women's plight.

1. Duality: Achebe is a strong proponent of the Igbo notion of duality. Leonard in *The Lower Niger and its Tribes* discusses the Igbo principle of dualism thus: ". . . no matter how much a man may try to do the right thing, the right in the opinion of others is not the absolute, irrefutable right that can stand its ground, without either question or argument" (131). Achebe's essay "Chi in Igbo Cos-

mology" deals extensively with the Igbo notion of duality *(Morning Yet,* 159–75 [130–45]). This notion discourages viewing life as simple and absolute. The Igbo notion of duality is well expressed in the proverb quoted by Achebe, "Wherever Something stands, Something Else will stand beside it". Explaining this proverb to Moyers, Achebe said, "It means that there is no one way to anything. The people who made that proverb, the Ibo people, are very insistent on this; that there is no absolute anything, even good things . . . their world is a world of dualities. It is good to be brave, they say, but also remember that the coward survives the brave man . . . " ("Chinua Achebe," 2). Against this belief in the diversity and multiplicity of things, including gods, inflexible action and dogma appear absurd and "blasphemous" to Achebe. The implications are considerable and add to our understanding of his novels. Achebe will frequently draw our attention to the disastrous consequence attendant on stiff absolutism, and conversely, the redemptive value of flexibility and open–mindedness. He will always provide his heroes with alternatives and options and will demonstrate with emphasis how their failure to explore these alternatives largely contributes to their doom.

2. Moderation and balance: In addition to dualism, the Thomistic principle of balance and moderation underlies Achebe's redemptive thoughts. Achebe's position is akin to that of St. Thomas Aquinas who, following Aristotle, maintains that virtue stands at the middle. An echo of this classical principle may be found in Shakespeare's *As You Like It,* "Those that are in extremity of either are abominable fellows, and betray themselves to every modern censure worse than drunkards" (IV:i, 5–7 [725]). There is often a sense of denunciation of extremists and fanatics in Achebe's novels. Achebe will always create foils whose moderation counterbalances the protagonist's extremism, and really points the correct way to redemption. For example, Okonkwo's extremism is counterpoised with Obierika's common sense and moderation, which is indirectly suggested as the better course. Achebe's discussion of the dynamics of community and individuality in his works is yet another example of his emphasis on balance: "Community and individuality are the twin poles of man's search for fulfillment. It has never been a simple question of a choice of one and rejection of the other but of a balance between them" ("The Uses of African Literature," 12).

3. A related theme that is also highlighted in his works is that of gender. Achebe believes that every human being possesses the masculine and feminine principles. For a more satisfactory and fulfilled personality, there is need to balance the two, and this is one of the ways redemption is suggested in his novels. Achebe's treatment of reality as a complexity, his quest for the middle position, and his constant juxtapositional presentation of opposites—these all contribute to Achebe's overall image as a realistic writer.

4. Achebe draws our attention to the plight of women in Africa. Often he is seen to present the case as it is. He is dealing with a society where women are, by modern standards, suppressed. Okonkwo's wives in *Things Fall Apart* and Clara in *No Longer at Ease* are typical examples of oppressed women. Achebe is however not interested only in the oppressed woman. He also presents us with pictures of the rebellious woman, the potent woman, and the inspired woman. Although not a feminist, Achebe interestingly goes beyond the traditional African view that has women play subordinate role to men, and elevates them to a higher pedestal in which they become symbolic healers and redeemers of society. This redemptive role, though mildly present in his earlier novels, is prominently explored in his last novel, *Anthills of the Savannah*.

5. Finally, redemption in most cases is not a direct attainment in Achebe's novels; it is often offered inferentially. The closest Achebe comes to offering solutions directly is in Ikem's address on the national and ideological issues in his speech to a university audience in *Anthills of the Savannah*. One theme strongly present in all his novels, albeit submerged, is the need to resort to traditional values as a form of redemption. The loss of these values is seen to be responsible for the multitude of problems facing African countries; restoration of these values, and a blending of these with correct ethical values newly acquired from contact with Western tradition is a highly prized form of redemption underscored in all of Achebe's novels.

THINGS FALL APART

Things Fall Apart was written to redeem the Igbo, and, ultimately, the African from the dark image of colonial distortion, for, as we have seen earlier, the duty of the writer is to restore dignity to his own people, to help them get on their feet again. Accordingly, Achebe takes us back to the past to show that the Igbo past "was not one long night of savagery from which the first Europeans acting on God's behalf delivered them" ("The Novelist as Teacher," *Morning Yet,* 72 [59]). On the contrary, it was a heroic past dominated by characters like Okonkwo, a proud and industrious figure who, by dint of hard work, rose from poverty to eminence, a man whose faith and devotion to the ideals of his society led him to fight to a finish defending those ideals. This hero of the past, in all his glories, is held up to the present as a model of courage, hard work, strength, determination, and commitment to societal values. The society that produced him is also a source of pride, a people worthy of emulation. A stable society that respected age and revered merit, that offered maximum protection to the individual through its gods, the common will, its laws and sanctions, a democratic society that could boast of its rich arts and culture, such a society is revealed in *Things Fall Apart* as a model for a disorganized and disoriented present, and as a show–piece to those who had been fed with misinformation about the Igbo past.

   This past, however harmonious and balanced, was not inclusively wholesome, and by pointing out its imperfections and suggesting better alternatives, Achebe performs his avuncular role in society. As he states in "The Role of the Writer in a New Nation," "the past needs to be recreated not only for the enlightenment of our detractors but even more for our own education" (Killam, 9).

   Achebe chooses a period in the past when things are falling apart. The disintegration of the pre–Western culture seems inevitable. The title of the novel is taken from Yeats's "The Second Coming" and suggests the poet's interpretation of history which presents "defeat as inevitable, victory as impermanent, and the contending forces as phases of a single, inexhaustible creative energy" (Stock, 86). In Yeats's view, every civilization is built by the "cumulative mind" found in the tradition and sustained through the hierarchy of values operative in that tradition. As long as "the hierarchy holds its own integrity," the civilization will hold out against chaos which is always "beating on its own wall." However, within every civilization there are frustrated elements or foibles which constitute, as it were, cracks within the walls, and eventually expand to form the "opposing gyre." These cracks will in time be wide enough to let in the "chaos" or the "mere anarchy" that will destroy the civilization. Thus, every civilization begins, expands, and explodes; none is ever static, and none is ever evolving toward "an inclusive perfection." As one civilization ends, another begins on its ashes, and the cycle continues in the form of history.

Like Yeats, Achebe believes that a civilization collapses as a result of forces operating from within and from without. The Igbo civilization, which Umuofia symbolizes, is portrayed in its idyllic form in the first thirteen chapters. The tribe has, however, already developed cracks in its walls and is heading toward its final demise, that is, toward a collision with an outside force (Western civilization) in which it will be overwhelmed. Hence, in this novel, Achebe works out the dynamics of disintegration as he shows how external and foreign pressure, colonialism and Christianity, speed up an already disintegrating system. Achebe, however, does not lament the passing away of old ways. In "The Role of Writer in a New Nation," he argues that human values are never "fixed and eternal," rather they are "relative and in a constant state of flux" (Killam, 10). Consequently, a people's cultural life must be subject to the inevitability of change. This is a centripetal theme in *Things Fall Apart*. The novel affirms that cultural transition is a "historical imperative" and demands a flexible and open mind. For survival or success in the changing process, there is need for accommodation and readjustment. Hence, the road to redemption lies in reading correctly and sensibly the writing on the wall, and having enough common sense and flexibility to adapt. The resolution of these issues is dealt with implicitly in *Things Fall Apart*. By showing us what went wrong with the hero and the community, Achebe educates us on how to avoid the errors of the past; hence, the portrayal of past failure holds redemptive value for Achebe's contemporaries.

Okonkwo was a man driven by fear to extreme reactions. The fear of failure made him hate everything that his father represented: weakness, gentleness, and idleness. He became obsessed with manliness, and this forced him into situations that his society disdained: "He ruled his household with a heavy hand. His wives, especially the youngest, lived in perpetual fear of his fiery temper, and so did his little children" (9 [16]). The simple emotion he displayed openly was anger, because to exhibit "affection was a sign of weakness; the only thing worth demonstrating was strength" (20 [30]). He suppressed the "women stories" which his son Nwoye loved to hear. Such stories would make Nwoye weak, improvident, and unable "to feed the ancestors with regular sacrifices," and that would threaten Okonkwo's "dynasty." Okonkwo, therefore, insisted on "masculine stories of violence and bloodshed" (37 [52]), stories about "tribal wars or how, years ago, he had stalked his victim, over-powered him and obtained his first human head" (38 [53]).

In trying to suppress gentleness, Okonkwo lends himself to violence. To show how the streaks of violence and destructiveness are intrinsic to his character, the nar-

rator associates him with the symbolism of fire and fire–related images. At the beginning of the novel, his ascendance to fame has Promethean overtures: "Okonkwo's
fame had grown like a bush–fire in the harmattan" (3 [7]). Fire imagery invests
Okonkwo with power:

> Okonkwo was popularly called the "Roaring Flame." As he looked into
> the fire he recalled the name. He was flaming fire. How then could he
> have begotten a son like Nwoye, degenerate and effeminate? . . . He,
> Okonkwo, was called a flaming fire. How could he have begotten a
> woman for a son? (108 [143])

The effect of the fiery images in this passage is reinforced by contrasts. Okonkwo's
utterances and threats are sometimes described in metaphors of thunder; for example,
in the *ogbanje* scene, when the "truth" was not fast coming out of Ezinma, Okonkwo
"roared at her" and "swore furiously." And while Okagbue tried gentle persuasion,
"Okonkwo stood by, rumbling like thunder in the rainy season" (58 [79]).

Often the violence is expressed in concrete actions. He beats his wives (21, 27–28
[31, 39]), attacks his son Nwoye for converting to Christianity (107 [141]), cuts down
Ikemefuna (43 [59]), and when he fails to mobilize Umuofia to go to war, he single–
handedly kills the white man's messenger (144 [188]) and subsequently kills himself
(146 [190]). All these acts of violence proceed from Okonkwo's paranoia and his
blind commitment to the cult of virility.

The irony in Okonkwo's denial of the feminine principle is that he is unknowingly
denying an essential part of his nature, for there is that soft (feminine) part of him
which he cannot divest, in spite of his emphasis on strength. According to the narrator, Okonkwo may never show any emotion openly except that of anger, yet he has
love and compassion, and it is this soft part of his nature that sustains our sympathy
for him. Okonkwo can be thunderous with Ezinma, yet he is loving and caring when
struggling to save her from *iba* or malaria. During the New Yam Festival he fired a
gun at Ekwefi, but he also followed her to the cave in the dead of night to protect her
from harm (76 [103–03]). Again, when Ikemefuna was under attack, the feminine in
Okonkwo compelled him first to withdraw to the rear, and later to look away from the
matchet about to strike his "son" down. For three days after the incident, he brooded
over the event, and for two days he refused to eat. Okonkwo's doom is partly due to
his failure to tap the feminine resources in his nature. Nevertheless, Achebe sees a
possible blending of the masculine and feminine as redemptive

Okonkwo, on the contrary, consciously dissociates himself from any feminine
qualities for fear of being tainted with the fate of his father. He consistently mistrusts
and opposes actions associated with femininity. He judges actions and feelings by one

criterion: manliness. Whatever he admires is "manly," and whatever he condemns is "womanly." His affection for Ezinma is diluted by her gender: "He never stopped regretting that Ezinma was a girl. Of all his children she alone understood his every mood. A bond of sympathy had grown between them as the years had passed"(122 [158]). He regards soft feelings of tenderness, brotherhood, and tolerance as womanly:

> Even as a little boy he had resented his father's failure and weakness, and even now he still remembered how he had suffered when a playmate had told him his father was *agbala*. That was how Okonkwo first came to know that *agbala* was not only another name for a woman, it could also mean a man who had taken no title. And so Okonkwo was ruled by one passion—to hate everything that his father Unoka had loved. One of those things was gentleness and another was idleness (10 [17]).

For Okonkwo, the men who refused to participate in the killing of Ikemefuna were "effeminate men" and, by implication, despicable. He is incensed that his son Nwoye should join the Christians whom he regards as "a lot of effeminate men clucking like old hens" (108 [142]), and he is disgusted with the rulers and elders of Mbanta, his motherland, for their cowardice in refusing to chase the Christians out of their village with whips. No wonder he refers to them as "a womanly clan" (113 [148]). In all these cases, Okonkwo is seen to despise the feminine principle contrary to the ethos of his society.

Generally speaking, Umuofia subordinates women to a secondary place where they exist merely to serve the will and needs of men. As we learn from one of Achebe's explanations: "No matter how prosperous a man was, if he was unable to rule his women and his children (and especially his women) he was not really a man. He was like the man in the song who had ten and one wives and not enough soup for his foo–foo" (37 [52]). The world of Umuofia is definitely a man's world. Yet the feminine principle pervades the spiritual and moral life of this society. In it, Ani, the Earth goddess, is the final arbiter of all moral conduct, and also "the source of all fertility." Okonkwo's offenses against Ani (the beating of his wife during the Week of Peace, the killing of Ikemefuna, and the accidental killing of Ezeudu's son, regarded as a feminine crime) earn him the serious disapprobation of the clan. For his feminine crime, he is forced to take refuge in his motherland, which is the society's mandate for the atonement of the crime. It is significant that the Oracle of the Hills and the Caves has a feminine name, Agbala, and has a powerful priestess, Chielo, whom Okonkwo himself fears and respects. The entire clan has much trust in this Oracle; hence, it must be consulted before the clan is committed to war: "And there were, indeed, occasions when the Oracle had forbidden Umuofia to wage a war. If the clan had disobeyed the Oracle, they would surely have been beaten, because their dreaded *agadi–nwayi* [old woman] would never fight what the Ibo call *a fight of blame"* (9 [16]). While women do not enjoy equal treatment with men in Umuofia, the feminine principle operates in the culture with its own authority.

Manliness is prized as a positive attribute in Umuofia. However, its value is not accentuated to the degree of Okonkwo's obsession. His mania contradicts the standard values of his society. The killing of Ikemefuna illustrates the contradiction between Okonkwo's actions and the values they are meant to defend. Ezeudu, who brought the news to Okonkwo that the Oracle of the Hills and Caves had "pronounced" the sacrifice of Ikemefuna, is described as the oldest man in the village and "the great and fearless warrior in his time" who "was now accorded great respect in all the clan" (40 [55]). It is significant that this manly but highly revered spokesman of Umuofia would repeatedly advise Okonkwo to avoid involvement in the death of Ikemefuna who regards Okonkwo as father. Okonkwo's "cultic obsession" with manliness has him defy the traditional value embodied in Ezeudu's advice. Hence,

> As the man who had cleared his throat drew up and raised his matchet,
> Okonkwo looked away. He heard the blow. The pot fell and broke on the
> sand. He heard Ikemefuna cry, "My father, they have killed me!" as he
> ran towards him. Dazed with fear, Okonkwo drew his matchet and cut
> him down. He was afraid of being thought weak (43 [59]).

Okonkwo's devotion to manliness is a perversion which has turned him into a menace to his society. His participation in the killing haunts him for three days and yet does not change him. To awaken the strength, fortitude, and masculinity that slumbered after the event, he says to himself: "When did you become a shivering old woman . . . you, who are known in all the nine villages for your valour in war? How can a man who has killed five men in battle fall to pieces because he has added a boy to their number? Okonkwo, you have become a woman indeed" (45 [62–63]). The conflict of the masculine and feminine principles in this novel is not without significance.

In *Things Fall Apart* Achebe "teaches" that the "effeminate," the "womanish," in other words, love, affection, and mercy, are redemptive values essential for the well–being of the individual and the community. This idea is symbolically expressed in the folklore about the Earth and the Sky (38 [52–53]). The tale is prefaced by the passage in which Okonkwo urges his boys to stay in his *obi* to listen to his "masculine stories of violence and bloodshed." Nwoye, we learn, has preference for feminine stories like the tale of the Earth and the Sky. The masculine Sky withholds rain from the feminine Earth, causing drought and great suffering. The Earth sends the Vulture to plead with the Sky, and the Sky finally relents. The Vulture, who pleads for mercy, stands for the female principle (Weinstock and Ramadan, 129–30). The rain symbolizes the feminine qualities (tenderness, love, and mercy). The conflict between the Sky and the Earth reflects or symbolizes the conflict in Okonkwo. His attempts to stifle the feminine quality in himself and others (the boys) is compared to the Sky's withholding rain, an essential source of life. The outcome, Achebe seems to point out, is a dreary life of "stony Earth" and "the suffering of the sons of men." The very "rain" which Okonkwo withholds, Christianity will in time dispense in abundance. Achebe therefore uses this simple but symbolic tale as a warning both to Okonkwo and Achebe's audience: to stifle the feminine principle is destructive; to release it is redemptive.

In another strain, yam is a masculine symbol: "Yam stood for manliness, and he who could feed his family on yams from one harvest to another was a very great man indeed" (23 [34]). We also learn that "yam, the king of crops, was a man's crop" (16 [25]). We recall that early in Okonkwo's career, because the Sky withheld the rain, the Sun (another masculine symbol) roasted all the yams he had planted (17 [25–26]). Owing to his resilience and to the seed–yams he had borrowed from Nwakibie, Okonkwo had other yams to sow. Ironically, when the rain fell after the severe drought, it was torrential and utterly destructive. "For days and nights together it poured down in violent torrents, and washed away the yam heaps. Trees were uprooted and deep gorges appeared everywhere" (17 [26]). The resultant poor harvest led one man to commit suicide. This interplay of symbols foreshadows future events relating to Okonkwo and his clan. The suppression of the feminine principle in the individual or in society will precipitate a crisis, and the solution will not be salutary but catastrophic. As Weinstock and Ramadan observe, in *Things Fall Apart,* Christianity is always associated with water images (129). When Christianity arrived, its effect was torrential. It furthered the disintegration of the traditional society.

Fixation is a vice in Achebe's order of redemption. The problem with Okonkwo is not his indissoluble attachment to traditional values, but his narrowness of vision in relation to other perspectives. He is fixed and unrelenting in his commitments. Whether in obeying the Oracle, or in defending the traditional ways against the onslaught of colonialism and Christianity, Okonkwo is unbending. When he returns from exile and notices all of the changes in Umuofia, for example, the introduction of the Christian Church and the white man's government, the only solution he offers is war: "What is it that has happened to our people? Why have they lost the power to fight?" (124 [161]) Despite the odds, he fights against the Christians and the white man's government, blind to the enormous power of his enemy, deaf to all warnings, especially about how the white man wiped out Abame (124 [161]). Inflexibility and bigotry, resulting from his failure/phobia, become his major flaws. He thus "represents the narrowness of tribal life carried out to an extreme even for his time and place" (Weinstock, 20). In depicting him that way, Achebe "teaches" that such vices are damaging to a people's cause.

In his novel, Achebe points the way to redemption by creating characters whose redeeming virtues are contrapuntal to the hero's vices. Okagbue is one such character. In his appearances, he acts cool–headedly compared to Okonkwo's fiery outbursts. During the search for Ezinma's *iyi–uwa*, Okonkwo threatens, roars, and rumbles "like thunder in the rainy season," but Okagbue retains his calm and patience, gently probing the little girl: "Leave her to me," he tells Okonkwo, "in a cool confident voice" (57 [77]). Okagbue, we are told, is famous in Umuofia for his knowledge in matters of *ogbanje* or reincarnation. When Okonkwo threatens to "beat sense" into Ezinma for her reluctance to reveal where she hid her *iyi–uwa*, Okagbue says to him, "I have told you to let her alone. I know how to deal with them" (58 [78]). Okonkwo is essentially trying to use force or "manliness" to resolve a matter of life and death. The solution ultimately comes, not from his thunderous threats, but from the gentle (watery) manners of Okagbue through whose persuasion Ezinma reveals where she hid her *iyi–uwa* (59 [79]). Okagbue possesses the virtues which Okonkwo requires, a combination of patience and tactics.

Obierika is another character whose actions often represent the "other alternative," the redemptive alternative. Strength, manliness, and masculine ideals are, doubtless, respected values in Umuofia. Okonkwo accepts these values in a literal sense. Obierika, his foil, is, however, more subtle and more pliable. Unlike Okonkwo, he understands that culture is both compliant and ambivalent, and that reality is "at once simple and extremely complex." Achebe is best identified in this novel with the character of Obierika (Achebe, Interview with Jeyifo, *Contemporary Nigerian Literature,* 13). Achebe employs Obierika to express his views more directly; through Obierika he corrects the imbalances in the hero and suggests more realistic solutions to problems. Obierika's reaction to Okonkwo's murder of Ikemefuna not only brings out the contrast between the two characters, but also underscores the correct course, which is the more flexible way of interpreting the traditional codes. For Okonkwo, if the Oracle has decreed that Ikemefuna die, no one should question the authority and the decision of the gods. But Obierika has the wisdom to discern some flexibility in his society's code of values: "If I were you I would have stayed at home . . . if the Oracle said that my son should be killed, I would neither dispute it nor be the one to do it" (46–47 [64–65]). Obierika knows that tribal gods respect the dictates of the individual's conscience, and that blind obedience could lead to abominable acts with tragic consequences: "What you have done," he tells Okonkwo, "will not please the Earth. It is the kind of action for which the goddess wipes out whole families" (46 [64]). This echoes a previous warning from Ezeani, the priest of the earth goddess, after Okonkwo broke the Week of Peace by beating his wife: "The evil you have done can ruin the whole clan. The earth goddess whom you have insulted may refuse to give us her increase, and we shall all perish" (22 [32]).

Okonkwo's uncompromising attitude alienates himself from his people who themselves are flexible and compromising. It is true that in matters affecting the stability of the clan (relationship to their gods, for example), their laws are firm and abiding, yet in general they are more flexible and accommodating than Okonkwo. They accommodate, for example, weak and effeminate men like Unoka, Okonkwo's father. Umuofia adapts to changing situations, as Ogbuefi Ezeudu testifies, when he comments on Okonkwo's violation of the Week of Peace. From what he heard from his father, in the past, a violator was "dragged on the ground through the village until he died." With time this mode of capital punishment gave way to a system of fines. In Obodoani, the custom is still severe, and Ezeudu condemns it: "They have that custom in Obodoani. If a man dies at this time he is not buried but cast into the Evil Forest. It is a bad custom which these people observe because they lack understanding" (23 [33]). Umuofia is responsive to change, especially when their decision does not conflict with the will of the gods.

The need for compromise as a means of redemption is a theme to which Achebe constantly returns in this novel. In some instances, he juxtaposes two contrasting attitudes in order to highlight this compromise. Uchendu and Okonkwo, for example, react differently to Obierika's tale of the killing of the white man on the iron horse in Abame, which sparked off a harsh reprisal in which large numbers were killed. Uchendu reacts with disdain: "Never kill a man who says nothing. Those men of Abame were fools. What did they know about that man?" (98 [129–30]). Okonkwo reacts differently: "They were fools. . . . They should have armed themselves with their guns and their matchets even when they went to market" (99 [130]). As usual, Okonkwo supports violence as a solution to the problem. Uchendu, on the other hand, has common sense to place blame upon the people of Abame for their irresponsible action. Obierika, Achebe's persona, contemplates the consequences: "They have paid for their foolishness. . . . But I am greatly afraid. We have heard stories about white men who made powerful guns and the strong drinks and took slaves away across the seas, but no one thought the stories were true" (99 [130]). Obierika implies that the strength of the white man makes it imperative for Abame and Umuofia to approach him cautiously, and to compromise, where possible. Accepting Obierika's views, Uchendu adds an interesting comment akin to Emerson's doctrine of compensation: "The world has no end, and what is good among one people is an abomination with others" (99 [130]). He illustrates this view with the case of the albinos who, though regarded as aliens, yet find accommodation in Igbo society. In effect, Achebe assumes that "the world has no end"; that there are other peoples, other cultures, other views, and it is foolish to refuse to accommodate these other systems, for, according to Umuofia's proverb: "Let the kite perch and let the eagle perch too. If one says no to the other, let his wing break" (14 [22]).

In another incident, Achebe juxtaposes two extreme positions in order to highlight the middle course. When an early Christian zealot killed a sacred python in Mbanta, a confrontation broke out between Mbanta people and the Christians. Among Mbanta people themselves, there was a discussion on how to deal with the issue. Okonkwo "who had begun to play a part in the affairs of his motherland" took an extreme position, demanding the use of violence in solving the problem: "Until the abominable gang was chased out of the village with whips," he argued, "there would be no peace" (112 [148]). Many of the assembled rulers and elders chose the opposite course, preferring to leave the gods to fight for themselves. For Okonkwo, this position smacked of cowardice, the type of reaction he expected from a "womanly clan" but never from Umuofia, his fatherland. Ironically, Umuofia, itself, will in turn refuse to go to war; thus it will disappoint Okonkwo. At the end of the deliberation, the Mbanta people decided on a middle course, to ostracize the Christians. Although Okonkwo "ground his teeth in disgust" at such a decision, it ultimately proved to be a wise one, for no bloody fight ensued, and besides, "the gods were still able to fight their own battle," for Okoli, the offending Christian, suddenly fell ill and died (114 [150]). The compromise had worked.

Paradoxically, the coming of the white man to Umuofia has a positive value, which itself is redemptive. As we have noted earlier, Achebe subscribes to the Yeatsian theory of the inevitability of change in the history of any civilization. *Things Fall Apart* deals with a crucial period in the history of Umuofia when the old civilization approaches the brink of disintegration. Obierika rightly identifies the major source of this disintegration as the white man: "The white man is very clever. He came quietly and peaceably with his religion. We were amused at his foolishness and allowed him to stay. Now he has won our brothers, and our clan can no longer act like one. He has put a knife on the things that held us together and we have fallen apart" (124–25 [162]). But the coming of the white man is an historical imperative, an event Umuofia could not countermand. Umuofia had reached a point where, in Yeats's words, "the centre cannot hold." Like a blighted tree, Umuofia, already fractured by internal flaws, stood tottering at the mercy of any storm. Once threatened by the white man's government and religion, it succumbed.

Yet, the white man's mission was ultimately redemptive. Umuofia was already sick and had to be "doctored." Apart from the many acts of brutality the society embraced, like abandoning twins in the forests, mutilating *ogbanje* children after death, abandoning victims of swelling sickness to die in the forest, the society of Umuofia is shown to have failed to extend protection to the weak, the poor, women, and the outcasts (*osu*). Monstrous injunctions of the gods were promptly executed without human consideration, and contravention of certain laws drew terrible penalties. Okonkwo's seven years of exile for the accidental shooting of his friend's son is a typical example of such harsh penalties. In addition to the sentence of exile, his houses were set ablaze, his barns destroyed, and his animals killed by the men of Umuofia who stormed his compound, dressed like warriors. Obierika, one of the participants in this exercise, was later moved to question traditional justice:

> Obierika was a man who thought about things. When the will of the goddess had been done, he sat down in his *obi* and mourned his friend's calamity. Why should a man suffer so grievously for an offense he had committed inadvertently? But although he thought for a long time he found no answer. He was merely led to greater complexities. He remembered his wife's twin children, whom he had thrown away. What crime had they committed? (87 [117–18])

Obierika acts as Achebe's mouthpiece in this analysis. The passage is a direct commentary on society's inhumanity. This inhuman practice places Umuofia in a morally vulnerable position, which the missionaries could readily exploit upon their arrival.

Apart from Obierika, Nwoye also questioned his society's traditional practices. He was never impressed by the clan's celebration of strength and masculinity. His taste was a far cry from that of his father who prepared him for a "manly" life by telling him stories of violence and bloodshed. But Nwoye preferred "women stories." Greatly disturbed by the death of his "brother" and mentor Ikemefuna, a death for which he held his father suspect, and worried about the clan's insensitive and chilling practice in connection with the abandoned twins he had chanced upon crying in the thick forest, Nwoye became alienated from his people. The coming of Ikemefuna had significantly boosted his morale and given him fulfillment. It had made him "feel grown up" and "seemed to have kindled a new fire" in him (37 [51]). When he sensed that Ikemefuna had been killed, "something seemed to give way inside him, like the snapping of a tightening bow" (43 [59]). The death of Ikemefuna signaled his final break with the traditional Umuofia society. Henceforth, he became a quiet rebel against the traditional norms. It also explains his rejection of Okonkwo who epitomized the cruelty in these norms. The coming of the Christians to Mbanta led him to discover in them what he had lost in the deceased Ikemefuma, a brotherhood. His decision to become an early convert is based upon "natural law" and prefigures his recognition of a higher moral ethos.

Christianity was for Nwoye a redemptive event. Redemption is Christianity's fundamental mission. Christ is the symbol of redemption, especially as he fulfills the prophecy of Isaiah: "*to bring the good news to the afflicted. / He has sent me to proclaim liberty to captives, / sight to the blind, / to let the oppressed go free*" (Lk 4:18–19; Is 61:1–2). Achebe sees Christianity as largely contributing to the destruction of the traditional system, but also as redeeming the victims of the old system. The conversion of Nwoye to Christianity is explained by its synaesthesia:

> It was not the mad logic of the Trinity that captivated him. He did not understand it. It was the poetry of the new religion, something felt in the marrow. The hymn about brothers who sat in darkness and in fear seemed to answer a vague and persistent question that haunted his young soul—the question of the twins crying in the bush and the question of Ikemefuna who was killed. He felt a relief within as the hymn poured into his parched soul. The words of the hymn were like the drops of frozen rain melting on the dry palate of the panting earth (104 [137]).

In Nwoye, the convert, the life of cruelty and insensitivity, represented with images of barrenness, gave way to a new life of poetry and brotherhood, represented with images of rain. Christianity, therefore, gives life and hope. For Okonkwo, Christianity was "womanish" because it signifies those values which he despised—love, affection, gentleness, and mercy. But it is precisely these values for which Nwoye had yearned and now found in Christianity. Many others in Umuofia felt as Nwoye and saw Christianity as a refuge for the oppressed and the underdogs: the so–called *efulefu* or "worthless, empty men"; the *osu* or outcasts who were virtually ostracized from society which would not allow them to marry nor permit them be married to free–borns; parents of twins; and those held in contempt because they had taken no titles (110–13 [144–49])..

The missionaries, themselves, included people who exhibited exemplary qualities. An example is Mr. Brown who displayed the vitality of Christian faith in his reverence for his fellow man. He educated the people and cared for their welfare. His willingness to listen to the people and learn from them about their own culture enabled him to carry out his mission in a very hospitable manner. He not only cared for the people's spiritual welfare by building new churches, he also cared for their material progress; hence, he built a school and a hospital. Consequently, "his mission grew from strength to strength" (128 [166–67]).

The colonial administration also made a positive contribution, despite the oppression it represented. The aim of the colonial government, as stated by the District Commissioner, was to grant protection to all the people, irrespective of age or rank, and to promote peace and justice. Addressing the six elders of Umuofia who had been arrested as a result of the violence against Christians before humiliating them, he said: "We have brought a peaceful administration to you and your people so that you may be happy. If any man ill–treats you we shall come to your rescue. But we will not allow you to ill–treat others. We have a court of law where we judge cases and administer justice just as it is done in my own country under a great queen" (137 [178]). The new administration, therefore, aimed to introduce a system which would grant equal treatment to all and curb the excesses based on superstition, fear, and brutality. In carrying out its aims, the administration may have faltered, as discussed earlier in chapter two, yet it is significant that its primary purpose was the institution of law and order and fair treatment to all. The ultimate beneficiaries of the new system would be those who felt unfairly treated in the tribal system. Another redemptive aspect of the new administration proved to be the material benefits it introduced into Umuofia for which it won the loyalty of many men and women: "The white man had indeed brought a lunatic religion, but he had also brought a trading store and for the first time palm–oil and kernel became things of great price, and much money flowed in Umuofia" (126 [163]). The people enjoyed the social uplift resulting from the economic progress introduced by the colonial administration. This partly explains why they did not feel "as strongly as Okonkwo about the new dispensation," and also why it proved difficult for Okonkwo to mobilize them to fight the white man.

Achebe sees the family, particularly the extended family, as the vehicle of redemption. He devotes much space to the family because of its privileged role in society. Okonkwo's family receives the greatest attention. From the art–loving but improvident Unoka, Achebe takes us to Okonkwo and his family. We see them in their moments of joyful celebration (the wrestling and the locust episodes) and also in their moments of crisis (wife–beatings, Ezinma's illness, the exile, and Nwoye's separation). In *Things Fall Apart,* the family functions as a citadel of moral support in times of crisis. Mgbafor sought the solace of her family when her husband Uzowulu persisted in beating her. Her family provided a haven and responded by punishing Uzowulu with a sound beating and a refusal to pay back his bride price. At the *egwugwu* tribunal, her family sat beside her and spoke on her behalf. Okonkwo himself derived support and empathy from his family. After the devastating harvest in his early career, his father, Unoka, consoled him with these words: "Do not despair. I know you will not despair. You have a manly and a proud heart. A proud heart can survive a general failure because such a failure does not prick its pride. It is more difficult and bitter when a man fails alone" (18 [27]). This consolation is ironically prophetic, for, in the end, Okonkwo will act alone and fail. During his exile, his family's support was of immeasurable value, as it really was all through his life. However, a "crack" (using Yeats's term) was introduced into the family by Okonkwo, himself, when he killed Ikemefuna who had been integrated into the family. From that time on, Nwoye dreaded him and later deserted him.

Obierika's family is more ideal, and Okonkwo could not help admiring its harmony (45–46 [63–64]). In Obierika's home, Ndulue's family was discussed as a model in which the husband and wife were a great support to each other. According to Obierika, Ndulue and Ozoemena "had one mind"; Ndulue could not do anything without telling Ozoemena. They loved each other in life and death. When Ozoemena heard that Ndulue was dead, she first made sure the story was true, and then, immediately, she too died. Her death was a "willed response to her husband's death." Okonkwo, in his characteristic way of viewing reality only in terms of gender, is disappointed in Ndulue confiding in his wife Ozoemena and says: "I thought he was a strong man in his youth" (48 [66]). Ndulue was a great warrior in his days, and yet unlike Okonkwo, he was able to balance the masculine and the feminine principles in himself. As Iyasere observes: "The union in life and in death of Ndulue and Ozoemena is a symbolic dramatization of the union of the masculine and the feminine attributes in a great man" (104). Redemption may be found in such a union, a point which Achebe achieves through contrast. The Ndulue episode arises on the very first day Okonkwo attempts to shake off the psychological effects of the death of Ikemefuna. Okonkwo is a great warrior who kills his "son" and terrorizes the other (43 [59–60]). Haunted by his deed, he visits his friend Obierika to resolve his psychological dilemma. In Obierika's peaceful home Okonkwo listens to the story of Ndulue and Ozoemena, a story of union in love. The peace and unity in Ndulue's family contrasts with the division and insecurity in Okonkwo's family and Okonkwo's self. Unfortunately, because of foolhardiness, he is unable to perceive the redemptive symbols contained in Ndulue's episode, just as he will turn a deaf ear to the wise and redemptive advise from his maternal uncle, Uchendu.

Uchendu's relationship with Okonkwo stresses the redemptive merit in the extended family system. Okonkwo's exile to his motherland proved a traumatic experience. Uchendu provided him practically all he needed for resettlement, and constantly appealed to him to feel at home among his kinsmen in order to overcome his sorrow. During Okonkwo's thanksgiving and farewell feast, in the presence of his maternal *umunna* (descendants of common ancestors), Uchendu led the prayer, and prayed to the ancestors, not for money or wealth, but for more kinsmen. He added: "We are better than animals because we have kinsmen. An animal rubs its aching flank against a tree, a man asks his kinsman to scratch him" (117 [154]). The oldest member of the *umunna* also emphasized the need for the protection of kinsmen. His fear of disintegration represents Achebe's stylization of the plight of his own generation: "I fear for you young people because you do not understand how strong is the bond of kinship" (118 [155]).

A stronger link may be found in the maternal relationship (a far more redeeming link) than in one's paternal *umunna*. Uchendu argues: "A man belongs to his fatherland and not to his motherland. And yet we say Nneka—'Mother is Supreme'" (94 [123]). He believes that a child belongs to its father, but when beaten by its father, it seeks refuge in the mother's hut. In time of crisis, the motherland provides protection and offers healing. Uchendu explains to Okonkwo: "A man belongs to his fatherland when things are good and life is sweet. But when there is sorrow and bitterness, he finds refuge in his motherland. Your mother is there to protect you. . . . And that is why we say that mother is supreme" (94 [124]). In motherhood we find the feminine principle most intensely represented. Uchendu is fully aware of Okonkwo's alienation from his clan as a result of his "manly" conduct, and he deliberately attempts to persuade him to rely on the feminine principle enshrined in motherhood to solve his problem. The exile might have served as a healing experience for Okonkwo, had he understood "how it symbolized man's need of the tender and consoling qualities which are the woman's side of his nature" (Stock, 89). His seven years of exile passed by without subduing or pacifying him. He returned to Umuofia unchanged, unredeemed, still clinging to his idea of manliness.

Things Fall Apart deals with the twilight of an integrated, though fragmented ("cracked" to use Yeats's term), African world at the moment of its confrontation with the European world. It also dramatizes conflicts (personal and cultural) resulting from this confrontation. The tragic nature of the confrontation is signified in the actions of those who, blind to the inevitability of change and the immense power of the white man, resist with violence. Achebe shows in this novel that in such a situation, redemption lies in accommodation and compromise, flexibility and balance. Hence, while men of action like Okonkwo perish in their narrowness of vision and blind resistance, more flexible and accommodating men like Obierika survive.

It is possible to outline Achebe's intent concerning those internal fractures that caused the Igbo culture to implode, as it were, in the face of the invasion of Western culture. In essence, it is foreshadowed in the deteriorating relationship between the members of the male line of Okonkwo's family. Each breaks from the other. There is, in fact, no personal or spiritual relationship from one son to the other. We detect only a biological relationship through the physical mother. There is a total absence of a cultural mother (as was explored above). What must be probed at this point is a phenomenon central to the cultural control of an Igbo society, namely, the use of titles.

In Igbo society it is clear that male aggression is necessary for vitality. If one recalls the story of the Sun and the Earth, male aggression is the synergistic force of the society. The question is how to preserve the vitality of the aggression without letting it become male dominance. We have already indicated that, on a personal interior level, this is experienced in the "acceptance of the feminine" within the individual. Practically, however, on the social level, male aggression was controlled by the conferring of titles. To acquire a title one had to be courageous in achievement (for example, feeding one's family against all adversity), but also one must have been willing to forego or sacrifice one's possessions. Without these conditions no title could be granted. The title gave one's argument a greater weight in assemblies of the community. It was an ingenious system. One gave up possessions (and thus one's material strength), and, though diminished in terms of wealth, one had a greater say in the governance of the community. Thus, domination over the community through wealth or achievement was checked, yet, at the same time, the vitality of the individual could be channeled to continue to work for the community. Perhaps, an ageless wisdom had created this system because it was seen that he who is aggressive in besting the challenges within his society will eventually desire to dominate over the society. The aggressive person left to his own devices would one day want to control exclusively. The title system presumed that if one lived with the "weakness" of his wisdom and will alone, the aggressive male would come to discern those qualities necessary to govern a community. As was said before, on a personal level, this "living with weakness" is what is concretely meant as "accepting the feminine."

This system, of course, was responsible for the understanding of the Igbo that "among the Igbo there is no king." In any event, through the conferring of titles we perceive how the dialectical poles of cosmological dualism and the individual with the society are integrated harmoniously. In short, moderation and flexibility are the values which Achebe understands as redemptive, and they are inculcated in a single system for male socialization. However, the story of the Sun and Earth adumbrates the failure of this clever system. The story presupposes that the male principle always exercises aggression. The aggression is of two types. The first scorches the earth; the second floods her. Either is a violent act. Most certainly both are forms of domination, and both manifest egotism in the extreme. The moral of the story is that the proper admixture of strength and tenderness will produce a harmoniously productive coexistence. Domination is avoided and life is assured. The system of titles presumes the same "natural" aggression of Igbo males. The title system further assumes that the experience of "weakness" by the male will, in fact, help him to identify with the "weakness" of the Earth in the story and, therefore, find moderation in duality as the puissance of life. This yields two exceptions:

1) when a man will not work to achieve titles, or
2) when a man acquires the titles for their own sake as an instrument for dominance.

The first man is weak, passive, or, as he would have been called by the Igbo, "womanly." Unoka, Okonkwo's father, represents the first exception. In this case, the system of titles may well so suppress male aggression, that the individual is belittled, and, eventually, all vitality is taken out of him. Or, Unoka, by natural temperament, may simply be slothful. As the Igbo say, "there is always another at your side," which is their belief that there is a dynamism in dualistic opposites. In other words, such a situation of over dominance, will produce metaphysically its opposite: the aggressive male, who dominates through violence including overstepping all laws which will, in turn, stamp out vitality (fertility) itself. Okonkwo symbolizes the second exception. The title system will have no effect in channeling his aggression.

For Achebe, the relationship of Father to Son is perceptible through their position in regard to titles (which, in effect, is the experience of "weakness" that transforms aggressive dominance to life giving vitality). Between Unoka and Okonkwo (Father to Son) there is no relationship except as dualistic opposites. Yet, this bond is precisely the relationship that is absolutely fundamental to the existence of any society. In *Things Fall Apart*, this relation is broken, that is "cracked". It is essential to see the symbolism here. Unoka, by dint of an indolent nature or by intimidation in the face of the title system, is at the end of the Igbo title system. Okonkwo is the "primitive" or *original* Igbo male (a throwback to the beginning of time) for whom the title system was invented. We see the END and the BEGINNING of the Igbo male line in juxtaposition to the title system. In short, the title system itself had become bankrupt. Further, Achebe is making an anthropological statement and expressing a moral fact. Okonkwo is "old Adam" (cf. *Anthills*, 89, where Achebe, in Ikem's letter, identifies the Genesis myth with the Creation Myth of the Igbo), the original egotist, whose destiny is to fail time and again. He will dominate through force of will. He will de–stroy what he has been given stewardship over. Morally, Achebe infers that when humans cede their redemption to a system, they should expect nothing more than to become a product of that system, as is the case of the indolence of Unoka.

It is to the credit of Achebe's literary genius that we are given a glimpse of the future generation. Okonkwo has two sons: the first is his "spiritual" son, Ikemefuna; the other is the son of his loins, Nwoye. Clearly, the future was to have two parts: those who would follow the Igbo tradition, and those who would be absorbed into the West. Yet, in the killing of Ikemefuna by his "adopted" father, it is clear what the future of the Igbo would have become given the bankruptcy of the title system: male would dominate male. The spiritual reign of the Igbo would die in an internecine struggle for power through domination and violence. Nwoye breaks with his father Okonkwo and embraces the traditions of the West. This announces another fracture in the familial relation that forms the clan. By his conversion, Nwoye "adopts" a new Father, the Christian God, and embraces a new Mother (nurturer of culture), Victoria. In either case, be it Ikemefuna or Nwoye, the Igbo culture, its balance, and its harmony, die. While Nwoye perceived redemption in the values of Christianity, Nwoye's conversion is not redemptive. Infected by the same inflexibility as his father, he rejects all things Igbo. He has only replaced one system with another. Thus, while redemption lies at the heart of this novel, the tragedy of *Things Fall Apart* is not only that sympathetic characters cannot achieve moderation and flexibility in themselves, but also the culture of the Igbo is lost through their mismanagement.

Perhaps, only as a presage to his future novels, Achebe chronicles the past as pregnant with lessons for a future society that will have to struggle to rediscover its identity. Not only on a moral level but also symbolically, Achebe has couched his narrative in images that deal with redemption. Okonkwo is the archetype of "old Adam" who will continue to reside within Achebe's male characters from novel to novel, though most particularly in *Anthills of the Savannah*. Male domination will be portrayed in images of scorching heat or torrential rain. Further, the penchant to cede redemptive value to systems, be they political, military, or revolutionary, will also conclude in "things falling apart."

Confronted with this pessimistic ending, can the theme of redemption survive? It brings to mind the words of Jesus that these things are "being fulfilled today even while you are listening" (Lk. 4:21). Achebe's novel itself is both a prophecy and a hope for his own society, the heirs of the Igbo. If Africa does not revisit and recover its traditional past where once its ancestors struggled with their interior "demons" in order to experience harmony and balance, it is condemned to repeat the same pattern of:

1) domination by the forces meant to give vitality, or
2) oppression through the systems it creates.

This is Achebe's prophecy. His hope is that the present generation can still return to its past, accept it, and see within its tradition what must be understood about the African spirit to better discern its complexity.

ARROW OF GOD

Arrow of God is Achebe's third novel. Like *Things Fall Apart*, it deals with the effect of "culture–contact" on an Igbo society. *Things Fall Apart* focuses on the initial contact between Umuofia and the British, whereas the later novel shows how the Umuaro clan adjusts to the new system. The course of this adjustment introduces conflicts, mostly as a consequence of British rule. Some examples are:

(a)   The conflict between Winterbottom and Ezeulu, between the British administration and the native authority, or between the western and the indigenous culture;

(b)   The conflict between Ulu, represented by his Chief Priest Ezeulu, and Idemili, represented by his priest Ezidemili;

(c)   The domestic conflicts between Ezeulu and his sons;

(d)   The conflict in Ezeulu himself as he tries to differentiate between his personal power and his public responsibility;

(e)   The conflict Ezeulu experiences in defining the limits of his authority and his confidence in the strength of his God's authority.

It is clear from these examples that Ezeulu is the center of action in *Arrow of God*. Achebe considers him as a man with a redemptive mission. His failure to achieve this epiphany bespeaks his shortcomings. His failure has a wider implication for the entire clan. Our discussion will concentrate on the activities of the main character, Ezeulu.

Ezeulu plays a prime redemptive role by virtue of his office as the Chief Priest of Ulu. He is "the keeper of collective security." Although from the beginning of the novel he is aware of the breakdown of solidarity among the Umuaro clan, which he attributes to "the new age" (14), he is fully conscious of the immense redemptive power that attends his office:

> In the very distant past, when lizards were still few and far between, the six villages—Umuachala, Umunneora, Umuagu, Umuezeani, Umuo–gwugwu and Umuisiuzo—lived as different peoples, and each worshipped its own deity. Then the hired soldiers of Abam used to strike in the dead of night, set fire to houses and carry men, women and children into slavery. Things were so bad for the six villages that their leaders came together to save themselves. They hired a strong team of medicine–men to install a common deity for them. This deity which the fathers of the six villages made was called Ulu. Half of the medicine was buried at a place which became the Nkwo market and the other half thrown into the stream which became Mili Ulu. The six villages then

took the name of Umuaro, and the priest of Ulu became their Chief Priest. From that day they were never again beaten by an enemy (14–15).

This historical review makes it clear that the federal union of the six villages was based on the need for security and that Ulu came into being solely for the purpose of protection. In addition to providing security, Ulu acts both as "the guardian of social well–being" and the keeper of seasonal calendar. His Chief Priest offers sacrifice on behalf of the people, and he prays for their well–being. After announcing the new moon and eating one of the sacred yams, he prays for fruition in his petition at the shrine of Ulu:

> *As this is the moon of planting may the six villages plant with profit. May we escape danger in the farm—the bite of a snake or the sting of the scorpion, the mighty one of the scrubland. May we not cut our shinbone with the matchet or the hoe. And let our wives bear male children. May we increase in numbers at the next counting of the villages so that we shall sacrifice to you a cow, not a chicken as we did after the last New Yam feast. May children put their fathers into the earth and not fathers their children. May good meet the face of every man and every woman. Let it come to the land of the riverain folk and to the land of the forest peoples* (6).

According to Mbiti, the priest in African traditional religions has multiple duties including "making sacrifices, offerings, and prayers, conducting both public and private rites and ceremonies, and, above all, fulfilling their office as religious intermediaries between men and God" (*Concept of God in Africa* 220). Ezeulu fulfills all these and more. He is a unique figure, being half man and half spirit. Furthermore, he is the scapegoat who bears the sins of the people and undergoes ritual purification and cleansing in order to help them avert disaster. Achebe gives us a detailed sample of such a purification ritual in his description of the Festival of the Pumpkin Leaves (71–74). Ezeulu comprehends his redemptive role:

> Yes, it was right that the Chief Priest should go ahead and confront danger before it reached his people. That was the responsibility of his priesthood. It had been like that from the first day when the six harassed villages got together and said to Ezeulu's ancestor: You will carry this deity for us. At first he was afraid. What power had he in his body to carry such potent danger? But his people sang their support behind him and the flute man turned his head. So he went down on both knees and they put the deity on his head. He rose up and was transformed into a spirit. His people kept up their song behind him and he stepped forward on his first and

decisive journey, compelling even the four days in the sky to give way to him (188).

Given the origin of his god and the nature of his office, Ezeulu has the religious, as well as redemptive, duty to protect his people. He is expected to be the symbol of unity in the their traditional governing structure. But as we shall see, he fails in this redemptive role owing to internal and external factors. His failure has tragic consequences for himself and the culture he represents. The main irony in this novel is that the Chief Priest of Ulu ends up no longer as the provider of unity and security, but as the enemy of the people.

The white man's administration was a shattering blow to the traditional authority of Ezeulu and his god. As we saw earlier, the six villages had created Ulu and united under him to preclude the threat of Abam warriors and slave hunters. The colonial government abolished slave trade and, through its "pacification," ended the "unpredictable predations of marauding [Abam] slave raiders," with the result that the traditional institution created to ensure collective security weakened and old resentments resurged. As Ezeulu knows, "the priests of Idemili and Ogwugwu and Eru and Udo had never been happy with their secondary role since the villages got together and made Ulu and put him over the older deities" (41). While serious external threats (like the Abam incursions) existed, these gods were contented to acquiesce and accept the leadership of a protective and unifying god, Ulu. But when the threat abated, they began to rear their heads in revolt. It is no wonder that the authority of Ulu is challenged by the priest of Idemili using the demagogue Nwaka. In one of his inciting speeches, he repudiates the right of Ulu to lead Umuaro:

> Nwaka began by telling the assembly that Umuaro must not allow itself to be led by the Chief Priest of Ulu. "My father did not tell me that before Umuaro went to war it took leave from the priest of Ulu," he said. "The man who carries a deity is not a king. He is there to perform his god's ritual and to carry sacrifice to him. But I have been watching this Ezeulu for many years. He is a man of ambition; he wants to be king, priest, diviner, all. His father, they said, was like that too. But Umuaro showed him that Igbo people knew no kings. The time has come to tell his son also.
>
> "We have no quarrel with Ulu. He is still our protector, even though we no longer fear Abam warriors at night. But I will not see with these eyes of mine his priest making himself lord over us. My father told me many things, but he did not tell me that Ezeulu was king in Umuaro. Who is he, anyway? Does anybody here enter his compound through the man's gate? If Umuaro decided to have a king we know where he would come from. Since when did Umuachala become head of the six villages?

> We all know that it was jealousy among the big villages that made them give the priesthood to the weakest. We shall fight for our farmland and for the contempt Okperi has poured on us. Let us not listen to anyone trying to frighten us with the name of Ulu. If a man says yes his *chi* also says yes. And we have all heard how the people of Aninta dealt with their deity when he failed them. Did they not carry him to the boundary between them and their neighbours and set fire on him? I salute you" (26 – 27).

There is no doubt that this speech from an enemy is highly demagogic, yet it shows the extent to which traditional authority, represented by Ulu and his Chief Priest, has come under fire. It reveals the crisis of authority which has arisen in Umuaro as a result of structural changes wrought by the colonial administration, the Christian church, and the new economic forces. Later, when war broke out between Umuaro and Okperi, it was the colonial authority that superimposed order. This was a war Ezeulu could not prevent in spite of his authority and engaging rhetoric. As the warring parties surrendered their guns to the white man, it became clear to the Umuaro people that "the exercise of judicial coercion and violence" had shifted from its traditional base to the colonial. Moreover, when Ezeulu testified against his people before Winterbottom, he was perceived (at least by his enemies) no longer as the hub of unity, but as the "friend" of the white man.

All said, Ezeulu deserves credit for the way he handled some of the conflicts that engulfed him. In dealing with the white man, for example, he outclassed his counterpart in *Things Fall Apart* (Okonkwo) who chose to fight and perish rather than accept colonial rule. Ezeulu wisely compromised (if only to learn the "trick" of the white man) by sending his son to learn the ways of the white man, or, put simply, the power of his technology. He also acted with honor in dissuading his people from fighting a war of blame, and telling the truth before the District Commissioner. His rejection of the chieftaincy offer, which would have subverted his religious authority, was heroic. If the novel had ended at the stage where he was released from detention, Ezeulu would have been remembered as a hero who remained incorruptible in his struggle for truth and justice. Unfortunately, Ezeulu left Okperi with bitterness and swore vengeance against his people for abandoning him at the critical moment. Like Okonkwo, who returned from exile to plunge into a fight against the new forces, Ezeulu returned from detention resolved to fight his enemies to the bitter end, and these happened to be his own people. The weapon he used in this fight was the authority he had exercised over the traditional calendar. Two months of detention postponed the timetable of the agricultural calendar he maintained by eating the ritual yams. While in detention, these sacred yams had not been touched. When he returned, he refused to an-

nounce the Feast of the New Yam until he had eaten the remaining yams. Until the
yams were eaten, they could not harvest their crops, and a new planting season could
not commence. Because of his action, the people were subjected to immense suffering and a threat of famine. For salvation, they turned to the Christian God. They sent
their sons with yam offerings to the Christian harvest festival, and "thereafter any
yam harvested in their fields was harvested in the name of the son" (230).

Ezeulu's hubris is his failure to act within the limits of his power. Although he is
aware of the enormous power he wields as the Chief Priest, he is haunted by the fear of
losing it. His obsession is evident in the following self–conscious and deeply psychological analysis:

> Whenever Ezeulu considered the immensity of his power over the year
> and the crops and, therefore, over the people he wondered if it was real. It
> was true he named the day for the feast of the Pumpkin Leaves and for
> the New Yam feast; but he did not choose it. He was merely a watchman.
> His power was no more than the power of a child over a goat that was
> said to be his. As long as the goat was alive it could be his; he would find
> it food and take care of it. But the day it was slaughtered he would know
> soon enough who the real owner was. No! the Chief Priest of Ulu was
> more than that, must be more than that. If he should refuse to name the
> day there would be no festival—no planting and no reaping. But could he
> refuse? No Chief Priest had ever refused. So it could not be done. He
> would not dare.
> Ezeulu was stung to anger by this as though his enemy had spoken it.
> "Take away that word *dare*," he replied to this enemy. "Yes I say
> take it away. No man in all Umuaro can stand up and say that I dare not.
> The woman who will bear the man who will say it has not been born yet"
> (3 – 4).

His confusion as to the precise limit of his power in relation to the power of Ulu is
rooted in his obsession. This confusion will continue until the revelation toward the
end of the novel when Ezeulu is made to know that he has been too presumptuous to
claim to be fighting for Ulu.

> "Ta! Nwanu! . . . Who told you that this was your own fight?" . . . " Be-
> ware you do not come between me and my victim or you may receive
> blows not meant for you! Do you not know what happens when two ele-
> phants fight? Go home and sleep and leave me to settle my quarrel with
> Idemili, whose envy seeks to destroy me that his python may again come
> to power. Now you tell me how it concerns you. I say go home and sleep.
> As for me and Idemili we shall fight to the finish; and whoever throws
> the other down will strip him of his anklet!" (191)

With this warning, Ulu makes it clear that Ezeulu is overstepping his boundaries, and should beware. But Ezeulu does not heed the warning. He interprets correctly that the fight was between the gods, and he was but a mere "arrow in the bow of his god." Yet, the Chief Priest, "half man and half spirit," does not know where to draw the line between Ulu's interest and his own obsession for vengeance.

His personal interest drives him into bitter contention with his people under the cover of executing Ulu's will. No matter how persuaded of his struggle in behalf of Ulu, deep in his heart he is driven by personal interests to a no–compromise confrontation with his people for failing to support him in his fight against the white man. Umuaro as a whole had become his enemy. On the day of his release, he declared war against his enemies, saying: "I am going home to challenge all those who have been poking their fingers into my face to come outside their gate and meet me in combat and whoever throws the other will strip him of his anklet" (179). Ironically, he is here uttering Ulu's challenge: "whoever throws the other down will strip him of his anklet" (191). This suggests that unconsciously Ezeulu, in his mad pursuit of vengeance, is turning himself into a god (Ulu); he is usurping the power of Ulu, and there lies his hubris.

This threat is fully executed using a most destructive weapon—the refusal to announce the Feast of the New Yam until he has eaten all the remaining yams. In other words, Ezeulu has decided to strike where it aggrieved most—to disturb the flow of Time or the seasonal rhythm and thereby cause untold suffering and possibly death, for he authorizes "no planting and no reaping" while the feast is yet unannounced. His people will have to suffer hunger in their long wait to harvest their yams, the symbol and source of life. Ezeulu himself is fully aware of the gravity of his act; he knows that no Chief Priest ever subjected the people to such extreme austerity by refusing to announce the feast (3). But the proud and stubborn Ezeulu (212) is the type of priest who "leads a god to ruin himself" (213) by sheer obstinacy.

Ulu the redeemer–protector is transmogrified into Ulu, the destroyer, by his Chief Priest. Bearing in mind that the Igbo society turns against a god that fails to deliver the goods, the stage is set for the death of a god and the culture it represents. Nwaka had already hinted at this reaction when he cited the case of Aninta where the people destroyed their god who had failed them (27). When Ulu through his Chief Priest failed to fulfill his redemptive role, that is, to provide unity and protection, the people did exactly what the underdog had done in Umuofia of *Things Fall Apart*— they turned to the Christian God for redemption. In this way, they demonstrated to Ulu and his Chief Priest that ultimate power lies with the people.

This apocalyptic alteration of the most profound beliefs of the society has moral, as well as political, overtones. First, no individual, no matter his position and function in society, should consider himself more important than his society. Achebe has always believed in the uniqueness and importance of the individual, but, he feels, "this uniqueness and importance is limited by the importance and the will of the community" (Egejuru, 122–23). Both Okonkwo and Ezeulu fail to find a balance between their individuality and the society. Okonkwo's extreme individualism drives him to sing outside the choir and to perish; Ezeulu's independence is antithetical to the beliefs of the people. Having antagonized the people by pushing his personal cause past through the communal interest, he finds himself completely alienated from the people:

> But the heaviest load was on Ezeulu's mind. He was used to loneliness. As Chief Priest he had often walked alone in front of Umuaro. But without looking back he had always been able to hear their flute and song which shook the earth because it came from a multitude of voices and the stamping of countless feet. There had been moments when the voices were divided as in the land dispute with Okperi. But never until now had he known them to die away altogether (219).

As if to compound his problem, at this critical moment of his isolation Ulu struck a deadly blow upon his Chief Priest with the sudden death of his beloved son, Obika. Before his mind snapped, Ezeulu interpreted this punishment as "the collapse and ruin of all things" (229). The lesson is clear: no individual is above his god and his community. In the view of Umuaro leaders, the case of Ezeulu justifies the ancestral wisdom "that no man however great was greater than his people; that no man ever won judgment against his clan" (230).

Second, Achebe believes that flexibility, reconciliation, and devotion to the commonweal are redemptive values needed to resolve the crisis of transition in Umuaro. Ezeulu should have listened to the wise advice from his friend Akuebue, from his own six ritual assistants (203), and from the ten titled elders of Umuaro (205). These tried in various ways to persuade him to relent in his anger, to shorten his pride and call the Feast of the New Yam. But Ezeulu, like Okonkwo of *Things Fall Apart*, remained unflinching. The titled men, representing the entire clan, warned him of the "fear and anxiety in Umuaro which if allowed to spread might spoil something" (206), and they advised him to find a way out of the problem (an alternative) so as to save the harvest and the people (208). They even took the risk to empower him to eat the yams to free himself of guilt: "Umuaro is now asking you to go and eat those remaining yams today and name the day of the next harvest ... if Ulu says we have committed an abomination let it be on the heads of ten of us here" (208). Despite such pleadings and reassurances, Ezeulu remained intractable.

At such a crucial time, Achebe suggests, the practical solution lies in the bending of wills, in compromise and reconciliation. External threats call for reconciliation and unity. This is a lesson Ezeulu failed to grasp in detention where John Nwodika faces him as the epitome of good–will and reconciliation. John abjured old scores between his village and Ezeulu's, and treated him like a friend and a father: visited him often, consoled him, brought him food, and cheered him. The first day, Ezeulu would not taste the food, still suspicious of Nwodika, but the next day, he changed his mind, having "seen enough of the man's mind to know he had no ill–will" (165). Thus, at Okperi, under the threat of the white man, the two foes fraternized. When Ezeulu returned to Umuaro, people poured in to visit and welcome his return; in two days he counted fifty–seven visitors, among them, two or three from Umunneora, the enemy village. The good–will shown by this people encouraged Ezeulu to consider possibilities of reconciliation (187).He began to notice that not everyone was opposed to him, and that the bulk of the "ordinary people" had nothing but good–will toward him. Ezeulu's experience of the warm reception by the people afforded him a golden opportunity to reconcile himself with his people. Pride intervened, and he failed to grasp the opportunity. He could never forgive the people for supporting Nwaka against him in the market place. In Ezeulu's revenge, no one was to be spared, for "he knew he could say with justice that if one finger brought oil it messed up the others" (187).

The Christian church benefited from the crisis of division in Umuaro. When the people made their yam offerings to the Christian God, the door was swung open for mass conversion. It confirmed Ezeulu's utterance that "when two brothers fight a stranger reaps the harvest" (131). However, the Christian church did not just play a passive role in the entire drama of events. Just as in *Things Fall Apart*, Christianity came on time to supply the security which the old dispensation failed to provide. With many symbolic signs, the narrator makes us understand that the Christian God was all along an active and a winning participant in the battle of the gods. We notice such participation, for example, when Oduche, the new convert, imprisoned Idemili's sacred python. Again, it is evident when Nwafo and Obiageli sent the python running for life merely by reciting "Python run! There is a Christian here." The incident greatly entertained Ezeulu who "broke into a long loud laughter," elated that in the encounter with the Christian God, his enemy, Idemili was the loser. Neither were Ezeulu and his god spared. Once, as Ezeulu sat in his *obi* thinking of the festival of the Pumpkin Leaves, the church bell rang and his thought shifted from the festival to Christian matters (42). His children interpreted the bell as saying: "Leave your yam,

leave your cocoyam and come to church," and Ezeulu termed it a "song of extermination" (43). The bells thus adumbrated the extermination of the tribal ways which he
fully represented. As the crisis over the announcement of the festival drew to a cres-
cendo, Ezeulu, pressed by the leaders, consulted Ulu, and we read: "As Ezeulu cast
his string of cowries the bell of Oduche's people began to ring. For one brief moment
Ezeulu was distracted by its sad, measured monotone and he thought how strange it
was that it should sound so near—much nearer than it did in his compound" (210). In
such ways as this, the Christian God through psychological portents had made his
presence felt all the time. When consulted, Ulu turned down the people's request, but
soon, the Christian God, viewed as closely stalking Ulu, would grant their request for
salvation.

The unity of its members partially explains why Christianity triumphed over the
old dispensation. Although the members may have disagreed over issues from time to
time, they always found a compromise. For example, Moses Unachukwu and Goodcountry are poles apart on the Christian attitude toward the sacred python. While
Goodcountry advocates killing the animal, Moses believes it should be left alone, if
only to avoid the crisis of division the act could effect (47–50). These two pillars of St.
Mark's C.M.S. church had clashed over the issue on occasions. Once, Moses publicly
challenged Goodcountry on the question of the python and received a public rebuke
and humiliation (214). Aware of the danger involved in Goodcountry's war against
the royal python, Moses appealed to a higher authority, the Bishop. The Bishop, already under pressure from the colonial Administration "to apply the reins on his
boys," came down firmly on Mr. Goodcountry. He wrote a soothing letter to
Ezidemili, the priest of Idemili, "assuring him that the catechist would not interfere
with the python." He also prayed for the day the priest and all his people would be
converted to the true religion (214). Because of the Bishop's letter, many natives,
including prominent leaders like Nwaka, began to send their children to school. Thus,
unlike the vengeful Ezeulu, who absolutely refused to compromise his position, the
Christians were prepared to explore alternatives in order to mend fences, and the result proved highly rewarding. In the end the Christian God wins the battle of the gods
through flexibility and compromise. Inspired by the sudden and impressive increase
in his school enrollment—a consequence of the Bishop's conciliatory move—Mr.
Goodcountry moved to take advantage of the crisis over the New Yam Feast and invited "our heathen brethren" to the Christian harvest. This is yet another remarkable
occasion in which a fanatical catechist was obliged to bend his will. However, the
offer was perceived as redemptive and swung the loyalty of Umuaro from their worship of a sadistic Ulu to a charitable and empathetic God.

If we interpret *Arrow of God* as a writer's attempt to teach, then we need to ask the critical question: what is Achebe teaching his contemporaries by the tragic story of Ezeulu? To answer this question, we need to keep in mind the significant parallel between the transitional period in which Ezeulu lived and Achebe's post–colonial era, that is to say, between the past and the present. Both periods are marked by two ambivalences: transition and crisis. The post–colonial Africa is unstable because of the crisis of leadership and the struggle for power among political parties. For Achebe, "the reality of Nigeria today is an important factor. The African in Nigeria is as important to me as the Ibo man in the nineteenth century" (Egejuru, 80). Achebe seems to offer the case of Ezeulu as a paradigm of how self–serving rigidity is bound to lead to destruction. In a period of transition, one must anticipate crises. Differences in ideologies are necessarily indigenous to the adjusting process. Achebe maintains that in such situations flexibility and compromise, rather than obstinacy, are necessary for personal peace and group progress. Above all, the people must be served. Their will must prevail, not anybody else's, regardless of position and authority. Arrow of God, therefore, dramatizes the failure of a hero in leadership and redemptive roles. It also postulates realistic means of redemption in transitional periods. The story of Ezeulu teaches contemporary aspirants to leadership in Africa the attitudes they must avoid and the values they ought to embrace.

NO LONGER AT EASE

Achebe's second novel, *No Longer at Ease,* was published in 1960, the year of
Nigeria's independence. It deals with events of the late 50's, when Britain was preparing to transfer power to Nigerians. The novel presents an inside picture of life in
pre–independence civil service. It also deals with the mode of adaptation by a people
who had accepted Christianity and Western life–style but had not totally abandoned
their traditional ways. The story centers on the life of Obi Okonkwo.

The central character is the son of Isaac Okonkwo and the grandson of the hero of
Things Fall Apart. Recognized as a highly intelligent young man, Obi won a loan–
scholarship from the Umuofia Progressive Union of Lagos, and was sent to England
to study law. In England he shifted his field to English, and after earning his bache-
lor's degree, he returned to Nigeria where he accepted a post in the Civil Service as
the Secretary to the Scholarship Board, a job that had previously been exclusively
held by British officers. For a time, Obi's high principles enabled him to ward off
numerous temptations to bribery and corruption from scholarship seekers. Unfortunately, his salary was not able to off–set mounting financial and social pressure, and
he slackened from his high ideals and began surreptitiously to take bribes. He was
trapped, tried, sentenced, and humiliated. His relationships with Clara, his own parents, and the Umuofia Progressive Union are subplots that parallel and give new life
to the action of the main plot.

The title, which points to the major conflict in the novel, is taken from T.S. Eliot's
poem, "The Journey of the Magi" (69):

> We returned to our places, these Kingdoms,
> But no longer at ease here, in the old dispensation,
> With an alien people clutching their gods.
> I should be glad of another death.

In Eliot's poem, the Magi return home a changed people after their journey to Beth-
lehem to witness the birth of Christ. They are "no longer at ease" as they discover that
the traditional society to which they were accustomed does not coincide with their
Christian experience. They have become strangers in a world that has changed for
good. Achebe's novel describes a parallel situation where the new clashes with the
old, and the characters are inextricably caught up between the two. More especially,
Obi Okonkwo, the principal character, has journeyed to England and acquired new
habits. Upon his return home, he finds the demands of two cultures divisive and tear-
ing him apart. The old and the new struggle for dominance within his psyche with
tragic consequences. Obi, though an intensely individualized character, represents

the young educated Nigerian a few years before independence. Equipped with knowledge of two traditions—European and tribal—Obi is well conditioned to be a model to a people who are faced with the crisis of culture collision. By examining Obi's role in the novel, we shall see how he failed to play a redemptive role because he lacked the moral fibre required to implement his high ideals and because he was not able to blend the good features of each of the two cultures.

The case of Obi Okonkwo is an example of how idealism is tempered by grim reality. Obi returns from England filled with high ideals about the future of his country. In England, his nostalgia for his native land occasioned his composition of a number of romantic verses about Nigeria. One of them reads:

> 'How sweet it is to lie beneath a tree
> At eventime and share the ecstasy
> Of jocund birds and flimsy butterflies;
> How sweet to leave our earthbound body in its mud,
> And rise towards the music of the spheres,
> Descending soft with wind,
> And the tender glow of the fading sun' (14–15 [23]*).

This poem is characterized by its "negritude." It reveals Obi's idealized picture of his country while he was abroad. He strongly believed at the time that as an educated young Nigerian he was duty–bound to save his country from corruption and moral decadence. His return to Nigeria restores reality. Obi is confronted with lazy and corrupt Customs officials: "Customs formalities here took thrice as long as at Liverpool and five times as many officials" (27 [35]). To Obi's shock and disappointment, a young Customs official asks two pounds as a bribe for Obi's radiogram. Obi is equally shocked and disappointed to discover the real picture of Lagos: slums, stench from a rotting dog abandoned in the street, and the night–soilman "swinging his broom and hurricane lamp and trailing clouds of putrefaction" (14 [23]).

Disillusioned by his country, Obi resolves to live by his principles. He is simple in dress as in speech. During the reception organized in his honor by the Lagos branch of Umuofia Progressive Union, Obi appears in shortsleeves because of the heat, and his English is spoken with common speech. He thus sharply contrasts with his hosts who wear flamboyant *agbada* and European suits in spite of the heat. The type of English they applaud is full of bombast and pedantry. Obi's sincere commitment to transform

---

* Citations to *No Longer at Ease* are first from the Heinemann African Writers Series edition (reset 1975 [republished 1987]) and then from the Fawcett (paperback) edition (1969).

his society is shown in his response to their welcome address in which he stresses the need for service to the country: "He told them about the value of education. 'Education for service, not for white–collar jobs and comfortable salaries. With our great country on the threshold of independence, we need men who are prepared to serve her well and truly'" (29 [37]). At this early stage, Achebe strongly identifies with Obi and uses him as his spokesman. Soon, however, Obi's virtuous self will yield to the grim reality of the new Nigeria. He will then cease to be Achebe's spokesman but will become his target.

The real Nigeria in contrast with the Nigeria of Obi's dream, offers a gloomy picture. Although independence is close, the signs are that the people are not fully prepared for self–government. This is evident in the corrupt practices that dominate their lives. Examples are not difficult to find. Obi's position in the Civil Service, Secretary to the Scholarship Board, is highly prized simply because, to many Nigerians, it is an avenue to enrich oneself through bribery. Joseph's colleague, for instance, expects Obi to take bribes: "'E go make plenty money there. Every student who wan' go England go de see am for house" (70 [77]). After Mark's abortive attempt to bribe Obi, the narrator lets us know that bribery has become a way of life in Nigeria: "He [Obi] had won his first battle hands–down. Everyone said it was impossible to win. They said a man expects you to accept 'kola' from him for services rendered, and until you do, his mind is never at rest" (80 [86]). We learn about a Minister of State who once said that taking bribes was not bad, but failing to perform the service for which the bribe was taken was unethical. Such comment reveals the extent of corruption in the country. Mark's failure does not end his attempts; he sends his sister Elsie to try other means. Elsie stands a better chance of getting the scholarship through the normal channel, because of her excellent grade at the School Certificate Examination. Nonetheless, she is worried that "people with Grade One are sometimes left out in favour of those with Grade Two or even Three" (83 [89]). Because she does not wish to risk refusal, she comes to Obi's home prepared to "do whatever you ask" to get the offer. Obviously, she is desperate enough to offer herself for the prized scholarship. Obi's friend Christopher (who typifies the common reaction of Nigerian officialdom to proposals of this sort) comments that he sees nothing wrong with sex bribery (110–11 [116–17]). The Nigeria of *No Longer at Ease* is perverted through and through. Bribery is common practice among the Police, the Customs, and the Civil Service. The case of Joshua Udo, a member of the Umuofia Progressive Union, reveals a lot more about corruption in public life. Joshua had bribed his way into the Post Office where he worked as a messenger. But for a long time he did not complete his bribe payment. To worsen matters, he slept on duty, thus offering his corrupt employer, the Chief

Clerk, a pretext to dismiss him. When he loses his job, Joshua appeals to Umuofia Progressive Union who in turn entreats Obi to use his position to get him a new job. Not much is said about politics in this novel, but the man who represents the budding politicians, the Honourable Sam Okoli, is himself corrupt and shallow–minded. He is presented as being overly preoccupied with women, cheap electronic gadgets, and the good life. Given all this background picture of corruption in the country, we see that the temptation to corruption was very high, though not "overwhelming" (81 [87]). Obi's fall is thus rendered plausible, but not justifiable.

Corruption in the Nigerian society is ubiquitous according to Achebe. Why would he lay so much emphasis on corruption in this novel? Roderick Wilson's reading of *No Longer at Ease* against the background of T. S. Eliot's "The Waste Land" and "The Hollow Men" is an appropriate context for dealing with this question. Wilson attributes the conflicts in the novel to the fragmentation of the individual and the society as a whole (162–66). For example, the Umuofia Progressive Union is a victim of the conflict of expectations. They grant a loan to Obi to enable him to earn a university education in England, and they also expect to benefit the Umuofia society, especially in winning land cases, acquiring education and employment for their sons and members. The Union anticipates a return from Obi also. They expect him to repay his loan, maintain a high standard of living commensurate with his new status, and fulfill all his financial obligations to his extended family, for example, to pay his brother's school fees and to bear the financial responsibility for his mother's funeral. They insist on Obi's maintaining a European life style, but at the same time, expect him to be traditional on the question of *osu*. The fragmentation extends to individuals; for example, Obi's friend and townsman, Joseph is both modern and traditional. In education, employment, and life style, Joseph is Westernized, but he is fiercely opposed to Obi's relationship with Clara because she is an *osu*. Obi's parents too are divided between their strong Christian belief and their traditional belief. The fragmentation in this society is explained by the so–called cultural collision.

What Achebe repeatedly insists upon in this novel is that the lack of a solid grounding in both traditional and Western values is largely responsible for the moral and cultural crises in the pre–independent Nigeria. The novel implies that the solution to the crises demands true adaptation, which involves exploiting the good in each culture. Commenting on the positive aspect of colonialism, Achebe once said:

> I am not one of those who would say that Africa has gained nothing at all
> during the colonial period, I mean this is ridiculous—we gained a lot.
> But unfortunately when two cultures meet, one might expect if we were
> angels we could pick out the best in the other and retain the best in our

> own. But this doesn't often happen. What happens is that some of the
> worst elements of the old are retained and some of the worst of the new
> are added . . . (Quoted by Killam, *The Writings of Chinua Achebe*, 4–5).

Obi Okonkwo therefore needs the affirmative values of Western education and the positive values of the traditional society to build a wholesome character. The fragmented society needs a blending of the positive values from both cultures to achieve wholesomeness.

To press this point, Achebe contributes concrete examples of what values should be possessed by those Nigerians who will be assuming the duties of their colonial counterparts. Hard work and devotion to duty are two outstanding qualities shown by the officials. Marie, the expatriate Secretary to Mr. Green, shows a remarkable combination of cheerfulness and efficiency in her work. As for Mr. Green, Obi's boss, his great devotion to duty, as well as his kindly heart, is deserving of honor and respect. Mr. Green, on the other hand, does not believe that Africans, including well–educated ones, could run modern institutions. Obi marvelled at the paradox he finds in his boss:

> Obi had long come to admit to himself that, no matter how much he dis-
> liked Mr. Green, he nevertheless had some admirable qualities. Take, for
> instance, his devotion to duty. Rain or shine, he was in the office half an
> hour before the official time, and quite often worked long after two, or
> returned again in the evening. Obi could not understand it. Here was a
> man who did not believe in a country, and yet worked so hard for it. . . .
> He continually put off going to see his dentist because, as he always said,
> he had some urgent work to do. He was like a man who had some great
> and supreme task that must be completed before a final catastrophe inter-
> vened (96 [102]).

The irony in the case of Mr. Green is biting. His continuing commitment and devotion at a time when the British are about to handover the reins of government is contrasted with the lack of serious commitment on the part of those Nigerians preparing to take over power. On the one side, this contrast raises considerable doubt regarding the readiness of the people for independence. On the other side, it suggests a solution to the general ethical depravity in the country. Achebe is therefore inferring that Western culture, as well as the colonial experience, possesses an immense treasure of values that should be implemented for responsible nation–building. The grim irony is that the people are more attracted to the "materialistic" (if not venal) elements of Western tradition. Umuofia Progressive Union's infatuation with meaningless bombastic English expressions, and "the Honourable" Sam Okoli's over–indulgence in petty, fanciful Western gadgets, are indicative of the kind of imitation of colonial governance that Achebe finds supercilious in light of the substantive offering of Western culture.

Obi's lot is that of many Nigerians who return from overseas equipped with technical knowledge and filled with goodwill in the hope of improving their country. However, they are soon disillusioned and frustrated by the rampant corruption of Nigerian society and the stagnation of its economy. Their enthusiasm dampens, and their slogan shifts from "I will change society" to "if you can't beat them, join them." Obi's fall is to be expected, given the corrupt social environment, as well as the mounting financial demands from the loan, tax, insurance, and the extended family. Notably, it is with much reluctance that Obi finally accepts a bribe. For a whole day, he refuses to touch the wad of notes, and the incident gives him a nightmare (153 [157]). When he accepts the twenty pounds that implicates him, "he seemed to have no choice" (154 [158]). The word "seemed" is carefully chosen and indicates Achebe's judgment, namely, that Obi could have avoided the scandal. Nevertheless, Obi excites our sympathy. As a representative of the educated elite that would replace the colonial elite, his fall becomes more resounding and tragic. In Achebe's proverbial language, "the [country's] only palm–fruit . . . [has got] lost in the fire" (6 [14]). "I cannot comprehend how a young man of your education and brilliant promise could have done this," said the presiding Judge during Obi's trial (2 [10]). This could equally be said to the whole of the failing generation of educated Nigerians on the "eve" of Nigeria's independence.

Corruption has received a lion's share of treatment in this novel, and it will be interesting to examine Achebe's hints toward its solution. A consideration of possible solutions is found in Obi's contemplation of the prevalent corruption in his society (40 [47–48]). He considers mass education to be one corrective measure but dismisses this resolution because such a remedy will take centuries to accomplish. Enlightened dictatorship is a scary solution. What about finding a meeting point between democracy, corruption, and ignorance? (40 [47]) Obi does not answer this question, indicating that he is inclined to accept this base solution. Achebe's suggestion is that the surest way to rid society of corruption is through individual effort. This is the implication of the argument between Obi and Christopher regarding the ethics of Elsie's choice to go to bed with Obi for her scholarship. Christopher, who had no problem with Elsie's desperate effort, argues that it is common practice and therefore is morally acceptable. "How do you know she did not go to bed with the board members?" he asks. Obi wisely responds: "But perhaps she will remember that there was one man at least who did not take advantage of his position" (110 [116]). This redemptive "one man," whose example would stand out for others, is the singular figure Obi aimed to be but failed.

Obi needs the fortitude of his grandfather to succeed. Achebe deliberately refers us to the period in Umuofia's history when traditional values held sway. The old man Odogwu recalls the period of greatness when "giants" lived in Umuofia. Odogwu sees the spirit of Okonkwo in Obi; he equates Obi's academic achievement with Okonkwo's heroic achievement of the past. This is, of course, Achebe's irony, for the reader knows well that Obi does not stand comparison with his forebear. The point however is that, had Obi been as strong and determined as Okonkwo, he would not have compromised his high principles. He would never have taken bribes nor would he have failed to marry Clara because of the hullabaloo about her being an *osu*. Obi cannot be Okonkwo because he lacks the moral character based on solid values that sustained the "giants" of old.

An incident situated in Isaac Okonkwo's house points to the solution of the problem of culture–conflict in the country. Obi had returned from England and paid a visit to Umuofia. Friends and kinsmen gathered in his father's house to rejoice with his family. An old man had asked Isaac to bring a Kola nut "to break for this child's return." Isaac, often "uncompromising in conflicts between church and clan," and sometimes tending toward fanaticism, refused to bring the kola nut that would be "sacrificed to idols in a Christian house." The old man left the room in protest and chose to sit outside (46–47 [54]). This conflict is a microcosmic representation of the larger conflict between the traditional and the Western cultures. Odogwu's solution of the conflict in Isaac's house reflects the kind of solution Achebe is advocating. Odogwu was known to be at peace with the two traditions. He offered to produce the symbolic kola nut, and, as he searched his goat–skin bag, "things knocked against one another in it— his drinking–horn, his snuff–bottle and a spoon" (47 [54–55]). The items in his bag signify a blending of cultures—the new and the traditional. His kind gesture worked the miracle on Isaac who changed his mind and served three kola nuts in a saucer. Odogwu insisted on adding his, thus making sure that the saucer contained a mixture of "Christian" and "heathen" kola nuts. Odogwu was the type of "heathen" who went to church at harvest, and one thing he was fascinated with was the Christian expression, "as it was in the beginning, it will be in the end." In blessing the kola nuts, Odogwu said a prayer that cheered every heart, Christian or "heathen": "'Bless this kola nut so that when we eat it, it will be good in our body in the name of Jesus Kristi. As it was in the beginning it will be at the end. Amen'" (47–48 [55]). Examined semiotically, Achebe is advocating a redemption after the spirit of Odogwu, which is at once open to Christian and traditional cultures. Kola nut among the Igbo signifies peace and friendship. The form and content of Odogwu's blessing brings together Christian and traditional elements, and the result is a union of hearts. Achebe is implying, therefore, that the problems caused by the culture conflict can be solved by exploiting the positive and efficacious elements from both cultures. This again calls for compromise and balancing. Isaac Okonkwo's near–fanaticism will not permit a balance, nor will the old man's uncompromising reaction. Odogwu's reconciling spirit is an index to peace, unity, and progress.

A MAN OF THE PEOPLE

We have already discussed this novel at length in chapter two. All that remains is to identify briefly one or two possible steps that Achebe thinks should help solve the crisis of corruption, greed, and mismanagement in the newly independent country. As mentioned in the second chapter, the military take–over at the end of the novel, so fraught with danger, is a most unpromising form of redemption. One suspects that the military regime will present another nightmare of corruption and misrule. Meanwhile, the two self–styled messiahs, Odili and Chief Nanga, have been shown to be unworthy of their claims; neither of the two is able to bring about any meaningful political changes in the country. Chief Nanga may, by sheer skillful manipulation, win the support of a politically ignorant people, but he is himself a political charlatan who lacks the vision and moral probity to qualify for leadership. Odili, in spite of his education and his claims as a social reformer, is incapable of providing the ethical leadership. He failed to win the support of the people, and he does not seem to be a sufficiently public–spirited individual. Max's claim to have the answer to the country's problems is tested during the campaigns, when he is bribed. At best, Max is a political theoretician. In this novel, Achebe is not as much concerned with pointing out the path to the solution as he is in pointing out the problems. There is, of course, the implied solution that goes with his rebellion; for example, when he attacks the people for their blind support of corrupt politicians, we know by implication that he expects them to reject exploitative politicians. In this third chapter, we are no longer interested in such implied antithetical solutions; we are concerned with more apparent solutions.

One positive clue toward redemption is the Josiah episode which has already received our attention in a different context. To appreciate how this incident serves as a metaphor for redemption, we shall re–examine its constructs in greater detail. The villagers of Anata are shocked by the abomination committed by Josiah, the greedy, profiteering local trader who had invited Azoge the blind beggar to his shop for food and drink. While Azoge was eating, the malevolent trader replaced his walking stick with another, intending "to make medicine for trade" with the blind man's stick. Josiah's goal was to turn the villagers into "blind buyers of his wares." The trick is discovered and a crowd of villagers is drawn to his shop, cursing, swearing, and condemning Josiah. In the end, the villagers boycott his shop forcing him to close it down, forcing his disappearance from the village.

One of the villagers, Timothy, utters the following condemnation: "Josiah has taken enough for the owner to notice." This statement is so pregnant with meaning that Odili reflects on it for sometime:

> I thought much afterwards about the proverb, about the man taking things away until the owner at last notices. In the mouth of our people there was no greater condemnation. It was not just a simple question of a man's cup being full. A man's cup might be full and none be the wiser. But here the owner knew, and the owner, I discovered, is the will of the whole people (97).

These words seem to be direct asseverations from the author. His emphasis is on the owner's knowing and condemning the evil one. The remarkable thing about the Anata villagers is that despite the influx of modern life style (they have shops, buses, etc.) and despite their Christian background, as is evident by their names, they yet retain some of the traditional ways. The villagers recognize an abomination and rise with one voice to condemn it. They also ostracize the culprit and in that way cure the evil. Again, the ethical will of the people triumphs over the mendacity and corruption of an individual.

In contrast, Josiah's counterpart, Chief Nanga, triumphs on the national level. With his ethic of the national cake supplanting the traditional ethics, the abomination he commits, far from earning him a boycott, earns him greater support from the people. With their traditional roots destroyed by the complexity of the modern state and Nanga's manipulations, the people lose the indispensable values of the past that could serve as a redeeming factor in their troubled world. It is significant that after Josiah disappears from his village, he is heard of no more until he resurfaces in Nanga's campaign rally where he plays a remarkable role of spotlighting in the crowd the intruding enemy, Odili. Achebe skillfully conjoins the villains toward the end of the novel. The distinction between them is that Josiah is accused and punished by the villagers, while Nanga is defended by the people. Nanga's apparent triumph bothers Odili as he comments:

> Although I had little hope of winning Chief Nanga's seat, it was necessary nonetheless to fight and expose him . . . In fact there was already enough filth clinging to his name to disqualify him—and most of his colleagues as well—but we are not as strict as some countries. That is why C.P.C. publicity had to ferret out every scandal and blow it up, and maybe someone would get up and say: 'No, Nanga has taken more than the owner could ignore!' But it was no more than a hope (121–22).

Lacking the old values, the people do not have the moral strength to "cry havoc" but rather fall easy prey to insidious political opportunists. The old values would also enable individuals to clean up their "filth" with honest practices and integrity. Achebe will return to this theme with greater emphasis in his last novel *Anthills of the Savannah* which we shall proceed forthwith to analyze. Meanwhile, we shall keep in mind that in *A Man of the People*, the action of Anata village stands out in the thick cloud of depravity as a piercing light of prophetic hope and as Achebe's parable for redemption.

ANTHILLS OF THE SAVANNAH

We recall that Achebe described his novels as "re–creations of the history of Africa in fictional terms." His focus is on Nigeria, although the themes he explores are universal (ie, have wider implications). In re–creating the national history of Africa, Achebe is all the time conscious of the special role he, as a writer, must play in society. For a full appreciation of his works, the reader must also be aware of this special role. Thorough understanding of *Things Fall Apart*, for example, demands an understanding of Achebe's attempt to restore his people's image and teach them how to avoid the errors of the past. Between the writing of his first novel and the last, the role of the writer in society had become Achebe's favorite topic in conferences and journals. In none of his novels is he more articulate on the subject than in *Anthills of the Savannah*. His concern with redemption is fully pronounced in this novel. It is his only novel in which a character is shown self–consciously and selflessly to explore solutions to his society's problems. Ikem's total commitment to redeeming his society cannot be matched by that of any character in Achebe's other novels. He is a typical writer trying to resolve the problems of the broken world around him.

With Ikem representing the modern and the leader of the Abazon delegation epitomizing the traditional, Achebe extensively discusses the nature and function of the writer. Some of his ideas correspond to those of other writers discussed in our first chapter. Even more interesting, Achebe deals directly with the redemptive role of the artist. Ikem, a poet, has already been distinguished as the author of a novel and a play. His most effective weapon, however, is his editorial–writing in the *National Gazette*. Through these editorials he exposes the "plain parasites" of the nation. The leader of the Abazon delegation is, himself, a story–teller; Ikem refers to him as such while addressing the students of the University of Bassa (141). The leader of the Abazon delegation is by description suggestive of traditional wisdom: a bearded old man, "tall, gaunt–looking and with a slight stoop of the shoulders" (112). He has an exceptional knowledge about the story and the story–teller, and he exhibits traits of inspiration. After a lengthy discussion on the story–teller, he confesses to have been "cackling away tonight like a clay–bowl of *ukwa* seeds toasting over the fire," and he also feels "like a man who has been helped to lower a heavy load from off his head." Again, he is "light–headed like one who has completed all his tasks and is gay and free to go" (115). Such cathartic experience is shared by prophets and artists. The agrarian images in his speech further suggest that he belongs to the tradition of the griot; however, the admixture of biblical images in his discourse reveals the Achebe in him.

According to the old man, the story–teller is a divinely inspired person. He is inspired by Agwu, the Igbo god of healers, who is also brother of Madness. Agwu is the inspirer of seers, diviners, and artists (114). Here we recall our discussion in chapter one where we mentioned Plato's idea of "the divine furor" in poets and Sidney's "force of a divine breath" which operates in the poet. Most writers see the poet as "vates," as one who has a prophetic role. For the old man too, story–telling is a prophetic vocation, and the story–teller is subjected to a divine transformation, the type of dramatic experience enjoyed by the Hebrew prophets: "Agwu picks his disciple, rings his eye with white chalk and dips his tongue, willing or not, in the brew of prophecy; and right away the man will speak and put head and tail back to the severed trunk of our tale" (115). The Old Testament prophet, Jeremiah, experienced a similar transformation from God: "Then Yahweh stretched out his hand and touched my mouth, and Yahweh said to me: / 'There! I have put my words into your mouth. / Look, today I have set you / over the nations and kingdoms, / to uproot and to knock down, / to destroy and to overthrow, / to build and to plant'" (Jer. 1: 9–10). The rite of initiation into the prophetic vocation is enacted in a slightly different manner in the case of Isaiah. The angel of Yahweh brushes Isaiah's lips with a red hot coal (Chapter 6), and, his sins thus cleansed, he thereupon fires his way into prophecy : "I then heard the voice of the Lord saying: 'Whom shall I send ? Who will go for us ?' And I said, 'Here am I, send me'"(Is. 6:8–9). Achebe's "vates" is closely related to the religious prophets, yet he is imbued with poetic imagination. He is "the liar who can sit under his thatch and see the moon hanging in the sky outside." In this visionary story–teller, the struggle of his society is "reincarnated." At this point, one can see the themes of rebellion and redemption defined in the role of the story–teller, especially given the fact that he embodies his people's struggle and is able to put head and tail to the severed trunk.

The old man further represents the story–teller as one with an important social responsibility. He is the cock that crows in the morning for the entire neighborhood, the cockerel that wakes the whole village, the bush–fowl that wakes the farmer to go to work (112–13). These agricultural images emphasize the voice or sound that summons society to act for its own good. Again, with the use of martial imagery, the old man underscores the saving role of the story–teller. According to him, those associated with war display various gifts from God: some have the gift of summoning people to fight, others have the gift of courage in battle, and some others, "when the struggle is ended . . . take over and recount its story" (113). Of these three roles—oratory, soldiery, and story–telling—the third is the most valuable for society, because the story is everlasting. From the story, society obtains direction and insight: "It is the story, not the others, that saves our progeny from blundering like blind beggars into the spikes of the cactus fence. The story is our escort; without it, we are blind" (114). Judging from the views expressed by the old man of Abazon, whom we know to be the author's spokesman, it is easy to see how Achebe fits into the category of writers across the centuries who perceive the unique role of the artist as that of enlightening, teaching, healing, directing, and, in short, redeeming society.

The reception of the six delegates from Abazon at Harmoney Hotel turns out to be an occasion of recognition for Ikem the writer. Somehow, it reminds us of the reception by the Lagos branch of the Umuofia Progressive Union in honor of Obi in *No Longer at Ease*. The difference between the two is, however, worth noting. The UPU members are disappointed in Obi, albeit by default, while the Abazon people are impressed by Ikem's fame and simplicity. The only complaint by the M.C., which the old man regards as unnecessary, is Ikem's inattendance at monthly meetings, "so as to direct their ignorant fumblings with his wide knowledge" (112). In his redemptive role, Ikem becomes the new Obi who courageously defends justice and who never compromises his high ideals. Because of his acid editorials, he is dismissed as the editor of the *National Gazette*. The controversy over his dismissal clears the ground for his invitation to lecture at the University of Bassa. Ikem seizes the occasion to talk about the role of the writer in society.

Ikem tells his audience that story–tellers (or artists) fight to preserve freedom and justice, and thereby constitute a threat to the forces of oppression. Story–tellers "threaten all champions of control, they frighten usurpers of the right–to–freedom of the human spirit—in state, in church or mosque, in party congress, in the university or wherever" (141). This is Achebe's Sartrean voice stressing the writer's involvement in the struggle for human freedom. It is also his recognition of the writer's Promethean role. Ikem further defines the solution the writer seeks for society: it is not stereotyped answers of the elitists, nor prescriptions, but questions. "A writer wants to ask questions. These damn fellows [elitists] want him to give answers," he says to the students (145). He concludes the lecture with an emphatic statement addressed to one of these elitists, the chairman of the occasion, himself a Marxist: "Writers don't give prescriptions . . . They give headaches!" (148). This is a clue to how we should approach Achebe, and indeed, artistic writers. Achebe seems to be replying to his critics who attack his "beautiful educational programme" (146) and are impatiently looking for one–track solutions. Achebe sees his role as opening up vistas that lead to solutions. As a writer, he raises questions that challenge our thinking (145), for thinking enables us to find solutions. His task is to show the light (being society's "mirror and lamp") and have the African pick his way through paths made visible. Artists provide society a mirror of reflection ; they present images that stir the mind and hopefully spur society to act. As Ikem puts it: "I want instead to excite general enlightenment by forcing all the people to examine the condition of their lives because, as the saying goes, the unexamined life is not worth living . . . As a writer I aspire only to widen the scope of that self–examination" (145–46). This purposefulness leads the reader to an important theme in this novel: self–redemption.

Self–redemption was a marginal motif in *No Longer at Ease*, but in this novel the subject of redemption receives detailed treatment. After independence, many African nations were plagued with the type of problems encountered in Achebe's novels —corruption, mismanagement, tribalism, and dictatorship. For apparent solutions, the modern "isms" have been advanced, especially by the intellectual elites in the universities, as the ultimate solution to the problems. Achebe rejects such text–book solutions as cheap and unrealistic. For a more realistic approach, he takes the reader to the scene of a university where the audience is engaged in an open dialogue with the artist, Ikem. Most members of this audience are oriented toward a Marxist solution. In this lecture–dialogue scene, Achebe critically examines some of the solutions being recommended for survival and for the resolution of African problems.

The bourgeoisie, or rather, the affluent, represented by the Bossa Rotary Club, offer their own solution: charity handouts to the poor. The club basked in self–adulation for their donation of a water–tanker to a slum district of Bossa. Charity handouts, Ikem points out, is "the opium of the privileged"; it offers no lasting solution. It is an opium because it quietens the conscience of the rich in the face of extreme poverty and hardship in the slums. Achebe believes that the "real solution lies in a world in which charity will become unnecessary" (143); in other words, the type of charity that will suffice is the eradication of the root cause of poverty.

Marxism, on the other extreme, is equally an unrealistic solution. The Marxist advocacy of a "democratic dictatorship of the proletariat" is ludicrous; hence, Ikem is quick to point this out with the quip: "I wouldn't put myself under the democratic dictatorship even of angels and archangels" (143). To begin with, the so–called proletariat, mostly comprising workers and students, are not among the oppressed or the deprived, nor do they qualify to speak for the peasants because they themselves, Achebe seems to suggest, are masked corrupt bourgeoisie who should take a large share of the blame for the country's problems. The workers are guilty of frequent strikes over trivial issues, and suffer absenteeism, low productivity, and ostentatious living. Some of them would go to any length to cover up their fraudulent acts, including burning down the entire Accounts and Audits Departments—an historical event recorded in Nigeria during President Shagari's regime. The workers are "parasites" of the nation; so too are the students who themselves are tribalistic, corrupt, and religiously bigoted. Achebe accuses Marxist ideologues of presuming to answer questions that have not been asked, "spouting clichés from other people's histories and struggles," which have no bearing on the African experience (146). They are unaware that "the oppressed inhabit each their own peculiar hell," which means that problems are Protean, and are borne out of distinct social, political, and historical background. Students, on their part, should beware of vacuous solutions "touted by all manner of salesmen," including artists: "You must . . . not swallow every piece of superstition you are told by witch doctors and professors. I see too much parroting, too much regurgitating of half–digested radical rhetoric" (148). With this type of attack on the academics, Achebe underlines the futility of proffering utopian solutions such as Marxism. As far as he is concerned, "man will surprise by his capacity for nobility as well as for villainy. No system can change that. It is built into the core of man's free spirit" (90); hence, the solution of the complex problems of the country goes beyond the doorstep of the "isms." It centers on the individual.

Individual reformation is a realistic solution that will ultimately lead to national reformation and redemption. This concept is contained in Ikem's letter to Beatrice. The letter condemns solutions based on empty theories and slogans. It also condemns self–righteous claims of orthodoxy. Neither orthodoxy , which often offers stilted solutions, nor revolution, which only serves as a temporary relief, is the right solution. The best solution is re–forming the individual, still apprehending that his personality is compounded by complex resources—genes, peers, environment, and "force of event." Like the psychoanalyst, "the most we can hope to do with a problematic individual psyche is to *re–form* it" (91), "for to do more, to overthrow the psyche itself [through Marxist indoctrination], would be to unleash insanity" (91). In the same way, society, which is "an extension of the individual," (91) has to be re–formed "around what it is, its core of reality; not around an intellectual abstraction" (91). Achebe is suggesting that solutions to African problems must take into account the African experience embodied in its history, traditions, religion, economy, and environment. Solutions based on borrowed garments of other peoples' experiences [Marxist, for example] are procrustean, superficial, and unrealistic.

Achebe's view on individual reformation is plausible for two reasons: (a) reformation of the individual leads to group reformation; (b) no system can function effectively when individuals are corrupt and depraved. People make and unmake systems; therefore, remedies are not embedded in systems but in "the core of man's free spirit" (90). Ikem, as Achebe's spokesman, says: "What is at issue in all this may not be systems after all, but a basic human failing that may only be alleviated by a good spread of general political experience, slow of growth and obstinately patient like the young tree planted by David Diop [the poet] on the edge of the primeval desert just before the year of wonders in which Africa broke out so spectacularly in a rash of independent nation states!" (128). Achebe's position could be summed up in Ikem's advice to his university audience: What is needed is self–redemption which calls for self–purgation ("to clean up your act"). In that way individuals would establish themselves on solid moral footing from whence they could redress national issues, especially those affecting leadership (148).

While authors generally focus on tribal leaders or persons of prominence, the plight of the people addresses fundamental problems that need to be remedied. The socio–political situation in contemporary African states, particularly Nigeria, parallels that of Russia prior to the Revolution. In the late nineteenth century Russia, the landowners and intellectuals lived affluently while the vast populace (the serfs) suffered hardship. Russian writers like Turgenev, Dostoevsky, and Tolstoi warned about the impending disaster that could result from the widening gap between the haves and have–nots. At present, in Nigeria, and in many African nations, there exists a yawning gap between the corrupt rulers and their oppressed subjects, and also between the rich and the poor. Achebe's concern about this disturbing situation is expressed in his characters. Some of these characters are caught up in contemplation over the problem, until Ikem plunges into action in search of solutions.

Identifying the problems and finding their solutions is a process of discovery, definition, reappraisal, and emendation. As Ikem debates the plight of the people, he first considers the cathartic effect, that the good humor of the suffering masses could produce positive results. He recalls the scene of the public execution by firing squad staged on the beach before an immense crowd. In that incident, the social gap between the comfortable affluent and the suffering masses was painfully noticeable from their seat assignments. The affluent class in their padded seats on a sheltered dais enjoyed the bloody spectacle along with the poor, scattered about the beach under the scorching sun. In other words, the poor and the rich watched the execution of the poor. Ironically, the oppressed masses were enjoying the spectacle with their exceptionally light humor. With the eye of an artist, Ikem feels differently as he ponders the issue:

> He [the oppressed] had learnt to squeeze every drop of enjoyment he can
> out of his stony luck. And the fool who oppresses him will make a par-
> ticular point of that enjoyment: "You see, they are not in the least like
> ourselves. They don't need and can't use luxuries that you and I must
> have. They have the animal capacity to endure the pain of, shall we say,

domestication." The very word the white master had said in his time
about the black race as a whole. Now we say them about the poor (37).

It is evident from this passage that mere good humor will only exacerbate the "stony
luck" which the oppressor foolishly misinterprets as being natural to the oppressed.
The so–called good humor then becomes a tragic humor, and much as it might accen-
tuate the resilience of the human spirit, if continues to disturb Ikem who perceives it
rightly as a sign of impotence on the part of the oppressed, and triumphant exploitation on the part of the oppressors.

Ikem's contemplation of the plight of the masses leads him to contemplate a personal solution: "He had always had the necessity in vague but insistent way, had always felt a yearning without very clear definition, to connect his essence with earth
and earth's people" (130). This yearning had led him into public life which was
marred for him by "the closed transactions of soldiers–turned–politicians." Now it
has become clear to him that his country's major problem is not corruption, not "sub-
servience to foreign manipulation," not capitalism, and not strikes and riots by workers and students: "It is the failure of our rulers to re–establish vital inner links with the
poor and dispossessed of the country, with the bruised heart that throbs painfully at
the core of the nation's being" (130–31). The main problem identified, Ikem seeks the
best means to resolve it personally. He must identify with this "core of the nation's
being," not in any pretentious way, but by being true to himself and still reach out to
help and receive help: "Like those complex, multivalent atoms in biochemistry books
I have arms that reach out in all directions—a helping hand, a hand signalling for help.
With one I shall touch the earth and leave another free to wave to the skies" (131).
Thus, through Ikem we come to understand another significant aspect of redemption
in this novel. It is the need for a link between the leaders, i.e, the chiefs and the intellectuals, and the common people. Distancing from the common people has been a key
problem in Africa from the colonials to their successors. Achebe is "teaching" his
people in this novel that true nation–building must develop a link between the rulers
and their subjects and also between the privileged and the unprivileged.

Of all the characters in the this novel, Ikem is most closely connected with "the
wretched of the earth." His fiancee Elewa, is of the low class by birth, employment,
and language. Her mother is a market woman who "can carry all her worldly wares in
one head–load" (144); she herself is "a half–literate salesgirl in a shop owned by an
Indian; living in one room with a petty–trader mother deep in the slums of Bassa"
(168); and her language is pidgin English. Ikem is a friend of taxi drivers who are
impressed by his humble life–style and especially by his allegiance to a "battered and
spluttering" car. His proximity to the ordinary people, this connection with the

"earth," distinguishes him from "the Mercedes–Benz–driving, private–jet–flying, luxury–yacht–cruising oppressor[s]." Sam, in contrast, is far removed from the common people. From his Presidential Retreat he can hardly feel the people nor know them, for, as the saying goes, "he who feels it knows it." When the common people take the initiative to establish contact with him, they are profoundly disappointed. Among those who accompanied the six Abazon delegates were "Abazon indigenes in Bassa: motor mechanics, retail traders, tailors, vulcanizers, taxi–and–bus–drivers, who had loaned their vehicles, and others doing all kinds of odd jobs or nothing at all in the city" (111). Sam shuns these people and so fails to establish a requisite human link. Achebe's valid argument is that no leader can know the people well unless he can establish direct contact with them. Through such contact Ikem gains first–hand knowledge of their problems and fights to alleviate those problems. The two taxi drivers testify on his behalf and praise him :

> "Ah. How I go begin count. The thing oga write too plenty. But na for we
> small people he de write every time. I no sabi book but I sabi say na for
> we this oga de fight, not for himself. He na big man. Nobody fit do fuck-
> all to him. So he fit stay for him house, chop him oyibo chop, drink him
> cold beer, put him air conditioner and forget we. But he no do like that.
> So we come salute am "(125).

Ikem could never become the spokesman of the common people if he had not reached out "to touch the earth."

Chris and Beatrice are also connected to the common people, though each in a unique way. Chris is originally so preoccupied with the affairs of a beaurocracy (which he defends and critiques at the same time) that he alienates himself from the people. But when hunted by the same system he served, he quickly discovers the common people and dies in defense of one of them. Beatrice begins her linkage, properly speaking, when she apologizes to her maid, Agatha and thereby resurrects her gloom into a "sunrise of smiles." After the deaths of Sam, Ikem, and Chris we see her become one with the common people as she involves herself with Elewa and the other members of the ecumenical gathering, benefitting from the redemptive implications of the ecumenical group.

Chinua Achebe has consistently shown interest in the plight of women in all his novels. He presents three categories of women: the oppressed, the rebellious, and the redeeming. Okonkwo's wives in *Things Fall Apart* represent the down–trodden women who have accepted men's tyranny with resignation. In *No Longer at Ease* Clara becomes a typical victim of oppression in modern Igbo society. As an *osu,* she is shunned, humiliated, and made to commit abortion. In *Arrow of God* we find an example of a rebellious woman in the person of Udenkwo. She resists her husband's attempt to exploit her. She refuses to allow him to use her cock for a sacrifice (193). In *A Man of the People*, Eunice fights back heroically. When her fiance, Max is run–over by Chief Koko's driver, she picks up her pistol and fires two shots into Chief Koko's chest, killing him (143). In *Anthills of the Savannah*, Comfort displays extraordinary prowess in the way she handles her fiance. For his silence when his aunt utters disparaging statements against Comfort, he is ejected from her flat; she defies all tribal inhibitions and marries a northerner (81). Udenkwo, Eunice, and Comfort epitomize the struggling, though courageously assertive, woman in a man's world. From the beginning, Achebe creates a unique female character. In his very first novel he draws on Chielo, the priestess of the powerful Oracle of the Hills and Caves whose approval must be sought before a war is fought. As Barthold observes, she "exemplifies the spiritual power of the Priestess, a power recognized and honored by the community, sanctified by ritual and invulnerable to the whims of individual men and women" (*Black Time*, 104). In times of crisis, she plays a redemptive role in the community. During Ezinma's illness, she plays such a role for Okonkwo's family; and one might note that in spite of Okonkwo's disregard for women, he shows exceptional respect for Chielo. Nevertheless, outside her prophetic moments, Chielo is a widow with two children. She shares the experience of the ordinary woman who lives in Umuofia's male dominated world. She shares a common shed with Ekwefi in the market (*Things Fall Apart*, 35 [48]) and is one of the women doing the cooking in Obierika's compound the day his daughter is married (80 [108]). Until his last novel, therefore, Achebe's women are more or less supernumeraries in man's theatrical world.

In *Anthills of the Savannah* something different happens. Achebe discovers the new woman and emphatically announces her role in post–independence African nations. Beatrice represents the new woman. She combines in her nature the old and the new, the traditional and the modern. She also has the power to redeem. She was the fifth daughter of a stern headmaster who was desperately in need of a son. Her mother was displeased when she was born, for she had preferred a son for her husband. At baptism she was named Beatrice Nwanyibuife ("a female is also something"). Nwanyibuife has a negative connotation; it is a defeatist or languid praise of the female. But Achebe shows that "Something" is important by linking her ontology to Idemili, the goddess of water and fertility, and by having her play a special role in the story of Kangan during the dictatorship of Sam. The name "Beatrice" means one who blesses, one who makes happy. After the death of the three key male characters, Sam, Ikem, and Chris, it is Beatrice who presides over the naming ceremony of Ikem's daughter and instills a new spirit into the group.

Beatrice's personality is indicative of her dual role. Her modern self operates side by side with her prophetic self, a duality not lost on Ikem: "Perhaps Ikem alone came close to sensing the village priestess who will prophesy when her divinity rides her abandoning if need be her soup–pot on the fire, but returning again when the god departs to the domesticity of kitchen or the bargaining market–stool behind her little display of peppers and dry fish and green vegetables" (96). This efficient career woman who had studied in London does sometimes "feel like Chielo in the novel, the priestess and prophetess of the Hills and the Caves" (105). In her dual role, she, more than any of the other characters in the novel, represents the link between Africa's traditional past and its Westernized present—a redemptive meld which, Achebe insists, is at the heart of the resolution of Nigerian identity. This linkage, lacking in Obi and partially responsible for his disaster, is accomplished in Beatrice.

In her prophetic role, she foretells of disaster in order to prevent it. In this, she is greatly indebted to "the divinity that controls [her] remotely," Idemili, the daughter of the Almighty, charged with the responsibility of "wrapping around Power's rude waist a loincloth of peace and modesty" (93). In the heat of action, Beatrice will endeavor to wrap modesty around Sam's rampaging Power. It was in her possessed moment that she boldly took Sam by the hand and led him to the balcony of the Presidential Retreat to warn him against betraying the country to foreign interests. In her Chielo mode, she also warns Chris of the impending calamity "building up for us" (105). Beatrice, in her redemptive role, is not only a Cheilo, but also an Esther. In confronting Sam, she sees herself fighting "like Esther for my long–suffering people" (74). Esther is the Old Testament heroine who saved the Israelites from their Persian oppressors. Beatrice is also compared to Zachary who provides the answer, or shall we say, the clue to the answer to a perplexing question. This allusion recalls Zachary, the father of John the Baptist, who had been struck dumb by an angel for doubting the omnipotence of God. Months later, the prophecy about the birth of John was fulfilled, and people assembled to name the child. The group at the naming ceremony, however, differed among themselves on the name the child would bear. Zachary given a tablet on which to write the name he preferred wrote, as he uttered the word "John," and with the utterance his power of speech was restored. Like Zachary, Beatrice remained flabbergasted and reclusive following the death of Chris. Significantly, her self–imposed retreat was dramatically broken in the midst of the debate between Emmanuel and Abdul. She "chipped in" with a salient question that sums up their debate: "What must a people do to appease an embittered history?" (204). Breaking her silence was like "the return of utterance to the skeptical priest struck dumb for a season by the Almighty for presuming to set limits to his omnipotence" (204). Beatrice's question is followed by the redeeming answer wrapped in action, the naming of Ikem's daughter in the context of a harmonious gathering (the details and implications of which we shall discuss later). In his narrative, Achebe has combined African traditional images with Christian–Biblical images to portray the redemptive role of the new woman, Beatrice.

Achebe creates a new role for woman in which she will no longer be the passive, suffering, and enduring woman. Her "Desdemona complex" must now yield to a new role defined and confirmed in action. As might be expected, Achebe uses Ikem the writer to announce the new role of the woman. Role defines identity; hence, Achebe's new role for the woman confers on her a fresh image. Achebe's use of the writer to identify this new woman and her special duty further underscores his conviction that the writer has to point the right direction for society. The new role is dramatically pronounced during Ikem's last and "epiphanic" visit to Beatrice, a visit rich in symbolism.

The visit takes place in August under a huge tropical storm. The characters encounter an "unseasonal tropical storm," for late October is the usual season for such a storm, and it often signals the end of the rainy season. Storms nomally usher in the rainy season between March and April, which is also the planting season. The storm here symbolizes the excessive and destructive male principle that threatens to devastate Kangan; it could also stand for Ikem's turbulent opposition to the forces of oppression. Being "unseasonal" indicates that its reference is out of the ordinary, not normal, something that the author wishes to suggest is not to be approved of. This storm that heralds Ikem's arrival portends the cessation of the long–time male domination and the beginning of a new era, an era of growth and fertility, not of strife and destruction, an era tempered by the feminine principle. After the blood bath in which the principal male characters are eliminated, the scene presents a mixed cast in which women play a prominent if not dominant role. Ikem presents a letter to Beatrice which recognizes her innovative role. The letter signifies, as it were, a changing of the guards. Henceforward, Ikem, who all along has been the voice of resistance against tyranny, will be phased out, while a new flower of hope, Beatrice, will flourish. The new woman is symbolized by the "hydrangea" which Ikem notices in Beatrice's parlor. The hydrangea is noteworthy for its large leaves and big flower clusters settled in one stalk. It is an attractive and decorative plant that gives a luxuriant look to any window or room. Will the new woman be a sign of unity and love? The following dialogue reveals a connection between the woman (Beatrice) and the flowers:

[Ikem]: ". . . Those are lovely flowers, what are they?"
[Beatrice]: "I have never known you to notice flowers or women's
clothes and rubbish like that before. What is the matter?
[Ikem]: "I'm sorry, BB, that's a lovely dress. And lovely flowers, what
are they? . . . I may not have noticed flowers before but I do now. It's
never too late, is it?" (86)

The purpose of his visit is to offer gratitude to Beatrice for the gift of "insight" on
"the role of the modern woman in our society" (88). It is not that Ikem has never recognized some kind of role for women in nation–building. After all, he "has written a
full–length novel and a play on the Women's War of 1929 which stopped the British
administration cold in its tracks" (84). This is a reference to the Aba women's riot of
1929 against the imposition of tax on women. The women asserted their historic role
when the men of their society could no longer resist colonial repression. Ikem had
based his understanding of women's political role on the traditional conception
whereby they were expected to intervene "only when everything else has failed";
hence, Ikem assigned to them "the role of a fire–brigade after the house has caught
fire and been virtually consumed" (88). In his symbolic letter, Ikem indicates that the
old perspective must now change. The mythical impression that blamed the loss of
paradise on the woman, as found in the Old Testament and African traditional my-
thologies, must now accept a new standard. Likewise, the late chauvinism, masked in
empty and meaningless glorification as happens in the New Testament and modern
Africa, must be dispensed with. This later version of degradation translated motherhood into an object of exaltation, hardly useful in "the practical decisions of running
the world." According to Ikem, the Christian ethos that elevated woman to the status
of the Mother of God and the Igbo reverence of the woman as signified by the nomen-
clature *Nneka* or Mother is Supreme are simply another expression of the same
stereotypical oppression. Women must now play a new role, and it is for Beatrice to
define it. Henceforth, "everybody had better know who is now holding up the action"
(90).

The visit marks a special moment in Ikem's struggle, the moment of recognition or
discovery. He has now come to realize that the redemption he so much toiled for has
been too masculine to be successful. It needs the balance of the feminine principle.
The reference to "Mother Idoto" at the end of Ikem's letter strongly links Ikem with
the poet Christopher Okigbo, the famous Nigerian poet and a close friend of Achebe.
We recall the opening lines of "The Passage," Okigbo's first poem in *Labyrinths*:

Before you, mother Idoto,
    naked I stand;
before your watery presence,
    a prodigal.

leaning on an oilbean,
lost in your legend.

Under your power wait I
    on barefoot,
watchman for the watchword
    at *Heavensgate*;

out of the depths my cry;
give ear and hearken . . .

(*Labyrinths*, 3)

This poem serves as an overture to the sequence of poems entitled "Heavensgate." In
the incantatory opening, the poet returns with a feeling of guilt to the neglected shrine
of Idoto, a riverine goddess in his village, Ojoto. In this and subsequent poems, he
celebrates the return of the "prodigal" (himself) from exile in an alien culture to his
native culture. In Okigbo, the return is seen as redemptive; it is a return from alienation to self–affirmation. In Achebe, we have a similar situation, although slightly different in matters of details. Ikem the poet abandons his former position that excluded
women in the scheme of things and returns to "the complex and paradoxical cavern of
Mother Idoto" to surrender to Beatrice, the daughter of Idemili (also a water goddess),
who is to be the new torch–bearer after he is gone. He returns to "Mother Idoto" to
confess that he has now gained a new insight into truth, namely, that the right solution
to the country's problems must center on individual reform, and that it must involve
the woman who signifies the feminine principle. Ikem further confesses that he
gained his awareness of the new role of women from Beatrice who has been aware of
it herself but who has not taken any positive action in relation to her new role. With
Ikem's letter, which acts as a moral goad, Beatrice now asserts her authority in the
naming ceremony.

    The naming ceremony of Elewa's baby–girl is held in Beatrice's flat at her own
initiation. In this ceremony, the new role of women is defined and given free expression. They are now bearers of traditional morals. Beatrice performs the ritual role traditionally reserved for men, and while not subsuming the role men play, adds a new
dimension, invigorating society with the strength, fortitude, endurance, and fruition

of the Earth Mother. Beatrice has not totally usurped the traditional role of men. It is not just Beatrice who names the child, but "all of us," in other words, "we the people," the whole group gathered there. Beatrice is their spokeswoman. Whereas the traditional ritual head, the Old Man (who is Elewa's uncle) would have named the child thus: 'You will be called Amaechina', Beatrice says, "We shall call this child AMAECHINA." The Old Man himself is aware of the change of emphasis. In his kola nut blessing, he says:

> "When I asked who named her they told me All of Us. May this child
> be the daughter of all of us."
> "*Ise!*"
> "May all of us have life!" (211).

The new leader in the naming ritual is a woman, Beatrice, described as "a captain whose leadership was sharpened more and more by sensitivity to the peculiar needs of her company" (212–13).

Ikem's posthumous child is female, yet she is given a male's name. Achebe is certainly not implying that women will now play the ritual role hitherto reserved for men. Achebe is not a feminist, and he is not interested in creating "macho" women. Already, Agatha is protesting her suspicion that her mistress is too manly: "Madam too strong . . . To strong too much no de good for woman" (213). Elewa balances the equation by explaining that being "too strong" is not good for men or women. Achebe knows too well that just as there are male tyrants, there could also be female tyrants. Yet he has a new role for women—to temper the strident masculinity of the African society with the feminine principle, to tame naked power, to blend and balance things out, to democratize by replacing the dictatorial absolute "me" with the democratic "us." The new role is to bring sanity to an "insane" world dominated by the masculine principle, to rebuild and heal the society devastated by male aggression and abuse of power.

Beatrice, the symbol of the new woman, bestows her love and understanding upon this group that represents a new hope for Kangan. Achebe's Beatrice comes close to Dante's Beatrice. Both are redemptive figures. In Dante's *Divine Comedy*, Beatrice signifies divine revelation. It is Beatrice who guides Dante through Earthly Paradise, where brotherly love and humility reign, to the celestial realm, where the dominant image is that of light. In *Anthills of the Savannah*, Beatrice plays a similar role by fostering the new spirit of love and humility in this micro–society. She guides the group through the dark tunnel of events to the light of understanding. There is need to emphasize however that she, like Dante's Beatrice, is the guide and not the light. It is the spirit of Ikem that engulfs the whole gathering, and Beatrice has no doubt that "he is floating around us now, watching with that small–boy smile of his" (206). Ikem is Achebe's model of a link between the privileged and the underprivileged. Ikem's example is at work here, although the group acts under the leadership of Beatrice. The new assembly becomes a congregation in which differences dissolve: differences between mistress and maid, intellectual and illiterate, urban and rural, military and student, civil servant and taxi driver, Pentecostal and Moslem. The new bond of friendship formed out of this linkage is stronger than kindred bond, for, according to Beatrice, "like old kinships," it is pledged on "blood casually spilt and profaned" (202). The new bond breaks the fetters of old stereotypes, prejudices, bigotry, and hatred. The traditionalists, represented by Elewa's mother and the Old Man, feeling the strength of the bond of unity in the gathering, become powerless and join the group. The old man praises their concerted action: "In you young people our world has met its match. Yes! You have put the world where it should sit" (210). The same old man affirms in his blessing that Kangan has seen too much fighting and killing: "But fighting will not begin unless there is first a thrusting of fingers into eyes. Anybody who wants to outlaw fights must first outlaw the provocation of fingers thrust into eyes" (212). Achebe suggests that this kind of ecumenical fraternization, which breaks boundaries of religion, tribe, and class, is the best way to prevent provocations that lead to fights.

The new order being created leaves considerable leeway for accommodation. The child is given a name that is similar in meaning to: "*The–remnant–shall–return*" which an Old Testament prophet gave his son (206). We shall later comment on the meaning of the "remnant," but what is important here is the blending of the Judeo–Christian concept with the African traditional concept. Such a blending appears also in the old man's kola nut ritual blessing and libation. Instead of the African palm wine, the group drinks beer and White Horse whisky. The old man himself in his ecumenical spirit is a reincarnation of Odogwu in *No Longer at Ease* whom we have discussed earlier. The spirit of adaptation displayed by the old man and all the members of the group opens the door for other forms of accommodation.

Achebe's favorite theme in *Arrow of God* resurfaces in this scene: that power belongs to the people. The trouble with many African states is that a handful of privileged people usurp power and lord it over others. While in power, they serve their own interests. As the old man puts it: "We have seen too much trouble in Kangan since the white man left because those who make plans make plans for themselves only and their families" (212). He further discloses that he has never entered a white man's house until this time: "May this not be my last time," he says. The "pompous asses," as Beatrice calls these power elites, like bottles, "are up there on the wall hanging by a hair's breadth, yet looking down pompously on the world." How fragile, Achebe seems to say, is power that wants the support of the people. Chris discovers the truth of this only too late. According to Beatrice, "Chris was sending us a message to beware. This world belongs to the people of the world not to any little caucus, no matter how talented . . . " (215). Thus, when the "last green bottle" falls, the African is left with the real owners of the nation—the people, and the future hope lies in their hands.

ANTHILLS OR THE REMNANTS

The title of Achebe's last novel, *Anthills of the Savannah* bears the theme of re-demption, although we do not discover this concept until we read Ikem's "Hymn to the Sun." We appreciate the full impact toward the end of the novel. Destruction and survival, crisis and redemption are woven into the title and sum up the action of the novel. *Anthills of the Savannah* is a novelist's reflection on the tensions, anxiety, and nightmare afflicting his society, his bold attempt to drill through the root causes, his design of possible solutions, and his reaffirmation of faith on man's ability to survive. As his characters pose piercing questions concerning the fate of their country, we gain insight into Achebe's preoccupation with the problems of Africa. Disturbed about the plight of his people, Ikem addresses the Sun in a Hymn and asks the following ques-tions: "Why have you brought this on us? What hideous abomination forbidden and forbidden and forbidden again seven times have we committed or else condoned, what error that no reparation can hope to erase?" (28). Beatrice too questions the rea-son for the tragic waste of lives in the death of Chris, Ikem, and others: Was all that attributable to human calculation or to predestination? "Were they [the tragic victims] not in fact trailed travellers whose journeys from start to finish had been carefully programmed in advance by an alienated history? . . . 'What must a people do to ap-pease an embittered history?'" (204). These and other related questions articulate the concerns of a writer committed to the destiny of his society. These are universal, per-ennial questions asked in various forms about the human condition. As we have ac-knowledged earlier, the role of the writer is to enlighten the society on how best to tackle such questions that relate to life, pains, suffering, and freedom. As we close the novel, a question remains on in our minds: what statement is Achebe making to his society? The last chapter, highly contrived with its symbolism, is the final layer of a palimpsest designed to assert his apocalytic sense of the defeat of the old system. The answer is contained in the title and in Ikem's "Hymn to the Sun."

The title is explained in the "Hymn to the Sun." The "Hymn" itself is an appeal to the Sun (addressed as the "Eye of God" and the "Great Messenger of the Creator") to spare the world of the terrible sufferings and death caused by the Sun's unrelenting heat. The Sun is presented as an agent of God's vengeance on the world. No amount of prayers and propitiatory offering can appease him. At one point, the writer [Ikem] begins to associate the god with greed: "Homeward–bound from your great hunt, the carcass of an elephant on your great head, do you now dally on the way to pick up the grasshopper between your toes?" (28). Because of the Sun's punishment, songbirds (often symbolizing artists in Achebe) have disappeared, leaving the morning as destitute as a penitent widow stripped of all her ornaments and jewelry. The Sun is warned to make sure that life cycle, along with seasonal cycle, will continue. The devastation is described as total, as the Earth itself catches fire and burns everything, so that soon "there was no fodder left to burn." This is the picture of drought, dearth, and death presented to us in a mythic and symbolic language. This picture of disaster recalls the wasteland image presented by the prophet Ezekiel and by the English poet T. S. Eliot. Achebe has always drawn inspiration from Eliot, Yeats, and the Bible. The picture Achebe paints here is that of a society reduced to a wasteland by the military junta led by Sam. The Sun's scorching heat, reminiscent of Okonkwo's untempered masculinity, is here a symbol of dictatorship, and the Sun itself is the dictator Sam.

The remnant motif of Ezekiel is expressed in the hymn and creates the grounds of hope. There are hints that life will continue in spite of the disaster. One example is the image of the trees which have become "hydra–headed bronze statues" but yet retain "residual features." These are compared to "anthills surviving to tell the new grass of the savannah about last year's brush fires." There is also the legend of the remnants of a terrible drought who in desperation abandoned their lands and possessions and headed south. They came upon the village of Ose, wiped them out, and settled in their land which they renamed Abazon. History now repeats itself as the same Abazon people are once again struck by a disaster. They cannot revert to their ancient method of solving their problem—migration and warfare; so, "they send a deputation of elders to the government who hold the yam today, and hold the knife, to seek help of them." As events unfold, we see how their peace overture is met with a hostile response from Sam's government. But then we are aware of their connection with Ikem whose spirit, as we have seen, will survive the dictatorship of Sam. It is from their leader that we get the suggestion that "the story" is "the anthill," for "it is the story that outlives the sound of war–drums and the exploits of brave fighters" (114). After the brush fires of Kangan, we know that it is only Ikem the poet, among the principal actors, whose "anthill–daughter" is celebrated by a group of survivors, the anthills of Kangan, who are left to reflect on the events and the future. This core group led by Beatrice looks toward the future with confidence. They are part of the "truth" which Chris beheld with a smile at the moment of death; they are the truth that Beatrice in her final epiphany beholds as "beautiful" (215). *Anthills of the Savannah* is, therefore, a writer's declaration of faith and optimism in the destiny of his people.

CONCLUSION

We maintain that literature and society are inseparable and that literature must address social issues. Writers are central figures in society, endowed with discrete talents to recreate the world with a view to addressing and improving it. With heightened sensibilities and extraordinary poetic imagination the "prophets" of letters see things wholly, and see connections, analogies, alternatives, and possibilities. They utilize God's gift of understanding and are compared to God in his ability to create, to the priest in his capacity to reveal divine mysteries to humanity and dispense God's wisdom to mankind, "preaching to all men in all times and places." "Soothsayers," they have direct access to truth. Illuminating society like a pillar of fire, they are qualified to give direction, direction toward the good or the ideal. They are also qualified to be the critics and the moral judges of society, thanks to their extraordinary insights into reality. Where society is fractured, writers are interested in reforming and rebuilding; they seek to restore lost perfection. Freedom is their primary goal, so too reconciliation and restoration of humanity to wholeness. They are sometimes Promethean figures, providing the fire of vision by which society is organized, rebelling against forces of negativism, and suffering for the good of society. They are teachers. Behind the mask of fiction is the voice of the master–writer guiding society toward the course of wisdom and truth, sometimes harsh, sometimes soothing, and sometimes ironic. All in all, redemption is what defines their role in society.

In order to enact their redemptive role, writers must be committed; their work must embody society's joy, fear, success, failure, hope, and aspirations. Writers of all times are seen to be conscious of their redemptive role in society. Contemporary African writers, particularly Achebe, have expressed the urgent need for the writers' involvement (at least in their works) in social and political issues. Fresh from the ordeals of colonialism, African countries are confronting gigantic problems connected with nation building. African writers have a responsibility to be involved in what Achebe described as the "big social and political issues of contemporary Africa" ("The African Writer and the Biafran Cause," *Morning Yet*, 113). To avoid such issues is to lose touch with reality, and, according to Soyinka, such avoidance could lead to vain literature of cultural definitions and metaphysical abstractions. In their redemptive role, contemporary African writers are continuing to adapt the form of the griot tradition. Griots were, for their societies, watchdogs, critics, chroniclers, the guardians of morality, and the inspired story–tellers.

Achebe addresses the social and political issues of his country in his novels and thereby demonstrates his concern for the redemption of his society. In our study, we examined his rebellion against colonialism, opposition to its claims and method. Colonial injustice, arrogance, and ruthlessness are exposed and condemned. The ironic treatment of the colonials' protective program of Indirect Rule is indicative of Achebe's contempt for some of their policies. These policies are adjudged to be doomed because they were fashioned for the convenience of the colonialists and not for the subjects. Achebe portrays the missionary proselytization as an arm of colonialism. The missionaries and administrators collaborate in their efforts to distort, demean, and frequently destroy tribal values and customs. While the administrators impose an alien political structure, the missionaries discredit the people's dieties and incite one segment of the people against the other in the name of pure religion. Achebe condemns the spurious claims of missionaries of their saving the people from wicked ways and false gods, from savagery and chaos. There is a suggestion in Achebe that if the missionaries could relate the values and customs they have in common with non–Christians and if they could be more compromising and accommodating, they would be more successful in evangelization.

Achebe's rebellion sometimes strikes both ways, hitting friend and foe. On the one hand, he rebels against the colonial defamation of the African image, and, on the other hand, he attacks Negritude's exaggerated presentation of the beauty of the African image. He thus maintains that a genuine commitment to redemption must present truth as it is. As a teacher, he is bent on pointing out to his contemporaries the errors and weaknesses of the past so as to prepare them for a better future. In his balanced portrayal of the strength and weaknesses of Okonkwo and Umuofia society in *Things Fall Apart*, Achebe reacts, by example, against Negritude's bona fide romanticization of African values.

Post–independence regimes in Africa proved a failure as bribery, corruption, and violence marred early attempts by politicians to manage the affairs of their nations. In *A Man of the People*, Achebe revolts against the political rogues, the Chief Nangas, for their self–aggrandizement and their total lack of concern for the welfare of the people. He also ridicules would–be leaders like Max and Odili—intellectual elite— for not having any defined program for the country. Ethically, they are as deplorable as the Nangas and the Kokos. The people, for their part, are vitiated and gullible, hav-

ing lost the moral sense of community and the integrity needed to repel political ro-
guery.

Military control is sad news, and Achebe indicates in his latest novel, *Anthills of
the Savannah*, that the self–styled redeemers in khaki had better remain in their bar-
racks. They are not only corrupt and degenerate as the politicians, they also terrorize
and brutalize the people. In the novel, Sam the leader is a tyrant, while his ministers
are sycophants, shaking like ninepins before his pompous presence. Rebelling against
military dictatorship, Achebe shows that tyranny unchecked turns monstrous and bru-
talizes the populace with state terrorism. Those who cooperate with dictatorship will
ultimately have to deal with its bitter after–taste, as Chris belatedly discovers. Military regimes promise not redemption, but violence, death and destruction.

Concern for society compels Achebe to rebel, but he always carries his message
beyond rebellion and proceeds to suggest possible solutions. As he explains in an interview with Bernth Lindfors, a writer's role "is more in determining than merely
reporting. In other words, his role is to act rather than react" (11). He sees the role of
the African writer basically as acting "to set the tone of what was going to happen,"
and having an influence in determining Africa's future. Hence: "I think our most
meaningful job today should be to determine what kind of society we want, how we
are going to get there, what values we can take from the past . . ." (12).

In his novels, Achebe attempts to work out practical means of redemption open to
his society. He teaches African societies the need for an accommodation of ideas, the
need for flexibility and open–mindedness. The course of nation building is complex
and difficult, but society must not be bogged down in one solution, for there are always alternatives to explore. The principle of moderation and balance must prevail
over bigotry and extremism. There is always a tendency for emergent nations to resort
to the masculine principle to resolve issues. But belligerence only leads to destruction
and death, as Achebe shows in *Things Fall Apart* and *Anthills of the Savannah*. The
blending of the masculine and feminine values is key to redemption. This is one great
lesson to be learned from the past, especially in the life of Okonkwo. The true redeemer is not the one thrust upon the people by tradition to force their will upon others, but
the one who is truly devoted to their well–being; hence, when Ezeulu and his god fail
to provide protection and unity, the Christian God supplants them and becomes the
new spring of hope. Flexibility, reconciliation, and commitment to the commonweal
are redemptive values stressed in *Arrow of God*. If African nations are to survive and
succeed, they must learn to come to terms with positive values from the traditional
and Western cultures. High principles, such as Obi Okonkwo held on his return from
England, must be sustained by a solid ethos. As Achebe shows in *Anthills of the*

Savannah, it is not enough for leaders to attain power with mere good intentions. Power can corrupt even the angels. Sam came into power with the least intention of steering his country toward dictatorship, yet he ended up as a dead tyrant. Therefore, linkage with the masses coupled with a genuine will to serve them offers the best safeguard against sliding into dictatorship. The answer to the widespread corruption in Africa lies in the reformation of the individual. One practical solution to Africa's multiple problems is the injection of the feminine principle into the national system, as Beatrice does at the end of the novel. Finally, Achebe teaches that no government will succeed in the post–independence African states unless it incorporates the will of the people in its program.

OPTIMISIM AND HOPE

Achebe's novels are replete with tragic events and generally end with the death or destruction of the protagonist. *Things Fall Apart* ends with the tragic death of Okonkwo, an Oedipal tragedy, reinforced by the irony of circumstance in which Okonkwo, desperately fleeing from the fate of his father, finally meets his fate in the evil forest. He rose very high in his community, but he was to be buried like a dog. In *Arrow of God,* the Chief Priest of Ulu, having "sacrificed" two of his sons (Oduche and Obika) to save his god and the traditional system, is himself "sacrificed" in the end, while his god loses to the Christian God. Achebe's most recent novel, *Anthills of the Savannah,* ends with the total elimination of the key figures, including Chris who dies under extremely absurd circumstances after Sam's dictatorship is overthrown. With his vision based on these and more tragic incidents, Achebe seems to be a pessimist, and we wonder how that position might affect his redemptive role in society. In *Critics on Chinua Achebe,* Agetua has noted that some critics believe that Achebe's first three novels "contain very little sunshine and hope" and that his main characters often "come to grief under circumstances which emphasize the cruel futility of things" (32). Is Achebe, therefore, a pessimist?

Achebe is certainly not a pessimist, for pessimism implies hopelessness and total darkness at the end of the tunnel, both of which are not reflected in his novels. As a realist interested in presenting both sides of the picture, Achebe explores the bright and the dark aspects of the human condition with no suggestion whatsoever that the dark experience is irremediable. Still, we have to contend with the fact that all his novels end unhappily. To begin with, an unhappy ending does not prove pessimism, just as a happy resolution might ultimately not indicate optimism. Nevertheless, Achebe's primary subject is Africa's past and present, and judging from the social and political condition of Africa as he realistically portrays it, a happy ending would sound absurd and illogical. "What about *Anthills of the Savannah,*" an objector might argue, "it ends on a note of celebration of life." The resolution of this novel, no doubt, is controversial; however, it seems that in spite of the last chapter, the novel still ends as a tragedy. The deaths of Ikem and Chris overshadow the celebration scene in the last chapter. More importantly, we are uneasily aware, that the celebration notwithstanding, the military is still in power, and the murderer of Chris and his type still loom large in Kangan. It is remarkable that after the naming ceremony in the last chapter, the group conversation winds up on the death of Chris, and the novel finally closes on that sad note. Structurally, therefore, the bright picture of the naming ceremony is parenthetically and paradigmatically sandwiched between two Chris episodes, one about his actual death (chapter seventeen) and the other about a powerful recall of his death. However, our position is that even the unhappy resolutions do not undercut the optimism in Achebe.

Achebe's optimism is revealed in his open–ended conclusions with a suggestion of action continuing with greater sunshine in the future. It is remarkable that each of his novels ends with an opening for a new beginning, thus confirming Achebe's firm belief in the strength of man's resilience. In *Things Fall Apart*, Okonkwo dies and his attempt to resist change fails, but the white man introduces the bible, Western technology, and new commerce, which signify a new beginning. In *Arrow of God*, Ulu yields his authority to the Christian God, and parents harvest their crops in the name of their sons (262) who have embraced Western education and the Christian religion. This, too, is indicative of a new beginning. *No Longer at Ease* closes with a remorseful protagonist, a moral change that reveals self–knowledge and the possibility of future improvement. The fall of the politicians and the advent of the military in *A Man of the People* create grounds for a new attempt at nation building. In *Anthills of the Savannah*, a new order could result from the ecumenical group. Although the sky is overcast with the continuing presence of the military, some brightness is already envisioned in the horizon.

Achebe does not consider himself a pessimist. He once declared: "If I were really as pessimistic as some people think, I wouldn't be writing. The bad news which I convey really comes ultimately from a belief that things could be better, which is an optimistic feeling" (Agetua, 35). Achebe's solid faith in society's ability to survive crises is the reason for his optimism. He believes in life's progressive pattern. According to him: "Creation is evolving, it is not yet ended. This is what I mean by 'Morning Yet on Creation Day'" (Agetua, 32). This title to one of his books expresses his hope. The failures and set–backs of African states at nation building, which Achebe dwells upon in his novels, should not be perceived as death–traps, but as fires of purification.

Achebe is attracted to tragic events because they make the story memorable (Agetua, 32). As he explains in an interview with Wren:

> I took to Hardy immediately. What appealed to me was his sense of reality, which is tragic; it's very close to mine. I think for the same reason I took to A.E. Houseman. There are a lot of funny things, a lot of comic things that happen in the world, and they're important. But I think that the things that really make the world, the human world, are the serious, the tragic. And this is, roughly, what Hardy says to me; this is what Houseman says to me. It is, you know, the man who fails who has a more

interesting story than the successful person. If you ask me why, I don't
know (61–62).

It is not Hardy's pessimism and sadistic imaginings that Achebe inherits, not even his
sympathy for his characters, but the tragic in human affairs, the serious aspect of life.
Achebe's optimism marks his point of departure from Hardy: "When we suffer hard-
ships and we are crushed, morally, mentally and psychologically . . . the writer comes
up . . . and he holds up some hope of a greater tomorrow whatever it is" (Jeyifo, *Contemporary Nigerian Literature*, 11). The dark side of Achebe's novels, including the
unhappy resolutions and tragic deaths are not signs of despair. Achebe strongly believes in survival, hope, and rebirth. He writes novels because he sees the "possibilities of man rising higher than he has risen at the moment" (Interview, Kalu Ogbaa,
4–5). Hence, Achebe's optimism serves his redemptive role. We shall now show how
this concept is reflected in his novels.

The hero of *Things Fall Apart* dies and is to be buried like a dog in the evil forest.
In addition, Umuofia community loses its autonomy to the British. Sad and disheart-
ening as all this may be for them, there is still room for hope. Okonkwo may have died
shamefully, yet he is "canonized" in the minds of later generations, which proves that
he has not died in vain. He alone earns a space in the book the District Commissioner
proposes to write (147 [191]). Okonkwo dies heroically refusing to be colonized, and,
therefore, dies a free man. Future generations remember him as a great man. In *No
Longer at Ease*, Odogwu mentions him as one of the "giants" of the past (49 [57]).
Okonkwo also survives in the values he stood for: hard work, devotion to the family,
and commitment to one's religious beliefs. His fear of failure and his blind insistence
on manliness, which drive him to destruction, stand out as lessons from the past. The
story of Okonkwo excites us, be it his success, failure, or destruction. Achebe explains in an interview with Egejuru:

> The important thing in my stories is not whether an individual is de-
> stroyed or not. What did he stand for? What was the destruction about?
> What are the echoes that are left in the society? When a man like
> Okonkwo crashes, there are echoes left by his death and these echoes
> continue to resound in the community . . . The story of Okonkwo is told,
> and in that telling of the story, something is reenacted (129).

Among those actions "reenacted" is man's resilience and his courage to fight and die
for his convictions. Echoes of Okonkwo provide reverberations of future hope. His
death signals the end of an epoch but it is not the end of the life of the community for
whom life will continue on a new note. Already, there is hope in the prospects of fu-

ture progress foreshadowed in the white man's establishment of churches, schools, hospitals, and modern trade.

Arrow of God ends with the destruction of the hero. Having willfully sacrificed his son, Oduche (to the Christian God), and also mysteriously sacrificed another son, Obika, to avert disaster, Ezeulu is himself sacrificed by a desperate god:

> But why, he asked himself again and again, why had Ulu chosen to deal thus with him, to strike him down and then cover him with mud? What was his offence? . . . When was it ever heard that a child was scalded by the piece of yam its own mother put in its palm? What man would send his son with a potsherd to bring fire from a neighbour's hut and then un- leash rain on him? Who ever sent his son up the palm to gather nuts and then took an axe and felled the tree? But today such a thing had happened before the eyes of all. What could it point to but the collapse and ruin of all things? Then a god, finding himself powerless, might take flight and in one final, backward glance at his abandoned worshippers cry:

> If the rat cannot flee fast enough
> Let him make way for the tortoise! (229).

Seen as a stumbling block, Ezeulu is sacrificed so that life may continue. His tragedy is his fall pursuing a tradition he was absolutely convinced was right. Yet Ezeulu's life is not totally tragic. His destruction leaves a trail of reminisces. The positive values for which he stood earn him a place in the roster of "giants". He was a priest who took his priesthood seriously. Perhaps he took it too seriously when he let his theology threaten life. His community elected to survive and did survive. We must keep in mind that in this novel, the community is more important than the individual, as Achebe himself has testified in an interview with Egejuru:

> Why did I let Ezeulu go so very quickly? My answer is that although Ezeulu is very important, he is not the most important thing in the book. His community is more important; the gods that took a hand in the story are more important than the human beings. So you have two categories that are more important than the individual (126).

Sad as Ezeulu's final destiny may be, there is something noble and honorable about his commitment to duty. This is the "good news" Achebe harvests from the past. The echo of the past fills the present with optimism. The Umuaro clan survives the ordeal inflicted on them by the intransigent Chief Priest. Christianity offers them new grounds for hope. The Christian God promises the redemption which Ulu failed to provide. Mahood has rightly called *Arrow of God* "a story of resilience"; it is resilience for the community and earth: both renew themselves (204). This is one aspect of optimism which, I grant, may not withstand a barrage of criticism from those who perceive the victory of the Christian God in the Battle of the Gods as a tragedy. There is a deeper structure that could be explored in the fate of Ezeulu in relation to the political gamble at a period of transition in Umuaro. As we have earlier noted, the parallel between the two eras at the time (Ezeulu's and Achebe's) cannot be disregarded in terms of political and social crises. What destroyed Ezeulu was not necessarily bad theology as his misconception of and greed for power. He had become too engulfed in his authority (or he had over–exaggerated it) so that he had become blind to the basic source of power in his society, namely, the people. Both Ulu and Ezeulu depend on the will and support of the people for their authority. And so, once this authority loses its foundation, which is the people, it is as good as dead. His defeat becomes inevitable. This defeat serves as a cautionary lesson to people in contemporary African politics: to subvert the foundation of the people's authority is suicidal. In the end, power will abide with the people and far from being destroyed, they will survive the crises caused by those who usurp and misuse the power which rightly belongs to the majority. The novel thus ends on a note of optimism, for the community learns, just as we do, that when one god fails, another will provide.

No Longer at Ease reveals a different type of optimism. It deals with the grave problems facing Obi Okonkwo. The good news is that he struggled; the sad news is that he proved to be a moral and ethical failure. The novel ends with a question: Why did Obi take bribes? "Everybody wondered why," and these include the Judge, Mr. Green, and even the members of Umuofia Progressive Union (154 [159]). *No Longer at Ease* is full of dark pictures of bribery, corruption, and inefficiency, all of which come together in the fall of Obi. But there is a positive side to this fall; it challenged the people to think. The courtroom was crowded with people because "the case had been the talk of Lagos for a number of weeks" (1 [10]). People wondered why a well educated man, so highly placed in the civil service, would suffer the loss of his respect by receiving bribes. In the words of the presiding judge: "I cannot comprehend how a young man of your education and brilliant promise could have done this" (2 [10]). Although Obi remained calm and unemotional during the trial, when the judge made this statement, "a sudden and marked change occurred," and he wept (2 [10]). "A marked change occurred," but it is hard to fathom the depth of this belated knowledge, to determine how deeply rooted is the change. Obi's weeping is the mask of self–pity and is by no means redemptive. We are left in doubt, in spite of his weeping, as to the extent his personal character has been improved by this experience. His sorrow raises false hopes of redemption. He lived very superficially, and his weeping is part of his superficial response to life. Having failed to live up to the demands of his middle class values, the values of the very class that would inherit the power of the colonial authorities when independence came, because he is a man incapable of living out his convictions, and because he is also incapable of making the right choice, he is abandoned in jail by Achebe where he rightly belongs. He has been set up as a paradigm of the disgrace inherent in modern African leadership which has avoided shouldering the responsibilities of power which require the exercise of sound ethical and moral judgements.

All said, there seems to be a sense of realization of wrong–doing for Obi and his community who are now forced to reflect on his life. Seen in the context of nation building, the story of Obi reflects the story of Nigeria, a country colonized and "trained" by the British. On the eve of independence, Achebe sees the pot–holes on the road to nationhood. Tested in the visionary light of the artist, the country's performance is failing. Asking 'why' opens a new window of optimism. Achebe, therefore, suggests that failure is part of development. The key issue is to find out why and continue from the point of recognition.

In *A Man of the People,* the overwhelming impact of corruption and violence is relieved by the psychological transformation of the the people after the coup. Once the politicians are rounded up and their misdeeds exposed, the people overnight turn against their former idols. As already pointed out, their inability to accuse themselves, to look inward for the solution to the issue of evil in society, points to a future problem. Nevertheless, some progress has been made. Evil has been exposed and virtue acknowledged. Chief Koko is condemned as a thief and a murderer, while Max is proclaimed a hero and a martyr (148). We are left with some hope that the military might redress the country's problems, yet in view of the possibility of a counter coup, that hope is tenuous. The good news in this novel is that Odili, who is honest and idealistic, though often naive, has learned a lesson from his mistakes, so that, if given a second chance, he might improve. There is no certainty about this ability to sustain one's integrity, given the corrupting influence of power. With hindsight gained from reading *Anthills of the Savannah,* we know that the intellectual elite failed when they came into power. Having said this, we must not forget that there are some good citizens in the country on whose actions future hope resides. Among these are Odili's father, a man of principle; Edna, who finally wins her freedom and chooses Odili for a husband instead of Nanga, and Eunice, who becomes an example of true friendship. Eunice played the "superwoman" to demonstrate her true love for Max. Dr. Makinde and his group are mentioned only briefly in the novel. They are uncorrupted, realistic, and bold enough to tell the truth and damn the consequences. Because of these characters, we are confident that all is not gone sour in the country, that ethical people still live in a corrupt country and could provide direction in the future. *A Man of the People* is a true mirror of politics in post–independence Nigeria. In attacking the short–comings in this country, Achebe hopes to restore order, and he discharges his role with optimism.

Anthills of the Savannah reveals the writer's role more overtly than any of Achebe's novels; it also proclaims optimism more openly. It deals with the crisis of dictatorship in an African country. The end is bloody with all of the key men perishing in violence. The death of Chris—"the last green bottle"—under peculiar circumstances, is likely to draw criticism from people who see the event as absurd and unnecessary. Chris's death brings a dark conclusion to the bloody saga and makes the concluding chapter look too artificial. Structurally and thematically, Chris's death is neither accidental nor absurd. From the beginning of the novel, Chris tries to avert the inevitable, and he fails twice. First, he wants to avoid confrontation with the dictator, unlike Ikem, who welcomes such confrontations. When Sam's authoritarianism becomes unbearable, Chris is compelled to rebel, although he cannot face the consequence, which is death, for by the law of tyranny, to challenge the tyrant is to deserve death. Second, Chris challenges Sam and flees for his life. Ironically, he flees to the North, a region of desolation. His attempt to escape is doomed by fate, for the farther he runs from death, the nearer he comes toward it.

Signs in the text show that Chris is fleeing toward destruction. The vegetation changes from the rich dense rain forests of the South [i.e., life] to a desert region where drought has dried up rivers and dust makes men look like corpses (194). Chris has moved from the coastal region to a "scrubland which two years without rain had virtually turned into a desert" (193). Every step he takes away from the South presents him with more signs of death and destruction. The security checks manned by blood-thirsty police and army men—agents of death—are death gates which give Chris "sharp anxiety." Significantly, "as the bus plunge[s] deeper into the burning desolation," Chris brings Ikem's prose–poem out of his pocket and begins to read it. It is the sight of "anthills in the scorched landscape" that sets him off reading the prose–poem (194). The indication is that Chris is fleeing to an arid area where people had deserted to avoid death. Shortly after reading Ikem's prose–poem and passing it to Emmanuel, he is gunned down by a corrupt and drunken policeman. Chris, "the last green bottle," dies laughing at himself. He has obviously discovered the futility of the system he has been part of, the dictatorial regime he has protected. The irony of his death lies in the fact that he died doing what he and his group had neglected, namely, connecting with ordinary people. His flight for life into the province had enabled him to make contact with a student leader, a taxi driver, poor children, and other low class people; thus, this experience "becomes a redemptive immersion in the suffering masses" (Updike, "Review," *The New Yorker,* June 13, 1988). Through suffering he gains knowledge and acts nobly in defense of a helpless girl. His death, as well as the deaths of Ikem and Sam, is an expiation for the regime's failure to establish inner links with the poor and dispossessed of Kangan. Tragic as their destruction may be, it represents the exit of an enlightened generation that was corrupted by power and failed to realize that "this world belongs to the people of the world not to any little caucus, no matter how talented" (*Anthills*, 215).

Achebe's vision of hope is displayed in the "anthills," the survivors, the remnants, who, as we saw in the foregoing chapter, meet in the naming ceremony of Ikem's and Elewa's child. The name given to the child, Amaechina, or May–the–path–never–close, bespeaks the "hope that springs eternal" (206). Carefully chosen, it clearly reveals the mind of Achebe about a society undergoing trial and at the verge of despair. For Achebe, the path may be slippery, often causing a fall, yet there is hope that something lasting will survive, and that after a series of tribulations, those redemptive ideals advocated by Ikem and rehearsed by the naming group, will take root. Then, in the words of the poet David Diop whom Achebe quotes in the epigraph to Chapter ten:

> Impetuous son, that tree young and strong
> That tree there . . .
> That is Africa your Africa
> That grows again patiently obstinately
> And its fruit gradually acquire
> The bitter taste of liberty

> David Diop, "Africa" (*Anthills of the Savannah,* 123)..

For survival to have any meaning, there must be a remembrance, a memory, a continuity, a story, a knowledge that others have suffered, battled, and died, that there had been a brush fire that devastated the savannah. According to an old Jewish aphorism, "remembrance is the secret of redemption" (Moyers, 5). In his novels, the writer, Achebe keeps remembrance alive, fans the embers of hope. Thus, redemption ultimately defines his role in society.

WORKS CITED

Abrams, M. H. *The Mirror and the Lamp.* New York: Norton, 1958.

Achebe, Chinua. "Africa and her Writers." *Morning Yet* (1975): 29–45; (1976): 25–38.

——————. "African Literature as Celebration," *African Commentary*, 1.2 (1989): 51–54.

——————. "African Literature as Restoration of Celebration." Petersen and Ruther-ford, 1–10.

——————. "The African Writer and the Biafran Cause." *Morning Yet* (1975): 137–47; (1976) 113–21. First published: *Kroniek van Afrika* 8 (168): 65–70; *Conch* 1 (1969): 8–14.

——————. *Anthills of the Savannah.* Garden City: Doubleday Anchor, 1988. Other editions include: London: Heinemann, 1987; African Writers Series, Oxford, Ibadan, Nairobi: Heinemann, 1988.

——————. *Arrow of God.* 2nd ed. New York: Doubleday Anchor, 1974. Other editions include: London: Heinemann, 1964; African Writers Series 16, London, Ibadan, Nairobi: Heinemann, 1965; New York, John Day, 1967; Anchor Literary Library. Intro. K. W. J. Post, Garden City: Doubleday Anchor, 1969; 2nd ed., London: Heinemann, 1974; *The African Trilogy.* London: Pan, Picador, 1988 (Contains *Things Fall Apart, No Longer at Ease, Arrow of God*).

——————. *Beware Soul Brother and Other Poems.* Enugu: Nwankwo–Ifejika, 1971. Rev. and enlarg. ed.: *Christmas in Biafra and Other Poems.* Garden City: Doubleday Anchor, 1973. Another edition is: London: Heinemann, 1972.

——————. "Chi in Igbo Cosmology." *Morning Yet* (1975): 159–75; (1976): 131–45.

——————. "Colonialist Criticism." *Morning Yet* (1975); 3–28; (1976): 3–24. Reprinted in *Hopes and Impediments* 68–90, 178–79.

——————. *Hopes and Impediments: Selected Essays, [1965–87].* New York: Doubleday Anchor, 1990. Other editions include: Oxford Ibadan, Nairobi: Heinemann, 1988; New York: Doubleday, 1989.

——————. Interview. John Agetua. "Interview with Professor Chinua Achebe, August 16, 1976." *Critics on Chinua Achebe 1970–76.* Ed. John Agetua. Benin City: John Agetua, 1977. 29–45.

——————. Interview. Chinweizu. "An Interview with Chinua Achebe." *Okike* 20 (1981): 19–32.

——————. Interview. Phanuel Akubueze Egejuru. "Writers Discuss their Works: Chinua Achebe." Egejuru, 121–32.

——————. Interview. Biodun Jeyifo. "Achebe." Jeyifo, ed.: 9–15.

——————. Interview. Bernth Lindfors. "Interview with Chinua Achebe." Lindfors *et al.* eds., 5–12. First published: "Achebe on Commitment and African Writers." *African Report* 15.3 (1970): 16–18; "Chinua Achebe: An Interview." *Studies in Black Literature* 2.1 (1971): 1–5.

—————. Interview. Bill Moyers. "Chinua Achebe." *World of Ideas*, #114. Public Affairs Television. Sept. 29, 1988. 1–6. [Transcript produced by Journal Graphics, Inc.]

—————. Interview. Lewis Nkosi. "Conversation with Chinua Achebe." Duerden and Pieterse, eds., 3–17. First published: *Africa Report* 9.7 (1964): 19–21; *Topic* 1 (1965): 8.

—————. Interview. J. O. J. Nwachukwu–Agbada. "An Interview with Chinua Achebe." *The Massachusetts Review* 28 (1987): 281–82.

—————. Interview. Kalu Ogbaa. "An Interview with Chinua Achebe." *Research in African Literature* 12 (1981): 1–13.

—————. Interview(s). Robert M. Wren. *Those Magical Years: The Making of Nigerian Literature at Ibadan: 1948–1966*. Time / Space Artists and Scholars 1. Washington: Three Continents, 1991: *passim*.

—————. *A Man of the People*. 2nd ed. African Writers Series. Oxford, Portsmouth, Ibadan: Heinemann, 1988. Other editions include: London: Heinemann, 1966; African Writers Series 31, London, Ibadan, Nairobi: Heinemann, 1966; New York, John Day, 1966; Anchor Literary Library, Introduction by K. W. J. Post. Garden City: Doubleday Anchor, 1967; New York: Doubleday Anchor, 1989.

—————. *Morning Yet on Creation Day: Essays*.[Rev. and enlarg. ed.] Garden City: Doubleday Anchor, 1975; Garden City: Doubleday Anchor, 1976. Another edition is: London: Heinemann, 1974.

—————. *No Longer at Ease*. African Writers Series 3, London, Ibadan, Nairobi: Heinemann, 1963. Reset 1975. Other editions include: London, Heinemann, 1960; Greenwich: Fawcett, 1960; New York, Ivan Obolensky, 1961; New York: Astor–Honor, 1961; New York, Fawcett, 1969; African Writers Series. Oxford, Portsmouth, Ibadan: Heinemann, 1987; *The African Trilogy*. London: Pan, Picador, 1988 (Contains *Things Fall Apart, No Longer at Ease, Arrow of God*).

—————. "Named for Victoria, Queen of England." *Morning Yet* (1975): 115–124; (1976): 95–103. Reprinted in *Hopes and Impediments* 30–39. First published: *New Letters* 40 (1973): 15–22.

—————. Newspaper article. *The Hartford Advocate* July 24 1989.

—————. "The Novelist as Teacher." *Morning Yet* (1975): 67–73; (1976): 55–60. Reprinted in *Hopes and Impediments* 40–46, 178. First published: *The New Statesman* 29 Jan. 1965: 27–31.

—————. "The Role of the Writer in a New Nation." Killam, ed., 7–13. First published: *Nigerian Libraries* 1 (1964): 113–19; *Nigeria Magazine* 81 (1964): 157–60.

—————. *Things Fall Apart*. Intro. and notes, Aigboje. African Writers Series 1. London, Ibadan, Nairobi: Heinemann, 1962. Reset 1976; New York: Fawcett, 1969. Other editions include: London: Heinemann, 1958; Greenwich: Fawcett, 1959; New York, Ivan Obolensky, 1959; New York: Astor–Honor, 1961; *The African Trilogy*. London: Pan, Picador, 1988 (Contains *Things Fall Apart, No Longer at Ease, Arrow of God*).

—————. *The Trouble with Nigeria*. African Writers Series. Oxford and Plymouth: Heinemann, 1984. Other editions are: Enugu: Fourth Dimension, 1983. London: Heinemann, 1983.

—————. "The Uses of African Literature." *Okike* 15 (1979): 8–17.

A. E. Afigbo. *The Warrant Chiefs: Indirect Rule in Southeastern Nigeria 1891–1929*. Ibadan History Series. London: Longmans; New York: Humanities, 1972.

Amadike, P. C. "Address to Convention of Nigerian Authors." *Okike* 20 (1981): 4–6.

Armah, Ayi Kwei. *The Beautyful Ones are Not Yet Born*. African Writers Series 48. London, Ibadan, Nairobi: Heinemann, 1969, reset 1975. Other editions include: Boston: Houghton Mifflin. 1968; African/American Library. Intro. Christina Ama Ata Aidoo. New York: Collier, 1969; London: Heinemann, 1969.

Awoonor, Kofi. *The Breast of the Earth: A Survey of the History, Culture and Literature of Africa South of the Sahara*. New York: Doubleday Anchor, 1976. Other editions are: New York, London, Lagos: NOK Publishers, 1975; Garden City: Anchor Doubleday, 1975.

Awoonor–Williams, George. "*George Awoonor–Williams*: 'From the Discussion' to Soyinka 'The Writer in a Modern African State'." Wästberg, ed., 31–32.

Bartold, Bonnie J. *Black Time: Fiction of Africa, the Caribbean, and the United States*. New Haven: Yale UP, 1981.

Bishop, Rand. *African Literature, African Critics: The Forming of Critical Standards, 1947–1966*. Contributions in Afro–American and African Studies 115. New York: Greenwood P, 1988.

Brutus, Denis. "*Denis Brutus*: 'From the Discussion' to Soyinka 'The Writer in a Modern African State'." Wästberg, ed., 33–34.

Camus, Albert. *The Rebel: An Essay on Man in Revolt*. Rev. Trans. Anthony Bower. New York: Vintage, 1956. First published as: *L'Homme révolté*. Paris: Gallimard, 1951.

Carlyle, Thomas. :"Lecture V. The Hero as a Man of Letters: Johnson, Rousseau, Burns." *On Heroes, Hero–Worship and the Heroic in History*. London: Chapman and Hall, 1897. 154–95.

Carroll, David. *Chinua Achebe*. 2nd ed. Macmillan Commonwealth Writers Series. London: Macmillan; New York: St. Martin's P, 1980. First edition: Twayne's World Authors Series, TWAS 101. New York: Twayne, 1970.

Cary, Joyce. *Mr. Johnson*. London: Gollancz, 1939.

Chinweizu, Onwuchekwa Jemie, and Ihechukwu Madubuike. *Toward the Decolonization of African Literature*. Vol. 1: *African Fiction and Poetry and their Critics*. Washington: Howard UP, 1983. Other editions include: Enugu: Fourth Dimension, 1980; London: KPI, 1985.

Clark, J. P. *Casualties: Poems 1960–68*. Harlow: Longman; New York: Africana, 1970.

Connolly, Thomas E. *Swinburne's Theory of Poetry*. Albany: State U of New York P, 1964.

Conrad, Joseph. *Heart of Darkness*. *Blackwood's Magazine* (February–April 1899). *'Heart of Darkness' and Other Tales*. Ed. Cedric Watts. World's Classics. Oxford and New York: Oxford UP, 1990.

Duerden, Dennis, and Cosmo Pieterse, eds. *African Writers Talking: A Collection of Radio Interviews*. New York: Africana Publishing Corporation; London: Heinemann. 1972.

Durix, Jean–Pierre. *The Writer Written: The Artist and Creation in the New Literatures in English*. Contributions to the Study of World Literature 21. New York: Greenwood Press, 1987.

Egejuru, Phanuel Akubueze *Towards African Literary Independence: A Dialogue with Contemporary African Writers*. Contributions to Afro–American and African Studies 53, Westport: Greenwood, 1980.

Ekwensi, Cyprian. *Beautiful Feathers*. London: Hutchinson, 1963. Another edition is: African Writers Series 84. London: Ibadan, Nairobi: Heinemann, 1971.

Eliot, T. S. *The Complete Poems and Plays 1909–1950.* New York: Harcourt, Brace & World, 1971.

Ellison, Ralph. *Shadow and Act.* New York: Random House, 1964.

Field, Margaret J. See Mark Freshfield.

Finn, Julio. *Voices of Negritude: With an Anthology of Negritude Poems Translated from the French, Portuguese, and Spanish.* New York: Quartet, 1988.

Freshfield, Mark. [*pseud.*] *The Stormy Dawn.* London: Faber and Faber, 1946.

Glicksberg, Charles I. *Literature and Society.* The Hague: Martinus Nijhoff, 1972.

Greary, William N. M. *Nigeria Under British Rule.* London: Frank Cass, 1965. First published: London: Methuen; Frank Cass, 1927.

Greene, Graham. *The Heart of the Matter.* London: Heinemann; New York: Viking, 1948.

Hill–Lubin, Mildred A. "Chinua Achebe and James Baldwin at the African Literature Association Conference in Gainesville." *Okike* 17 (1980): 1–5.

Huxley, Elspeth J. *The Walled City.* London: Chatto and Windus; Philadelphia: Lippencott, 1949.

Innes, C. L. and Bernth Lindfors, eds. *Critical Perspectives on Chinua Achebe.* Critical Perspectives 4. Washington: Three Continents P, 1978.

Iyasere, Solomon O. "Narrative Techniques in 'Things Fall Apart'." Innes and Lindfors, eds., 92–110. First published in *New Letters* 40 (1974): 73–93.

Jacobsen, Dan. "*Dan Jacobsen:* 'From the Discussion' to Soyinka 'The Writer in a Modern African State'." Wästberg, ed., 28–29.

Jeyifo, Biodun, ed. *Contemporary Nigerian Literature: A Retrospective and Prospective Exploration.* A Nigeria Magazine Publication. Lagos: Federal Department of Culture, 1985.

Jones, Eldred. "*Eldred Jones:* 'From the Discussion' to Soyinka 'The Writer in a Modern African State'." Wästberg, ed., 34–35.

Joyce, James. *A Portrait of an Artist as a Young Man.* New York: The Modern Library, 1928.

Karl, Frederick R. . "Introduction. The Novel as Subversion." *The Adversary Literature, the English Novel in the Eighteenth Century: A Study in Genre.* New York: Farrar, Straus and Giroux; Toronto: Doubleday, 1974. Other editions are: *A Reader's Guide to the Eighteenth Century English Novel.* New York: Noonday, 1974.; *A Reader's Guide to the Development of the English Novel in the Eighteenth Century.* London: Thames and Hudson, 1975. 2–54.

Killam, G. D. *The Writings of Chinua Achebe.* Studies in African Literature. London: Heinemann, 1969.

————, ed. *African Writers on African Writing.* Studies in African Literature. London: Heinemann; Evanston: Northwestern UP, 1973.

La Guma, Alex. "*Alex La Guma:* 'From the Discussion' to Soyinka 'The Writer in a Modern African State'." Wästberg, ed., 21–24.

Loader, William R. *The Guinea Stamp: A Novel.* London: Cape, 1956.

Leonard, Major Arthur Glyn. *The Lower Niger and its Tribes.* London: Macmillan, 1906.

Lessing, Doris. "The Small Personal Voice." *Declaration.* Ed. Tom Maschler. New York: Dutton, 1958. 185–201.

Lindfors, Bernth. "Negritude and After: Responses to Colonialism and Independence in African Literatures." *Problems in National Literary Identity and the Writer as Social Critic: Selected Papers of the Fourth Annual NDEA Seminar on Foreign Area Studies, Columbia*

University . . . 1980. Ed. Anne Paolucci. Whitestone: Griffon House for the Council on National Literatures, 1980. 29–37.

—————————, et al., eds. *Palaver: Interviews with Five African Writers in Texas.* Austin: African and Afro–American Research Institute, University of Texas at Austin, 1972.

Llosa, Mario Vargas. "Social Commitment and the Latin American Writer." *Lives on the Line: The Testimony of Contemporary Latin American Authors.* Ed. Doris Meyer. Berkeley: U of California P, 1988. 128–36.

Lowell, James Russell. *The Function of the Poet and Other Essays.* Ed. Albert Mordell. Boston: Houghton Mifflin, 1920.

Lucas, John. ed. *Literature and Politics in the Nineteenth Century: Essays.* London: Methuen, 1971.

Mahood, M. M. "Idols of the Den: Achebe's *Arrow of God.*" Innes and Lindfors, eds., 180–206. First published in *The Colonial Encounter: A Reading of Six Novels.* London: Rex Collings, 1976; Totowa: Rowman and Littlerfields, 1977. 37–64.

Mazrui, Ali A. *The Trial of Christopher Okigbo.* African Writers Series 97. London, Ibadan, Nairobi: Heinemann, 1971.

Mbiti, John S. *Concepts of God in Africa.* London: SPCK; New York: Praeger, 1970.

Mphahlele, Ezekiel. Interview. Phanuel Akubueze Egejuru. "Writers Discuss their Works: Ezekiel Mphahlele." Egejuru, 132–141.

Nagenda, John. "*John Nagenda*: 'From the Discussion' to Soyinka 'The Writer in a Modern African State'." Wästberg, ed., 24–25.

—————————. "*John Nagenda*: 'From the Discussion' to Nkosi 'Individualism and Social Commitment'." Wästberg, ed., 52–54.

Narasimhaiah, C. D. "Where Angels Fear to Tread: Chinua Achebe and Wole Soyinka as Critics of the African Scene." *The Literary Criterion* 23.1 & 2 (1988): 222–36.

New Catholic Encyclopedia. 25 vols. New York: McGraw–Hill, 1967.

The New Jerusalem Bible. Garden City: Doubleday, 1985.

Ngũgĩ wa Thiong'o. *Homecoming: Essays on African and Carribean Literature, Culture and Politics.* [Intro.J. P. Clark.] New York: Lawrence Hill, 1973. Another edition is: Studies in African Literature, London: Heinemann, 1972.

—————————. ["Interview"]. Wilkinson, ed., 122–35.

—————————. "*James Ngugi*: 'From the Discussion' to Soyinka 'The Writer in a Modern African State'." Wästberg, ed., 25–26.

—————————. "Wole Soyinka, T. M. Aluko and the Satiric Voice." *Homecoming,* 55–66. An earlier version appeared as: "Satire in Nigeria: Chinua Achebe, T. M. Aluko and Wole Soyinka." Pieterse and Munro, eds., 56–69.

—————————. "The Writer in a Changing Society." *Homecoming* 47–50.

Nkosi, Lewis. "Individualism and Social Commitment." Wästberg, ed., 45–49.

—————————. "*Lewis Nkosi*: 'From the Discussion' to Soyinka 'The Writer in a Modern African State'." Wästberg, ed., 26–27.

Obiechina, Emmanuel. *Culture, Tradition and Society in the West African Novel.* African Studies Series 14. Cambridge: Cambridge UP, 1975.

————. "The Writer and his Commitment in Contemporary Nigerian Society." *Okike,* 27/28, March 1988: 1–9.

Ofeimun, Odia. ["Interview"]. Wilkinson, ed., 58–74.

————. *The Poet Lied and Other Poems.* Longman Drumbeat 24. Harlow: Longman, 1980. New edition: Lagos: Update Communications, 1989.

Ogungbesan, Kolawole. "Wole Soyinka and the Novelist's Responsibility in Africa." *New West African Literature.* Ed. Kolawole Ogungbesan. Studies in African Literature. London: Heinemann, 1979.

Okara, Gabriel. See: Zabus, Chantal.

Okigbo, Christopher. *Labyrinths* with *Paths of Thunder.* African Writers Śeries 62, London, Nairobi, Ibadan: Heinemann, 1971. New York: Africana Publishing Corporation in Association with Mbari Publications, Ibadan, 1971. Reprinted in *Collected Poems.* London: Heinemann, 1986: 15–76, 87–99.

Petersen, Kirsten Holst and Anna Rutherford, eds. *Chinua Achebe: A Celebration.* Studies in African Literature [New Series]. Oxford and Portsmouth: Heinemann; Sydney, Coventry, Mundelstrup: Dangeroo Press, 1991. First published in *Kunapipi* (1990).

Pieterse, Cosmo and Donald Munro, eds. *Protest and Conflict in African Literature.* New York: Africana Publishing Corporation, 1969.

Sartre, Jean–Paul. "What is Literature." Trans. Bernard Frechtman (Corr. trans.). *What is Literature and other Essays?* 21–245, 333–48. Translation first published as: *What is Literature?* New York: Philosophical Library, 1949. Another edition is: New York: Harper and Row, 1965. First published in *Le Temps modernes* 17–22 (February–July), 1947; *Qu'est–ce que la litterature?* Collection idées. Paris: Gallimard, 1948; *Situations, II. Qu'est–ce que la litterature?* Paris: Gallimard, 1948. 54–330.

————. "Black Orpheus." Trans. John MacCombie. *What is Literature and other Essays?* 289–330, 348. Translation first published *Massachusetts Review* 6 (1965): 13–52. First published in Senghor, ed. ix–xliv, and *Situations, III.* Paris: Gallimard, 1949. 229–86.

————. *What is Literature and other Essays?* Ed. Steven Unger. Cambridge: Harvard UP, 1988.

Senghor, Léopold Sédar. *Chants d'Ombre.* Collection "Pierres vivres." Paris: Editions de Seuil, 1945.

————, ed. *Anthologie de la nouvelle poésie nègro et malgache de la langue français . . . précédée de Orphée Noir par J.–P. Sartre.* 4th ed. Pays d'Outre–Mer. Paris: Presses universitaires de France, 1977. First published: Colonies et empires 5 ser.: Art et littérature 1. Paris: Presses universitaires de France, 1948.

Shakespeare, William. *As You Like It. The Complete Works.* Ed. Stanley Wells and Gary Taylor. Oxford: Clarendon P, 1986: 705–33.

Shelley, Percy Bysshe. *Shelley's Poetry and Prose: Authoritative Texts, Criticism.* Ed. Donald H. Reiman and Sharon B. Powers. Norton Critical Edition. New York: Norton, 1977.

Sidney, Sir Philip. *A Defence of Poetry.* Ed. Jan Van Dorsten. Oxford: Oxford UP, 1966.

Simons, John D. *Frederich Schiller.* Twayne's World Authors Series, TWAS 603. Boston: Twayne, 1981.

Soyinka, Wole. "A Dance of the Forests." Oxford: Oxford UP, 1963; *Collected Plays* 1: 1–77.

—————. *Collected Plays.* 2 vols. Oxford: Oxford UP, 1973–74.

—————. "The Future of West African Writing." *The Horn* 4 (1960): 10–16.

—————. *The Interpreters.* African Writers Series 76. Intro. and Notes Eldred Jones. London, Ibadan, Nairobi: Heinemann in association with Andre Deutsch, 1970. Other Editions are: London: Andre Deutsch, 1965; New York: Macmillan, 1965; London: Panther Books, 1967; African/American Library. Intro. Leslie Lacy. New York: Collier, 1970; Fontana Modern Novels. London: Fontana, 1972; New York: Africana Publishing Corporation, 1972.

—————. Interview. Lewis Nkosi. "Wole Soyinka." Duerden and Pieterse, eds., 171–77.

—————. "Introduction." *Six Plays.* xi–xxi.

—————. *Kongi's Harvest. Collected Plays* 2: 59–141.

—————. *Madmen and Specialists.* London: Methuen; New York: Hill and Wang, 1971; *Collected Plays* 2: 214–76; *Six Plays*: 221–93.

—————. *The Man Died: Prison Notes of Wole Soyinka.* London: Rex Collings, 1972. Other editions are: New York: Harper and Row, 1972; Harmondsworth: Penguin, 1975; London: Arrow, 1985; Ibadan: Spectrum, 1988; New York: Noonday, 1988.

—————. *A Play of Giants.* Methuen Modern Plays. London and New York: Methuen, 1984.

—————. *Season of Anomy.* London: Rex Collings, 1973. Other editions are: New York: The Third Press, 1974; London: Arena, 1980; Panafrica Library, Walton–on–Thames, Surrey: Nelson, 1980.

—————. *A Shuttle in the Crypt.* London: Rex Collings, Eyre Methuen; New York: Hill and Wang, 1972.

—————. *Six Plays.* The Master Playwrights. London: Methuen, 1984.

—————. *The Strong Breed. Collected Plays* 1: 113–46. First published: *The Swamp Dwellers, The Trials of Brother Jero, The Strong Breed.* Ibadan: Mbari, 1963.

—————. "*Wole Soyinka*: 'From the Discussion' to Nkosi 'Individualism and Social Commitment'." Wästberg, ed., 51–52, 57–58.

—————. "The Writer in a Modern African State." Wastberg, ed., 14–21.

Stock, A. G. "Yeats and Achebe." Innes and Lindfors, eds., 86–91. First published: *Journal of Commonwealth Literature* 5 (1968): 105–11.

Stamp, Laurence Dudley. *An Intermediate Commercial Georgaphy.* London: Longmans, 1927. 10 editions by 1954.

Updike, John. "Review of *Anthills of the Savannah*" *The New Yorker,* June 13, 1988: 114–16.

Waggoner, Hyatt H. *Emerson as Poet.* Princeton: Princeton UP, 1974.

Wästberg, Per, ed. *The Writer in Modern Africa.* Uppsala: The Scandinavian Instutute of African Studies. New York: Africana, 1969. Another edition is: Nordiska Afrikaninstitutet. Uppsala: Almquist and Wiksell, 1969.

Weinstock, Donald, and Cathy Ramadan. "Symbolic Structure in *Things Fall Apart.*" Innes and Lindfors, eds., 126–134. First published in *Critique* 11 (1969): 33–41.

West, Michael Philip. *English Words for All Occasions.* London: Longmans, Green, 1933.

———————— and James Gareth Endicott. *New Method English Dictionary*. London: Longmans, 1935. 3rd ed., 1953.

Wilkinson, Jane, ed. *Talking with African Writers: Interviews with African Poets, Playwrights & Novelists*. Studies in African Literature [New Series]. London: James Currey: Portsmouth: Heinemann, 1992. First published: London James Curry; Rome: Bagatto Libri Societa, 1990.

Wilson, Roderick. "Eliot and Achebe: An Analysis of Some Formal and Philosophical Qualities 'No Longer at Ease'." Innes and Lindfors, eds.; 160–68. First published in *English Studies in Africa* 14 (1971): 215–23.

Wren, Robert M. *Achebe's World: The Historical and Cultural Context of the Novels of Chinua Achebe*. Washington: Three Continents P, 1980.

Zabus, Chantal. "Of Tortoise, Man and Language. An Interview with Gabriel Okara." *Critical Approaches to* Anthills of the Savannah. [= *Matatu* 8]. Ed. Holger G. Ehling, Amsterdam and Atlanta: Rodopi, 1991. 101–13.

Zall, Paul M. "Introduction." *Literary Criticism of William Wordsworth*. Regents Critics Series. Lincoln: U of Nebraska P, 1966. ix–xvii.